Grammar of the Edit

Tell more effective visual stories by learning the "grammar" of cinematic language with this elegant, accessible reference. The newly revised and updated fourth edition of *Grammar of the Edit* gives you the answers to the all-important questions of when to cut and why, and teaches readers the principles behind transitions, editing for continuity, selecting the best shots, editing sound, color correction, and more. Designed as an easy-to-use guide, *Grammar of the Edit* presents each topic succinctly with clear photographs and diagrams illustrating key concepts, practical exercises, and quiz questions, and is a staple of any filmmaker's library.

New to the fourth edition:

- an expanded companion website at www.routledge.com/cw/bowen, offering downloadable scenes and editable raw footage so that students can practice the techniques described in the book, and instructional videos showcasing examples of different editing choices and types of shot transitions;

- new and expanded quiz questions and practical exercises at the end of each chapter to help to test readers on their knowledge using real-world scenarios;

- updated topic discussions, explanations, illustrations, and visual examples;

- an all-new chapter on sound resources in filmmaking and audio-editing guidelines.

Together with its companion volume, *Grammar of the Shot*, the core concepts discussed in these books offer concise and practical resources for both experienced and aspiring filmmakers.

Christopher J. Bowen has worked within the motion media industries for over 18 years as a cinematographer, editor, director, and educator. Currently, he is an Associate Professor of Film Production and Visual Media Writing at Framingham State University. He is also an Avid Certified Instructor, Creative Director of his own media production company, Fellsway Creatives, and author of the companion text, *Grammar of the Shot*.

Grammar of
the Edit

Fourth Edition

Christopher J. Bowen

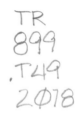

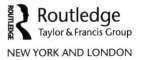
Routledge
Taylor & Francis Group

NEW YORK AND LONDON

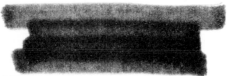

Fourth edition published 2018
by Routledge
711 Third Avenue, New York, NY 10017

and by Routledge
2 Park Square, Milton Park, Abingdon, Oxon OX14 4RN

Routledge is an imprint of the Taylor & Francis Group, an informa business

Third edition published by Focal Press 2013

Library of Congress Cataloging in Publication Data
A catalog record for this book has been requested

ISBN: 978-1-138-63219-6 (hbk)
ISBN: 978-1-138-63220-2 (pbk)
ISBN: 978-1-315-20840-4 (ebk)

Typeset in Univers
by Keystroke, Neville Lodge, Tettenhall, Wolverhampton

Visit the companion website: www.routledge.com/cw/bowen

Contents

Contents

Contents

Introduction

Today's world seems to be filled with screens, both large and small, that stream moving images. From the IMAX theater to the billboard near the highway to your UHDTV, laptop, or tablet to the smartphone in your pocket: all are capable of displaying motion pictures. And every moving image that you see on these screens has been edited. Movies, television shows, commercials, music videos, and web videos of all kinds have been cut down, re-ordered, padded out, massaged, sweetened, and tweaked to some degree or another – by an editor.

A writer creates the story, a director coaches the actors, a cinematographer creates the visual style of each shot, and an editor puts all of those pieces together. Being one of the last creative people to touch a motion media project, the editor truly is the final storyteller. That final version may be exactly what the creators set out to make, or it may be very different in mood, tempo, information content, or emotional effect. It is the skill, craft, and gut instinct of the editor that help to form the over-arching visual style, pacing, and coherence of story that are ultimately experienced by the audience. Editing is where you get to figure out how to make it all work together.

This book, *Grammar of the Edit*, Fourth Edition, continues the series' long tradition of introducing a beginner to the world of motion picture editing. The suggested guidelines, and general practices presented herein will provide a new student of this craft with a solid understanding of the established techniques and methodologies associated with the *what*, *how*, and *why* of the video-editing process.

The updated fourth edition has been thoughtfully redesigned, enhanced, and expanded. Many of the figures that illustrate the concepts have been replaced or refreshed. Each chapter begins with an outline of that chapter's contents, and ends with a detailed review section highlighting the main concepts covered by that chapter. Value-added sections called Exercises and Quiz Yourself conclude each chapter. They present ways in which you can immediately put into practice the techniques and guidelines discussed in the chapter, and offer a gauge to see how well you absorbed the information. Many new topics have been added throughout and most recurring topics have been rewritten and restructured for clarity and flow.

Regardless of the career direction in which the fledgling editor wishes to go, everyone needs to learn how to walk before they can run and this book should help to define the basic terms and clarify the common practices of editing. It does not mention specific video-editing software but it does discuss some issues inherent to the digital video medium. The terms "motion picture" or "motion media piece" may be used liberally to encompass a variety of live-action and animated project types, whether produced for the web, television, or movie theater. A particular genre of film or a specific type of television programming may be called out in an example to help to illustrate a unique point. The goal of this book is to inform a person who is new to editing about the accepted practices of the craft, the reasoning behind those practices, and how the audience interpret meaning, on several levels, from the edited piece. Good technique and not-so-good technique will be discussed and illustrated. In the end, you will find that there is no 100% right and there is no 100% wrong; there is only what works and what does not work – and why.

Acknowledgments

I wish to thank the supportive team of publishing professionals at Routledge/Taylor & Francis Group who helped to make this new and improved fourth edition a reality. I would particularly like to thank Simon Jacobs and John Makowski, who worked diligently to get this new edition off the ground. I hope our efforts continue to honor the legacy of Roy Thompson, who penned the first edition so many years ago. The goal we all share in producing this book is to get the pertinent information about editing motion media pieces into the minds and hands of the next generation of visual storytellers. I hope that this revised fourth edition continues to inform and inspire all of those readers who are just beginning their creative journey into the world of motion media production.

As an Associate Professor of Film Production and Visual Media Writing at Framingham State University, I benefit from being surrounded by fellow educators and a lively and engaged population of students in the communication arts. The environment fosters much innovation and many new approaches to teaching and learning about our discipline. I wish to acknowledge the support of my colleagues and the helpful contributions from all of my students over the years. The same goes for my experiences when teaching at Boston University and at the Boston University Center for Digital Imaging Arts. A collective thank you to everyone who has added to my growth as an educator and as a motion media producer.

As a media professional, I wish to thank my many collaborators and clients, who have helped me to continue learning and to explore new techniques in telling their unique stories.

I am also grateful to the fourth edition's proposal and manuscript reviewers for their helpful suggestions and critiques. A special thank you goes out to Katarina Damjanov, Adam Davis, David E. Elkins, Jeffrey Hill, and Juli S. Pitzer.

Additionally, I would like to thank my on-camera talent for their time and cooperation:

Zach Benard	Crystal Haidsiak
Rose32 Bread	Caitlin Harper
Wendy Chao	Timi Khatra
Jacob Cuomo	Emily Klamm
Hannah Daly	Hannah Kurth

Olivia Lospennato

Anthony Martel

Emma Nydam

Kelsey E. O'Connor

Elizabeth Proulx

Rajiv Roy

Alexander Scott

Stacie Seidl

Stacy Shreffler

Eliza Smith

Rachel Swain

Tucker, Ghost, Maera, and Jinx

The majority of images in this edition have been created by the author, but a significant set of new pictures have been donated by several of my students who now do visual communication, photography, and design work professionally. I would like to thank the following individuals for sharing their creative works and for also manufacturing topic-related images that help to illustrate the film language content in this book: Zach Benard, Anthony Martel, and Mike Neilan.

The line art diagrams and the majority of the hand-drawn illustrations are also by the author. Once again, I must offer my thanks and appreciation to Jean Sharpe, who donated her time and skills to illustrating much of the second edition; some of those illustrations are reproduced here to continue their useful purpose.

Finally, I acknowledge my family for their support and offer an extra special thank you to Emily Klamm, who has been there through the thick and thin of it all – again.

This book is for all people who wish to learn the basics about communicating visually through motion pictures – especially the editing process. I hope you have fun and enjoy the ride. If you would like to learn more about the topic, find additional resources, or contact the author, please visit the author's website: www.fellswaycreatives.com.

For Emily & Jinx & Sparky

Chapter One
Editing Basics

- A Very Brief History of Film Editing
- Basic Factors Affecting Editorial Choices
- Stages of the Editing Process
- The Basic Motion Picture Transitions

When you write something, like a paper for school or a blog post, you typically have a message in mind before you start writing. Then, to do the actual writing, you select words from your vocabulary and put them together in particular ways to construct sentences. If assembled correctly, these accumulated sentences will inform, entertain, or evoke emotional responses within the reader. A very similar process occurs when you edit a motion picture. You have to have a message (or story) in mind as you begin. Then, to do the actual editing, you select shots of visual and aural content and assemble them in a particular **sequence**. If done correctly, this motion media message will inform, entertain, or evoke emotional responses within the viewer. In order for your readers to comprehend your sentences, you must follow the known and accepted rules of grammar for your written language: word order, verb tense, phrase construction, punctuation, etc. There is also a similar grammar for the "language" of motion pictures. It governs how their images are recorded and how they are edited together – and audiences have learned how to "read" them.

In our companion book, *Grammar of the Shot,* the basic practices of structure, movement, and purpose in frame composition are discussed in detail. This text, *Grammar of the Edit,* presents the basic guidelines of motion media construction that will allow you to take those same shots and assemble them together into a meaningful story. As a creative motion media producer, you can choose to edit your visual elements however you wish, but it should be understood that there are certain basic guidelines that are commonly accepted in the entertainment and visual communication fields. The chapters of this book are designed to help you to understand the visual and aural materials that you will be working with and the basic grammar behind the editing process. Our goal is to help to get you set on a path to good editing practices.

A Very Brief History of Film Editing

Long before the existence of digital video and computer editing software, people used emulsion film to create the illusion of movement on a screen. Over 100 years ago, emulsion film strips and hand-cranked moving film cameras were leading-edge technologies, but the actual length of plastic film limited the duration of image recording time. Many of the original movies were merely **real-time** recordings of life's daily events.

Very quickly, the technologies advanced and motion pictures moved from being straight documentary recordings to more elaborately constructed fictional narrative stories. Longer strips of film allowed for longer recording times. As film's visual language began to develop, more shot variety was introduced and motion pictures grew in scope and sophistication. The "cutters" who once just assembled a few short strips of picture film took on a new role in the expanding post-production phase of filmmaking. Story structuring – or sometimes reconstructing – became the full-time job of the film editor.

Within just a few decades, a more complex visual language of motion picture photography and editing had evolved. Films were quickly becoming the largest entertainment and information medium on the planet. They were held in high esteem by many and denounced by others as a novelty at best and a corrupting distraction at worst. Motion pictures and how audiences perceived them became a source of study. Many theories about the social and artistic values of filmmaking, and the visual power of film editing especially, emerged from different cultures around the world.

At what point the editor cut the film and how the various shots were joined together were seen to have an effect on the viewing audience above and beyond the actual story. Editing was no longer just a means to physically trim the excess footage from a series of shots; it had become recognized as a powerful tool in the filmmaker's toolbox. Over time, the machines that took the pictures and performed the cuts evolved, but most of the basic parameters of visual grammar remained the same. Differing editorial styles have come and gone, but the core methods and intent behind the practice of assembling picture and sound elements are unchanged even today.

What Is Editing?

As a transitive verb, "to edit" can mean to review, refine, modify, eliminate, or assemble components into a new, acceptable form. It was first used broadly with the written word and is now also applied to moving picture and sound creations. For our purposes, the term "editing" (a noun) is the act of assembling individual clips of picture and sound into a coherent story of some kind. So an "editor" is a person who takes a bunch of picture and sound material, and reviews, refines, modifies, eliminates, and assembles those picture and sound components into a new, acceptable form or story.

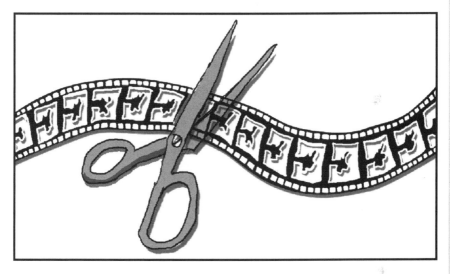

FIGURE 1.1   Initially, editing motion picture film required very basic technologies.

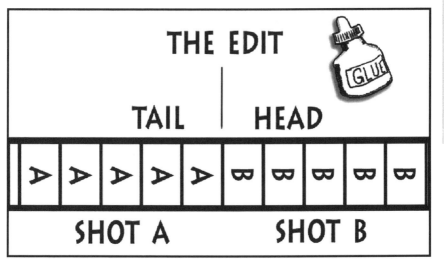

FIGURE 1.2   The head of the film clip for Shot B is edited onto the tail end of Shot A.

A Very Brief History of Film Editing

An **edit** (also a noun) is the place where you join together those clips, and transition from one shot to the next within that assembly. Put simply, an edit is a cut point: a place where one shot ends and another separate shot begins. The term "cut" stems from the days when motion pictures were shot and edited on very long strips of celluloid plastic emulsion film. Looking at the individual still frames on that strip of film, the editor would determine where to physically cut the film between pictures. A pair of scissors or a razor-blade "splicer" was used to actually cut the film at that point (Figure 1.1). Glue or tape was then used to join the different cut strips of plastic film together again (Figure 1.2). The cut or join becomes the point of transition from one shot to the next. The **straight cut** described here is just one way to move between shots. How, when, and why you choose to transition from one shot to another depends on many variables.

What Basic Factors May Affect Your Editing Choices?

Tools

The first factor you may wish to consider is what medium you are using to perform the actual edits: film, tape-to-tape video, or digital video-editing software. Each medium, and the devices that are used in the editing processes, can often dictate physical, time-related, or, certainly, financial limitations. At the time of writing, you would be hard pressed to find anyone who, on a large and consistent scale, still splices emulsion film prints or runs linear tape edit suites. The majority of editing, for all kinds of motion media projects, is now done almost exclusively on computers (desktops, laptops, tables, or even mobile smartphones).

If you only have access to very basic editing software, then do not worry; you are still able to effectively edit picture and sound elements to create a good story. More advanced tools can allow new editors to play with more bells and whistles, but at the core, you need to maintain good storytelling (or story-showing) methods, regardless of the type of project you are making. Don't believe the hype: the "latest and greatest" technologies do not automatically enhance the quality or value of your project. You may find, however, that it is necessary to have a recent operating system and a recent version of editing software in order to actually decode and play the video files generated by the many different digital video cameras in use today.

However, having some access to a decent computer and the video-editing software of your choice is actually very important to anyone's progression as a practicing video editor. If you do not have the tools, you cannot practice, and you cannot do the work; therefore your skills will not improve. Luckily, several of the major apps do allow for free trials or "limited-use" free versions of their fully functioning software. Certain apps, with rudimentary features, are free or relatively inexpensive for download and do a fine job at providing you the tools you will need to complete basic and intermediate video projects. Audio-editing applications are similarly available.

In this book, we will purposefully keep the discussions of editing grammar as generic as possible. We will do very little in the way of mentioning specific hardware or software, tool names, buttons, menu items, or keyboard shortcuts. There are, quite frankly, too many, and they are being modified or removed with each new version of each device or app. The general working practices presented here should apply to any medium or genre and to most editing devices or applications. Just be aware that certain terminology used in one medium may have its origins rooted in another and may vary from one software application to another and even from one country to another.

Project Type and Genre

A second factor that may affect your editing choices can be the kind of project that you are editing. Are you assembling picture and sound media for a documentary, a fictional narrative short film, a news package, a website's how-to video, a music video, a television commercial, a cousin's wedding video, or even an animated cartoon? Each type of motion media project may have a differing duration, call for certain editing styles, and use particular visual elements, transitions, etc. For instance, you may wish to use long, slow dissolves from one shot to the next in a moody music video, but you may not find it very beneficial to use them in a hard-hitting, factual news package. We will discuss dissolves in more detail later, but the example illustrates the importance of understanding the traditionally accepted guidelines of style for differing program types and for genres within those distinct kinds of programs.

The project's budget, scope, purpose, quality of resources, and turnaround time also play into the approach an editor can take. Personal or "no-budget" productions may require that you own your own computer and software and have access to a large number of available media file storage hard drives. Larger shows are edited in more professional editing facilities with very complex signal flow and shared network storage. Often, a project's budget also affects the scope (the length of the desired final edit), the quality of resources, and the time frame for completion. Short news pieces with only a few images and soundbites need to be cut together quickly to get to air. A feature film, especially a grand epic saga, may have tens or hundreds of hours of footage to comb through and assemble into a rather complex, multi-character storyline. This kind of project may take months of your life to finish.

What Basic Factors May Affect Your Editing Choices?

The particular type of project you are editing can also demand and/or influence many of the nitty-gritty editing choices you get to make. If you are cutting for an established TV show, it probably already has a template or formula to be followed. Watch enough "reality" and non-fiction TV and you'll quickly see the sections, patterns, and timings of each episode. A slow-moving drama may call for uninterrupted long takes of really strong performances by the actors. A promotional video for a motocross racing team may benefit from very fast cutting of short, action-filled clips accompanied by hard driving music and many visual effects (sometimes called **VFX** or **DVE**). Your own experimental film or a music video project could allow you total freedom when it comes to how you treat the visual and aural elements. For the purposes of clarity and simplicity, we will often focus on the grammar and practices associated with fictional narrative motion picture story-telling, but the general guidelines may apply to all forms of motion media.

Degree of Audience Manipulation

It is safe to say that almost all edited motion media projects are destined to be viewed by some kind of audience, whether on a social media stream, in a large movie theater, or along the aisles of a "big-box" store. The editor is the person who crafts that particular viewing experience for the intended audience. Often tied directly to the purpose of the project, the level of manipulation (and we mean this in a good way) invoked by the editor is variable. It's like taking the audience on a ride at an amusement park. Are you going to create an adrenaline rush like the corkscrew coaster? Is your project calm like the "kiddie karz?" Do you want to construct a mysterious and complex story full of false leads like the hall of mirrors or frightening jump scares like the spooky haunted house?

The **pacing** and **rhythm** you provide to the edited shots, scenes, and sequences help to control the audience's experience and their mental, physical, and emotional reactions to the story. If you present certain information in a certain order for particular durations on screen, you will get certain kinds of responses from the viewer. The need for and degree of audience manipulation comes from the **content** and **purpose** of the motion media project.

Are you editing an informational process or how-to video? Not so much direct manipu-lation of emotions needed there. Are you editing a short, funny video for a website? You might construct a set-up/pay-off scenario with comedic timing. A dramatic, action adventure story has all of the ups and downs of a roller coaster ride. Sustained tension needs a release. Suspense must end to feel completed. The script, the direction, and the performances (whatever the project might be) all add to the degree of audience manipulation that the editor constructs while assembling the picture and sound elements. Whether the goal of the project is to inform or to entertain, or a combination of both, the quality of the edited content allows the audience to engage with the material during the viewing experience – to think and to feel – in ways that you, the editor, want them to think and feel, when you want them to think and feel in those ways.

Other Factors

Another factor involved with over-arching editorial choices is your own level of creativity. Experience can help to give you speed of execution and some well-developed problem-solving skills, but any editor, regardless or age or time in the editor's chair, can come up with bold, fresh, and innovative approaches to stitching together a very effective final product. The right editor can breathe new life into almost any old, tired, or boring content, but an editor, no matter how skilled, may still have to deal with those potential limiting factors discussed above.

Additionally, if the project is not your own, then you may have to consider the viewpoints and input of other parties. The vision of the director and the not-so-subtle suggestions of a producer can (and will) influence the direction in which a project, or certainly portions of projects, may go. Yes, an editor performs the task of editing, but she or he does not always have control over the many variables that are at play during the post-production process. The goal, however, should always be to create the best and most genre-appropriate viewing experience for the audience, regardless of any limiting factors or challenges that may present themselves. Getting your next job may depend on it.

Stages of the Editing Process

As an editor, you will be tasked with creating motion media presentations that show coherent, meaningful, emotional, and/or informational stories to certain audiences. To achieve repeated successes with these finished sequences, you will, most likely, need to work through several stages of story development.

The editing process, more generally referred to as **post-production** (or sometimes just **post**), can range from being rather simple to extremely complex. The post-production period really encompasses any and all work on the project that comes after the shooting period (also known as **production**) is completed. Picture and sound tracks are edited together to show and tell the story, special visual effects are generated, titles/graphics/

Stages of the Editing Process

credits are added, sound effects are created, and music is scored and mixed – all during post-production. On smaller projects, one person may have to do all of this work, but on larger productions, several teams of creators and technicians work in various departments to complete each element and join each phase of the post-production **workflow**.

In the world of broadcast television editing, there are two main phases of post-production: the **offline edit** and the **online edit**. The offline phase builds out the show completely but is traditionally done at a lower image resolution so that the editing system can work faster. The online phase turns the completed sequence into a high-resolution/best-audio-mix program ready for television broadcasting. It looks and sounds as best as it can for the viewing audience and conforms to the technical specifications of delivery. Today, computer processors, graphics cards, RAM, and media drives can be very powerful; this, combined with tapeless video capture and more capable video-editing software, lessens the need for rigid offline-to-online conforming. Most professional and many amateur editors can work on high-definition media all of the way through the editing process, although large amounts of data storage hard-drive space are eaten up quickly.

The following is a list of the major steps involved in a post-production workflow that stresses the editing process for the basic picture and sound elements of a project (consider the acquisition to picture lock stages as the offline phase, and the finishing and mastering and delivery stages as the online phase):

- acquisition
- organization
- review and selection
- assembly
- rough cut
- fine cut
- picture lock
- finishing
- mastering and delivery.

Acquisition

Simply put, you must acquire the visual and audio media recorded by the production team and any other sources required for completing the edited project (i.e., still photos, music, graphics, etc.). Motion picture and sound elements, whether on emulsion film, analog tape, or digital tape, or as digital media files, must be gathered together for the duration of the post-production editing process. As almost all editing is done on computers, any source material not already in a digital format must be converted. If you are using a digital non-linear editing system to perform the edit, then you will have to import, capture, or "digitize" all materials as media on your storage drives. These media files must be protected and remain accessible by your editing software for the life of the project.

Organization

All of the minutes, hours, feet, reels, or gigabytes of picture, graphics, and sound elements should be organized in some way. If you do not have a clear system of labeling, grouping, or sorting all of the material needed for your project, you will eventually have a difficult time finding that particular videoclip or that special sound effect, etc. when you really need it. Having unique bins or folders for material arranged by date, subject, scene, etc. is wise on both short-term and long-term projects. Organization of source materials is not the most glamorous part of the editing process, but it can certainly make the difference between a smooth post-production workflow and a slower and more frustrating one. Many of the better editors and **assistant editors** are also highly prized for their organizational skills. Tame the chaos into order and craft the order into a motion picture.

Review and Selection

Once you have acquired and organized all of your elements, it will be necessary to review all of this material and pick out the best pieces that will work for your project. You will "pull the selects" and set aside the good stuff while weeding out the junk that you hope you will not have to use. Some editors place the "selects" (or copies of the good stuff) in their "working" bins or folders, while others might color code their clips according to usability. Labeling, in some way, the shots you would like to use will be important as you proceed with the edit. You would also be wise to not actually throw anything away (trash or delete) because you never know what might come in handy a day or a few weeks into the editing process. That one shot of the flag waving in the breeze may just save the entire edit, so keep it readily available even though you know it is not one of your original selections. Some editors create "master footage" sequences out of all of the good material so that they have a single source through which they can more easily scrub. This is faster than loading each individual clip in the source viewer.

Assembly

This process calls for assembling all of the major pieces of the project into a logical sequence of picture and sound elements. If you are editing a scripted story, you may initially try to follow that script as a blueprint for assembling the best selections of the various shots of the scenes that make up the motion picture. Some editors start off by following scripts with production notes or storyboards. If you are creating a documentary or even a music video, there is always some story that needs to be shown to an audience; assemble those raw parts into this skeleton version. Some editors even string together all of the good takes of a performance at the appropriate point of the assembly sequence in order to get a better feel for which take may work best, eventually keeping just the chosen one. No matter what genre the project, the story, in its longest and most rough-hewn form, takes shape now.

Rough Cut

This is the stage of the project's development where the majority of the "visual fat" has been trimmed and you are left with a presentation that is a long but functional version of the narrative, with many rough edges. Not every cut is perfectly timed; there are no finalized titles or graphics; effects, if any, are more or less placeholders; and the **audio mix** certainly has not been completed. You do have the timing of the main elements down to a good pace, however, and you, and others to whom you show the developing work, like how the story unfolds, although major restructuring of scenes may still occur if the flow does not feel right.

Fine Cut

You have worked, re-worked, and massaged the material of your project into a tight and finely tuned presentation. You like the order and timing of shots in each scene, the overall pacing fits the story, and the various elements work together as best as they can. There will be no major renovations from this point forward. You, and the majority of the people to whom you show the piece, all agree that only minor tweaks are required. This cut is fine.

Picture Lock

You have reached picture lock when you are absolutely certain that you will not make any more changes to the picture track(s) of your edited sequence. The timing of all

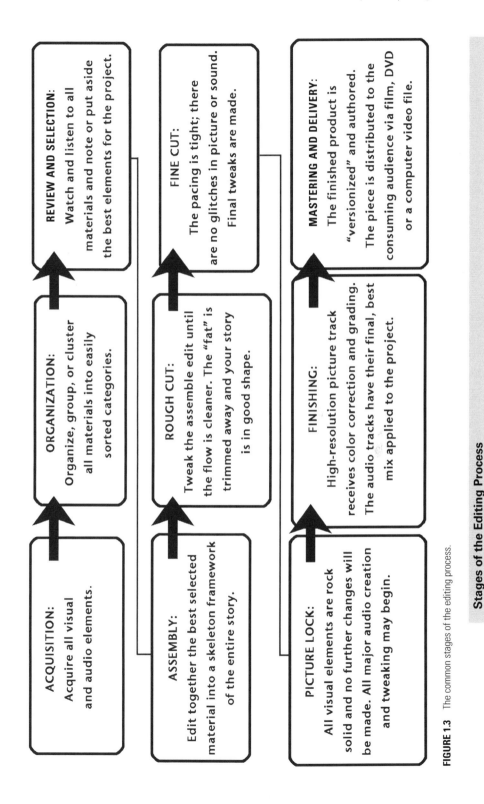

ACQUISITION:
Acquire all visual and audio elements.

ORGANIZATION:
Organize, group, or cluster all materials into easily sorted categories.

REVIEW AND SELECTION:
Watch and listen to all materials and note or put aside the best elements for the project.

ASSEMBLY:
Edit together the best selected material into a skeleton framework of the entire story.

ROUGH CUT:
Tweak the assemble edit until the flow is cleaner. The "fat" is trimmed away and your story is in good shape.

FINE CUT:
The pacing is tight; there are no glitches in picture or sound. Final tweaks are made.

PICTURE LOCK:
All visual elements are rock solid and no further changes will be made. All major audio creation and tweaking may begin.

FINISHING:
High-resolution picture track receives color correction and grading. The audio tracks have their final, best mix applied to the project.

MASTERING AND DELIVERY:
The finished product is "versionized" and authored. The piece is distributed to the consuming audience via film, DVD or a computer video file.

Stages of the Editing Process

FIGURE 1.3   The common stages of the editing process.

picture elements (shots, titles, black pauses, etc.) is set. Once you have locked the picture tracks (sometimes literally but mostly figuratively), you are then free to address your audio-mixing needs: final sound effects (SFX), level/panning tweaks, music scoring, etc. In the olden days of actual emulsion film "work print" editing, the picture track had to be locked at a precise duration so that each separately constructed audio track would **sync** up from the start frame. All computer editing software is so much more flexible that there is no longer an absolute need for picture lock, but keep in mind that any alteration to overall duration of picture tracks must still be altered on *all* corresponding audio tracks as well.

Finishing

This stage is sometimes called the online edit. If the offline edit has been done with low-resolution or proxy files, then these are swapped out for the highest-resolution video clips possible. Finishing is the stage where the color correction (also known as timing or grading) of the image is accomplished. Every clip of video is made to look as good as necessary according to the needs of the project (i.e., appropriate colors, saturation and **contrast** levels, etc.). The final mixed audio tracks are also in place in your timeline along with these "finished" video tracks.

Mastering and Delivery

All of your efforts in creating a well-edited piece will mean very little if you cannot deliver the show to the audience that need to see it. These days, this process may mean **rendering** everything and recording your finished sequence onto a master HD videotape, creating a cut list for an optical film print for projection in a movie theater, exporting and converting your story into a computer video file, or authoring onto a DVD or Blu-ray disc. Each medium would require a unique process and supporting hardware, software, and media. The end result is that you have a fully mastered original version of your show that you can then convert into other media formats and upload and/or **distribute** to various viewing outlets for audiences to enjoy.

You should now have a pretty good idea of what the basic editing or post-production workflow is for any project, whether large or small. You certainly may encounter projects that do not call for all of these stages of editing to be executed in a clearly delineated manner, but, for the most part, you will touch upon some combination of each of these stages as you work toward your finished sequence.

The Basic Motion Picture Transitions

The last topic for us to touch on in this introductory chapter on editing will be the edit point itself: the place where the two clips are joined together. Getting a handle on these terms now will help us to understand them better as they appear throughout this book. Chapter Six is dedicated to a more expansive exploration of these traditional editing practices.

In an edited sequence, there are four basic ways to transition from one shot or visual element into another:

1. **Cut** – An instantaneous change from one shot to the next. The last full frame of picture for a clip is immediately followed by the first full frame of picture for the next clip.

2. **Dissolve** – A gradual change from the ending pictures of one shot into the beginning pictures of the next shot. This is traditionally achieved via a momentary **superimposition** of the two shots where the opacity of the outgoing shot fades down and that of the incoming shot fades up simultaneously. As the end of the first shot "dissolves" away, the beginning of the next shot "resolves" onto the screen at the same time. Both images appear to be blended together on the screen for a very brief period.

3. **Wipe** – A line, progressing at some angle, or a geometric shape, moves across the screen removing the image of the shot just ending while simultaneously revealing the next shot behind the moving line or shape. The wiping shot replaces the previous shot on the screen over a brief duration where segments of both shots are partially visible.

4. **Fade** – (1) A gradual change from a solid color-filled screen (typically black) into a fully visible image, also known as a **fade-from-black** or **fade-in**; (2) a gradual change from a fully visible image into a solid color-filled screen (typically black), also known as a **fade-to-black** or **fade-out**.

The grammar of the edit has evolved in some ways since the early days of cinema, but these four basic transitions have remained the same. No matter what type of motion media project you are editing or what tool you are using to make it, a cut is still a cut. A dissolve is still a dissolve no matter what pictures you dissolve from and to. A wipe will literally wipe a new shot over the old shot. A fade-in still comes out of black and a fade-out still goes into black. The transitions have remained the same because their individual purposes have remained the same, and almost everyone around the world understands their grammar – or what it means when they see one being used at a transition point.

Later in this book, you will be able to explore a more in-depth analysis of these basic picture transitions and learn about audio transitions as well. For now, let us review the topics presented in this chapter, practice a few exercises, and quiz ourselves on some of the pertinent information. These concluding sections exist at the end of each chapter, so if you want to jump ahead and scan over these pages, you will have a solid understanding of the types of editing topics that we discuss, illustrate, and encourage you to think about and play with.

Chapter One – Final Thoughts: Editing Purpose and Process

Editing is required of almost every motion media project. Regardless of whether the "job" of the video is to inform, influence, or entertain, the greater or lesser effect of the overall messaging received by the viewing audience hinges upon the solidity and efficacy of the pictorial and aural presentation. Although several agents contribute important elements to the motion media piece, it is the editor who truly constructs the story and manages the final experience for the chosen audience.

Proven pathways in the post-production process exist to aid in this construction of the story. Organization is paramount. Moving the picture and sound assets through these steps helps the editor (and other post-production team members) to realize the precise story they have to tell, no matter how close or far that story may be from the original intentions of the project's initiators. When it all works well together, the editor forms a motion media piece that is a sort of waking dream for the audience. When the elements do not combine well, it can often feel more like a nightmare.

Related Material Found in Chapter Eight – Working Practices

At the end of each chapter in this book, you will find a concluding section like this that lists the numbers for corresponding working practices that are relevant to the chapter that you are just completing. The working practices are discussed and illustrated in Chapter Eight with a practical application in mind for the working filmmaker. You *do not* have to skip forward to read these elaborations now. You may cover them as you get to Chapter Eight or at any point you wish. We simply list these working practices now for your convenience.

#1, 2, 3, 4, 5, 7, 8, 40, 41, 42, 59, 60

Chapter One – Review

1. There are basic and widely accepted guidelines of visual grammar that govern the motion media editing process.

2. The grammar of the edit has evolved over a century of filmmaking, but the basics, covered in this book, have remained largely unchanged.

3. There are many factors that play a role in how a motion picture is edited, and the editor does not always have control over all of them.

4. The basic post-production workflow consists of the following stages: acquisition, organization, review and selection, assembly, rough cut, fine cut, picture lock, finishing, and mastering and delivery.

5. The four basic types of transition edits for picture tracks are cut, dissolve, wipe, and fade.

Chapter One – Exercises

1. Watch any movie, television program, or web video with the sound turned off. Take notes on what you see regarding anything to do with the images, such as how often the image changes and how many different types of images are used to show the program. Are graphics used (such as still photos, titles, or motion graphics)? When are they used and for what purpose, in your opinion?

2. If you can, experience the same movie, show, or video from Exercise 1 a second time, but face away from the images and only listen to the audio. Take notes on what you hear, such as quality of sounds, quantity of sounds, whether there is music, and when. In your opinion, do the sounds you hear support the story or message of the video? If so, how?

3. If you already have an editing project on your computer, open it and observe how you have organized your bins/folders/clips/sequences, etc. If you do not find much organization, figure out what you could do to better group together or arrange your video and audio assets – both on your hard drives and inside your editing project. Have you made a back-up of the original source files?

4. Think about your most recent editing project and map out all of the stages of post-production (as described in this chapter) that you went through. Did you have a different workflow? What might you try differently on your next project? What step(s) did you do that did not get mentioned in our list?

Chapter One – Quiz Yourself

1. In the early days of filmmaking, how did "cutters" physically attach one strip of plastic movie film to another?

2. What are two factors that can contribute to editorial choices that you may have to make?

3. Name the four basic types of transitions that can occur at an edit point on your picture track.

4. Subjective question: do you consider a dissolve between two shots or a fade-to-black/fade-from-black between two shots to be more dramatic? Why? What factors need to be taken into consideration?

5. List four ways that you could organize your video and audio clips in your editing project.

6. If you are in the assembly stage of post-production, what processes might you be executing at that phase of the edit?

7. During which stage of post-production would you color grade the video tracks and attend to the final audio mix?

8. Are there any key differences between the rough cut and the fine cut stages of the editing process? If so, in your opinion, what are they and do you think that they might exist for most projects?

9. Which transition typically uses a moving line or a geometric shape to help to switch from one video clip to the next in the sequence?

10. True or false: keeping each clip in a sequence on screen for the exact same duration is the best way to present most visual material to a modern audience.

Chapter Two
Understanding the Visual Material

- Basic Shot Types Used as Cinematic Language
- Shot Categories: Simple, Complex, and Developing

When you watch a stage play, a music concert, or a sports event in an actual public theater, club, or stadium, you generally only get to observe the actions of the performers from one static viewpoint. If any of these events are recorded and broadcast on television, the person watching at home, although missing out on the thrill of being at the live event, will benefit from having a more "intimate" viewing experience. This is due to the event's coverage by multiple cameras from varying positions and with differing lens **focal lengths**. The person at home "sees" more views and details on the broadcast images than the person at the actual event can see.

It is this same concept of coverage that allows people watching a motion picture to feel as though they are observing actual events unfolding before their eyes. They get to "see" more because the camera records the people, places, and actions from many different vantage points that show varying magnifications of detail. Typically, following the master scene technique, the production team photograph all of the important action from what they consider to be the most advantageous and necessary points of view. Each one of these camera views is called a shot.

These shots, or individual units of visual information, are eventually given to the editor during post-production. Even though the editor had no control over which shots were recorded on the film set or how they were composed, it will be his or her job to review all of the material and choose the best viewpoints and performances – to pull the selects – and to combine these various shots to show the audience the best presentation of the story, whatever it may be.

You may consider the individual shot types to be like a vocabulary of sorts: the visual phrases of our cinematic language. Knowing the "words" and their interpreted meanings will help an editor to construct visual "sentences" that may be more broadly understood by a diverse viewing audience.

The Basic Shot Types

Most editors get involved with a project only during post-production. Although many professional editors may have worked in production on a film set or in a television studio at some point in their careers, it is not that common for them to work both production and post-production jobs. What is common, however, is the need for editors to know certain production concepts and terminologies and be well versed in the visual grammar of film-making. Knowing the basic shot types and how to best juxtapose them during the edit is a key responsibility for the editor. He or she should know how to best show the story with these shots. As a review, we present the following section, which highlights and illustrates the main building blocks of cinematic language – the basic shots:

- the extreme close-up (XCU/ECU)
- the big close-up (BCU) (UK)/"choker" (US)
- the close-up (CU)
- the medium close-up (MCU)/bust shot
- the medium shot (MS)/mid-shot
- the medium long shot (MLS)/medium wide shot (MWS)
- the long shot (LS)/wide shot (WS)
- the very long shot (VLS)/very wide shot (VWS)
- the extreme long shot (XLS/ELS)/extreme wide shot (XWS/EWS)
- the two-shot (2-shot/2S)
- the over-the-shoulder shot (OTS/OSS).

Shot Descriptions

The basic shot types can be used to record subjects or objects of any size. For demonstrative purposes, we are going to focus our examples mainly on the framing of a human subject. Obviously, you will encounter these same shots framing non-human objects or even "empty" **film space** without any human figures present and you will understand them just the same.

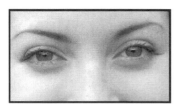

Extreme Close-Up

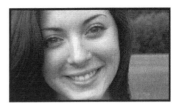

Big Close-Up/Choker

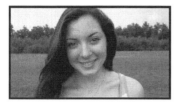

Close-Up

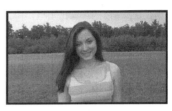

Medium Close-Up

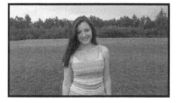

Medium Shot

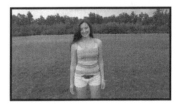

Medium Long Shot

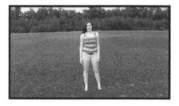

Long/Wide Shot

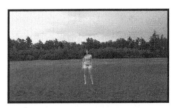

Very Long/Wide Shot

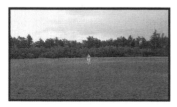

Extreme Long/Wide Shot

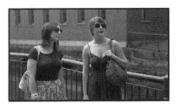

Two-Shot

The Basic Shot Types

FIGURE 2.1   The extended family of basic shot types from our cinematic visual language.

The Extreme Close-Up (XCU/ECU)

1. Purely a detail shot. The framing favors one aspect of a subject such as his or her eyes, mouth, ear, or hand. It may be a magnification of any object or item or just a part of an object or item.

2. Lacking any points of reference to the surrounding environment, the audience have no context in which to place this body part or object detail, so understanding will stem from how or when this shot is edited into the motion picture. It is often helpful, but not required, that the subject whose body detail is displayed in the XCU is shown before or after in a wider shot so that context may be established for the viewer.

3. This type of extremely magnified imagery can be used in documentary work such as medical films or scientific studies, more fanciful projects like music videos and experimental art films, or as appropriate in a fictional narrative story.

4. **Editor's Main Concerns?** Focus – Video clips of objects recorded with this level of magnification may have soft-focus issues due to a very shallow **depth of field** (especially if the subject or camera are in motion). Framing – Such extreme close-ups may suffer from poor framing or difficult-to-decipher imagery of unknown, enlarged subject parts.

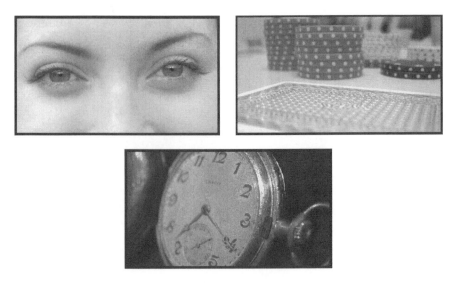

FIGURE 2.2 Examples of extreme close-up (XCU/ECU) shots.

The Big Close-Up (BCU) (UK)/"Choker" (US)

1. The human face occupies as much of the frame as possible and the image still shows the key features of eyes, nose, and mouth at once. The top of the frame is just above the eyebrows and the bottom of the frame is just below the lips.

2. Such an intimate shot puts the audience directly in the face of the subject. Every detail of the face is highly visible, therefore facial movements or expressions need to be subtle. Very little head movement can be tolerated before the subject moves out of the frame.

3. This shot is about who and how that who feels: angry, scared, joyful, etc.

4. **Editor's Main Concerns?** Framing – Beyond the possible issue of the lower lip/ mouth dropping below the bottom edge of the frame when the subject speaks, the entire "concept" of the BCU composition for a human face can be awkward. It is not a common framing in many genres of motion media productions, so make sure that its use has solid purpose in the visual design of your project. Make-up – Almost all performers (fiction or non-fiction) wear some sort of make-up to beautify or enhance their facial features. A shot this close (in UHD) could be ruined by improperly (or excessively) applied make-up.

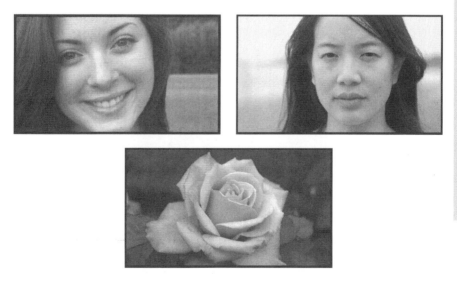

FIGURE 2.3   Examples of big close-up (BCU)/"choker" shots.

The Basic Shot Types

The Close-Up (CU)

1. Sometimes called a "head shot" because the framing is primarily the face, but it may cut off the top of the subject's hair. The bottom of the frame can begin anywhere just below the chin or, more traditionally, with the neck and some upper shoulder visible.

2. A very intimate full-face shot of a human subject showing all detail in the eyes. It conveys the subtle emotions that play across the eyes, mouth, and facial muscles of an actor. Health conditions and facial hair in men and make-up use in women are clearly visible.

3. The audience should be totally focused on the human face. An emotional connection to the on-screen subject can be easily made. A non-human subject will fill the frame, and should be easily identifiable.

4. Shows who but not so much where or when.

5. **Editor's Main Concerns?** Subject's **eye-line** – If using an **objective** shooting style (as for fictional narrative), do the subject's eyes look out of the frame in the correct direction, matching the context of film space in the wider shots of this character? If using a **subjective** shooting style (as for a news reporter or show host), do the subject's eyes look directly into the lens (connecting with the audience) or just awkwardly off the lens axis (not connecting with anything)?

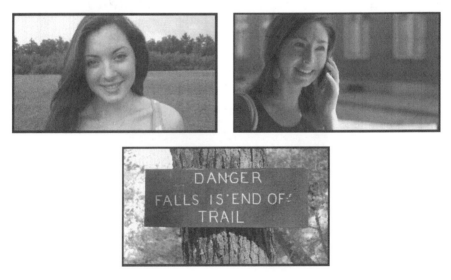

FIGURE 2.4 Examples of close-up (CU) shots.

The Medium Close-Up (MCU)/Bust Shot

1. Sometimes called a "two-button" for the tight bottom frame cutting off at the chest, roughly where you would see the top two buttons on a shirt. Definitely cuts off above the elbow joint. The bottom of the frame may be slightly different for men or women, depending on costuming.

2. The subject's facial features are rather clear. Where the eyes look is obvious, as is emotion, hair style and color, make-up, etc. This is one of the most common shots in filmmaking because it provides much information about the character while speaking, listening, or performing an action that does not involve much body or head movement.

3. The audience are supposed to be watching the human face at this point in the framing, so actions or objects in the surrounding environment should hold little to no importance.

4. Depending upon lighting and costuming, you may discern general information about where and when.

5. **Editor's Main Concerns?** Composition – Is the human figure frame left, frame right, or central? Is **continuity** of **screen direction** being maintained? Does the background compete too much with the subject? Is the depth of field too large?

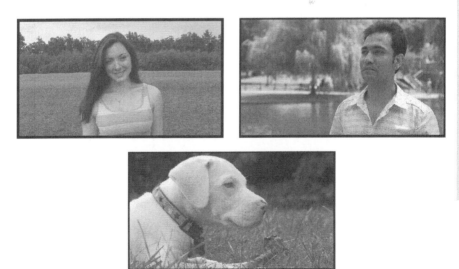

FIGURE 2.5 Examples of medium close-up (MCU) shots.

The Basic Shot Types

The Medium Shot (MS)/Mid-Shot

1. May also be called the "waist shot" because the frame cuts off the human figure near the waist.

2. The human torso is most prominent in the frame. However, the eyes and the direction they look, clothing, and hair color and style are all plainly visible.

3. Beware of the subject **breaking frame** (when an actor's body part touches or moves beyond the established edge of the picture frame).

4. Certainly shows who and also provides generic detail about where (inside or outside, apartment, store, forest, etc.) and when (day or night, season).

5. **Editor's Main Concerns?** Beyond subject movements breaking frame, watch out for matching **headroom** and **look room** (also known as **looking room)** in dialogue coverage shots that need to edit back to back in a scene.

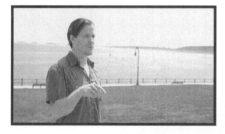
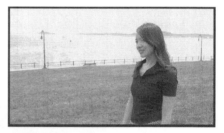
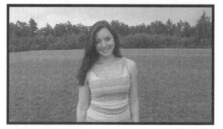
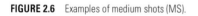

FIGURE 2.6   Examples of medium shots (MS).

The Medium Long Shot (MLS)/Medium Wide Shot (MWS)

1. The first shot where the surrounding environment occupies significantly more screen space than the subject. Traditionally framed such that the bottom of the frame cuts off the leg either just below or, more commonly, just above the knee. The choice of where to frame the leg may depend on costuming or body movement of the individual in the shot. If you cut the bottom of the frame above the knee, it is sometimes referred to as the "cowboy." (In classical Hollywood Westerns, it was important to get the obligatory "six gun" strapped to the hero's thigh in the shot.)

2. The human figure is prominent and details in clothing, gender, and facial expressions are visible. The environment is clearly conveyed and understandable.

3. Shows who, where, and roughly when.

4. **Editor's Main Concerns?** Awkward bottom of frame – Keep an eye on the subject's legs and costuming (especially when the subject is in motion). Is there an aspect of those elements that is distracting? Similarly, is there some sort of "slice" of distracting object hovering just inside the bottom of the frame? It may be possible to scale the image up slightly to remove these from view.

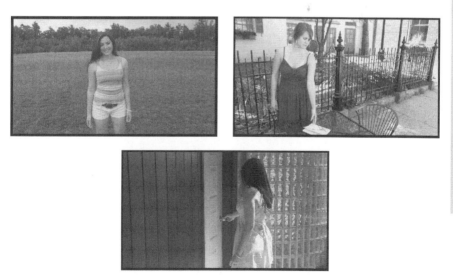

FIGURE 2.7   Examples of medium long shots (MLS).

The Basic Shot Types

The Long Shot (LS)/Wide Shot (WS)

1. This is usually considered a "full body" shot, wide but still in close to the figure. It often frames the feet just above the bottom of the frame and the head just below the top of the frame. It may often be noted as a generic wide shot (WS) as well.

2. The tall vertical line of the standing human figure attracts the viewer's eye away from the surrounding environment; however, a fair amount of the location is visible and should be considered important to the composition.

3. May work well for an **establishing shot** of a smaller **interior** location or a contained **exterior** area like a storefront doorway.

4. Shows where, when, and who. Gender, clothing, movements, and general facial expressions may be seen but real facial detail is somewhat lacking.

5. **Editor's Main Concerns?** Visibility of emotion — With the face being so small in the frame, try not to use the LS for highlighting emotion, unless the overall movements of the subject's body are being used to clearly convey that state.

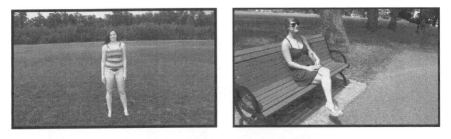

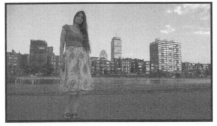

FIGURE 2.8   Examples of long shots (LS).

The Very Long Shot (VLS)/Very Wide Shot (VWS)

1. A proud member of the wide shot family.

2. Easily recorded in exterior locations but may be accomplished in interior shooting places where enough width and height exist within the studio set or location building.

3. The human figure is visible but only generalities of race, mood, clothing, and hair may be observed. The environment within the film space dominates much of the screen.

4. May be used as an establishing shot.

5. Shows where, when, and who (but usually they are too small to see real detail).

6. **Editor's Main Concerns?** Visibility of subject – Does the subject get lost among the background elements in the shot? Does the composition of the frame incorporate enough visual information to be useful to the audience?

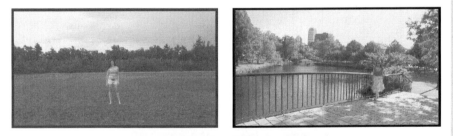

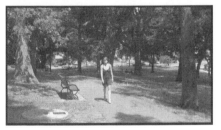

FIGURE 2.9   Examples of very long shots (VLS).

The Basic Shot Types

The Extreme Long Shot (XLS/ELS)/Extreme Wide Shot (XWS/EWS)

1. Also referred to as an extremely wide-angle shot.
2. Traditionally used in exterior shooting.
3. Encompasses a large field of view, and therefore forms an image that shows a large amount of the environment within the film space.
4. Often used as an establishing shot at the beginning of a motion picture or at the start of a new sequence within a motion picture. An XLS may be cut in whenever a very wide vista needs to be shown in the story.
5. Shows where (urban, suburban, rural, mountains, desert, ocean, etc.) and may show when (day, night, summer, winter, spring, fall, distant past, past, present, future, etc).
6. May show a lone stranger walking into town, or a massive invading army. Most often, the human figures in the XLS are so small that details are indistinguishable. General, not specific, information will be conveyed about a character.
7. **Editor's Main Concerns? Horizon line** – If it should be level, is this the case? Unwanted objects – Due to the potentially large number of objects visible in this wide vista of film space, is there an object that should not be present in this shot (a period-piece XLS showing a cell tower, or a billboard for an inappropriate product or business)?

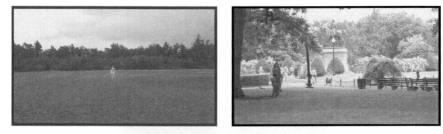

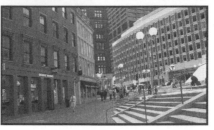

FIGURE 2.10   Examples of extreme long shots (XLS/ELS).

The Two-Shot (2-Shot/2S)

1. Contains two subjects who generally either face toward the camera (but not into the lens) or face each other and are seen in profile or 3/4 profile.

2. The framing depends on whether the subjects are standing or sitting, moving or static, or making gestures and performing actions. A medium two-shot (M2S) is common but allows for little gesturing or body movement. Medium long shot or long shot two-shots will allow more room around the subjects for movement or action.

3. The framing for tighter shots (MCU, CU) would entail extremely close proximity of subjects' heads, implying intimate connectivity or aggressive posturing like two boxers in a clinch. To see the faces of both subjects in a very tight two-shot, you would have to "favor" one body before the other, literally overlapping the people within the frame. The person closest to the camera and seen fully by the viewer is given favor. No overlapping is required if seen in CU two-shot profile, as in a kissing shot, a slow dance, or boxers before a match.

4. Adding persons creates a three-shot (3-shot), a group shot, or a crowd shot, depending on how many individuals are clustered together in the frame. The framing would be wider for the extra people who are added to the composition and the bodies would have to be staggered into the depth of the frame.

5. **Editor's Main Concerns?** Continuity – As we now have two or more persons in the frame, it becomes difficult to always match continuity of action, eye-line, etc. when you cut to other coverage shots of the same people in this scene.

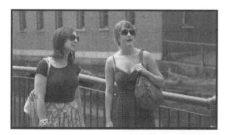 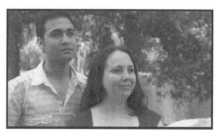

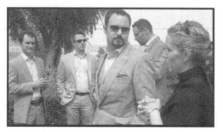

FIGURE 2.11   Examples of the two-shot, the overlapping two-shot, and the group shot.

The Basic Shot Types

The Over-the-Shoulder Shot (OTS/OSS)

1. A special two-shot in which one subject is favored by facing the camera (either frame left or frame right) and the other subject has his or her back turned toward the camera on the opposite side of the frame. The non-favored subject creates an "L" shape at the edge and bottom of the frame with the back of her or his head and shoulder; hence the name. The camera shoots over one subject's shoulder to frame up the face of the other subject for the viewer to see.

2. Due to the "shoulder subject" being partially cut off at the edge of the frame, the shot type used for the OTS shot may be as tight as a medium close-up – or maybe even a full close-up. Anything closer and the composition would alter the balance of the frame and the shoulder may get lost, creating what some may call a **dirty single**.

3. It is often helpful to have a decreased depth of field so that the portion of the shoulder subject visible in the corner of the frame is a bit blurry while the face of the favored subject is well focused. Having a well-focused back of the head may prove to be distracting for the audience. Editing software matte and blur effects can help with this if needed.

4. **Editor's Main Concerns?** Audio – You may need to layer in the audio from a good close-up shot for the subject whose back is to the camera. As his or her mouth is not visible, exact sync is not an issue, but beware of how the head and/or jaw move in conjunction with the differing voice track.

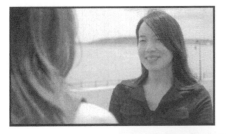
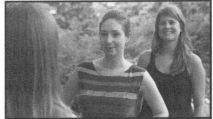
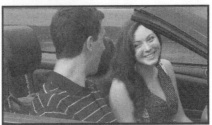

FIGURE 2.12   Examples of over-the-shoulder (OTS) framing.

Shot Categories: The Increasing Complexity of Motion Imagery

It is worth noting that all of the shot types outlined above have one thing in common: they belong to an over-arching shot category that we will call **simple shots**. They could, however, evolve into two other categories: **complex shots** or **developing shots**. Before we clarify what constitutes a simple, complex, or developing shot, we should give just a bit of attention to the four basic physical components of shot creation. How these elements are used helps to determine the category into which a shot may be placed.

1. LENS – Does the camera's lens move during the shot? Does the lens alter its light-gathering characteristics while the shot is being recorded? Lens movement, optical alteration of the angle of view, can only be achieved when using a **zoom lens** (or **varifocal lens**) with a stationary camera. So you have to determine if there is a zoom or a focal length change during the shot (Figure 2.13).

2. CAMERA – Does the entire camera body move during the shot? Essentially, is there a panning action or a tilting action executed while the camera is recording the shot? The camera mount (**tripod head**) would have to allow for these horizontal and vertical axis changes, but the camera support (**tripod**) would not be in motion (Figure 2.14).

3. MOUNT/SUPPORT – Does the camera's mount or support physically move the camera around the film set or location during a shot? In a television studio,

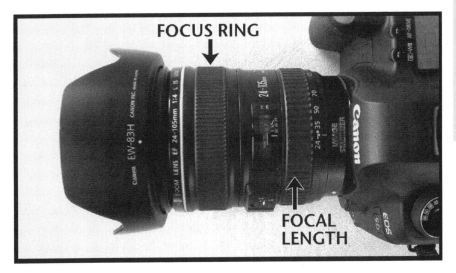

FIGURE 2.13   A camera lens with zoom or varifocal capabilities.

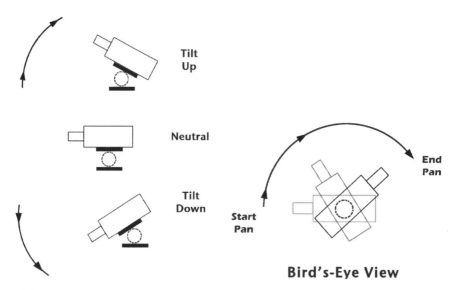

Bird's-Eye View

FIGURE 2.14 A camera mounted to a pan and tilt tripod head.

the camera is mounted atop a **pedestal,** which can boom up (raise camera height) or boom down (lower camera height) and roll around the smooth floor. On a film set, the camera can be mounted to a moving **dolly** on tracks or a **slider** (for **crab** or **truck** moves), attached to a **crane** or **jib arm**, suspended from cables, or carried with a Steadicam™, a drone, etc. (Figure 2.15).

4. SUBJECT – Does the subject being recorded move during the shot? The subject can be a person or many people, an animal, an animated object (something non-living capable of movement, like a remote-controlled toy car), or an inanimate object (something that does not move, like a brick or a pirate's treasure chest) (Figure 2.16).

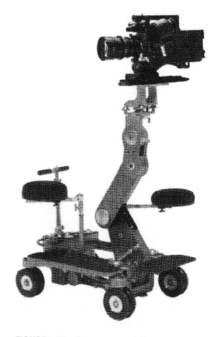

FIGURE 2.15 A camera on a dolly.

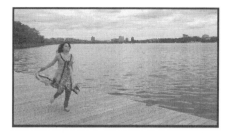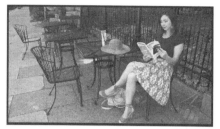

FIGURE 2.16   Subjects in motion and at rest.

Because you, as the editor, were not on set during production, you will not definitively know which shots contain these four elements. Most often, their presence or lack thereof will be noticeable to some degree because they all involve movement of some kind. What you should understand, though, are the basic categories that shots will fall into when one or several of the four elements are present. These three basic categories are simple shots, complex shots, and developing shots. Describing these over-arching shot categories now will help us in our analysis of editing them together – a topic we cover later in this book.

Simple Shots

- No lens movement   ✗
- No camera movement   ✗
- Mount movement   ✗
- Simple subject movement   ✓

Simple shots are just that: simple. They have no focal length changes (zooms). They have no **tilts** or **pans**. They show no camera body movement, as with a dolly or a jib. They do show the subject moving in simple ways across the screen, standing, sitting, speaking, gesticulating, etc. The basic shot types, discussed earlier, are all covered from a particular angle, with a set focal length on the lens and a **locked-off** mount. Whatever simple action unfolds before the camera, it happens within that set and finite framing. Often, simple shots can make up the bulk of fictional narrative motion picture content that is dialogue driven. Talking-head interviews for documentaries or news anchor MCU shots may be considered non-fiction simple shots (Figure 2.17).

Shot Categories: The Increasing Complexity of Motion Imagery

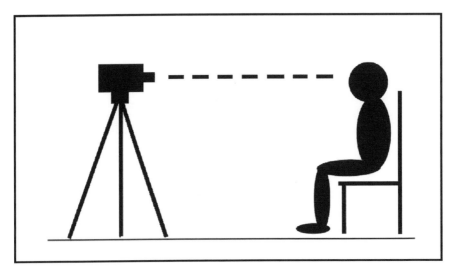

FIGURE 2.17 A simple shot has no lens, no camera, and no mounting or support movement but may have subject movement.

Complex Shots

- Lens movement   ✓
- Camera movement   ✓
- Mount movement   ✗
- Simple subject movement   ✓

A complex shot may contain:

- a pan (horizontal)
- a tilt (vertical)
- a pan and a tilt (diagonal upward or downward camera lens movement)
- lens movement (a zoom or a focus pull)
- lens movement and a pan (hiding a zoom by panning the camera)
- lens movement and a tilt (hiding a zoom by tilting the camera)
- subject movement and a pan to follow action
- subject movement and a tilt to follow action.

If a shot contains any combination of the three active elements (lens movement, camera movement, or simple subject movement), then it may be considered a complex shot.

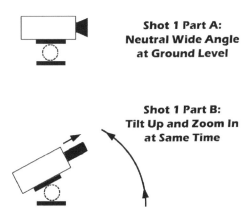

Shot 1 Part A:
Neutral Wide Angle
at Ground Level

Shot 1 Part B:
Tilt Up and Zoom In
at Same Time

FIGURE 2.18   A complex shot may combine a zoom with a camera tilt in order to follow subject movement.

If the complex shot does contain a pan or a tilt, then the production team should have ensured that it begins with a static start frame, goes through its move, and completes with a static end frame. The static start and end frames of these pan and tilt shots are very important to the editor. You will find that it may be difficult to cut from a static shot into a shot already in motion, or to cut out of a motion shot to a static shot. Entering or leaving movement at the cut can be very jarring for the audience. The best-case scenario is for you to be presented with pan and tilt shots that start and end with static frames and contain smooth, even movement in between. With complex shots containing subject and/or camera movement, it may be challenging to match continuity of action at the edit points (Figure 2.18).

Developing Shots

- Lens movement   ✓
- Camera movement   ✓
- Mount movement   ✓
- More complex subject movement   ✓

A developing shot incorporates movement of all four elements. As such, you can imagine that these shots are rather difficult to accomplish. Subjects may move in complicated blocking patterns on set, the camera is moved about following action (perhaps hand-held, on a dolly, a Steadicam™, or a drone, etc.), the lens may be re-focused or perhaps zoomed, and there will be a panning or tilting action at some point to maintain good composition.

Shot Categories: The Increasing Complexity of Motion Imagery

As an editor, you should watch these developing shots very carefully for quality assurance. They will most likely start and end with static frames, but the middle portion could be a hodgepodge of actions. Watch for proper focus, good framing, and smooth movements. These types of elaborate developing shots are designed by the filmmakers to be used as one stunning show piece, so there is often little actual editing that you may need to do beyond cutting the shot into the overall scene at the appropriate point. Cutting into and out of moving developing shots can upset the flow of the entire shot and take away from its effect on the viewing audience. This may be necessary for creative purposes, or if some of the action within the developing shot is not top quality – or if there is a lot of good coverage available to show a very dynamic action sequence.

A specific example of a developing shot is known as the "*Vertigo* shot." Alfred Hitchcock incorporated this type of in-camera visual effects shot in the 1958 Paramount Pictures release *Vertigo*. The camera either dollies toward a subject while simultaneously zooming wider or dollies away from the subject while zooming in. The goal is to keep the "foreground" object (the subject) the same size in the frame throughout the move. The result is a warping of perspective/magnification on the visible background elements in the shot. The audience are made to feel uneasy because of this unnatural visual trick. It is often used in filmmaking to indicate a disquieting, imbalanced, or freaky feeling for that character or within the narrative at that moment. This shot is sometimes called a "zolly" or a "dolly zoom."

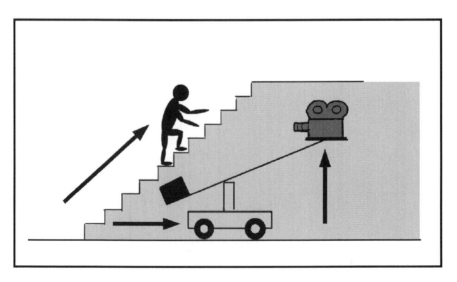

FIGURE 2.19 A developing shot follows complex subject action with lens, camera, and camera mount movements.

Keep in mind that the category names (simple, complex, and developing) are not the significant element here. The take-away for you should be the thought processes involved in analyzing the treatment of shot content that they denote. Watch shots for any sort of focal length changes, camera head movements (like pans and tilts), and subject movements. Additionally, you may also find shots where all of these aspects of the shot coverage and content exist plus there is major camera body movement (via support device movement) inside the one shot. These basic shot categories relate to the production team's chosen visual style(s) and will influence how you choose to work within (or around) both their treatments of the individual shot content and the overall visual style of the entire program.

Chapter Two – Final Thoughts: Camera Shots Are Your Building Blocks

When editors sit down in their chairs to begin work on a project, they usually do not know what the material that they are being tasked with editing will look like. Reviewing the video and audio assets is an important early step in the post-production process. Understanding the visual language of the basic shot types and being able to quickly categorize the shot style(s) of the director or director of photography will start the creative wheels turning in the mind of the editor. She or he can already begin pre-envisioning how the assembled piece might look. Figuring out how it all might sound is another thing all together, and we cover the types of audio files an editor may encounter in the next chapter. Then, in Chapter Four, after you've become comfortable with the visual and aural assets you will eventually have to work with, we present some criteria that may help you to assess all of this material and choose the best shots for the assembly.

Related Material Found in Chapter Eight – Working Practices

#14, 15, 16, 17, 18, 19, 20, 25, 26, 27, 28, 29, 30, 31, 33

Chapter Two – Final Thoughts: Camera Shots Are Your Building Blocks

Chapter Two – Review

1. An editor may show the actions of a scene unfold in different ways when presented with a good variety of coverage shots. If the editor lacks diverse or usable source material, his or her choices are greatly reduced.

2. The basic shot types are the extreme close-up, big close-up/choker, close-up, medium close-up/bust shot, medium shot/mid-shot, medium long shot/medium wide shot, long shot/wide shot, very long shot/very wide shot, extreme long shot/extreme wide shot, two-shot, and over-the-shoulder shot.

3. Simple shots are static shots with only slight subject movement.

4. Complex shots will contain a zooming focal length change and/or a pan/tilt action.

5. Developing shots have subject movement, lens movement, camera movement, and mount movement all within the single take of action coverage.

Chapter Two – Exercises

1. Watch your favorite movie or TV show and take note of how many CU, MS, LS, OTS shots, and two-shots occur. Which shot type is used more? At what points in the show do they get used? Do you notice a big difference in shot selection between theatrically released "big-screen" movies and "small-screen" TV or streaming media programming? How about among the different genres of shows you may watch?

2. Develop a very brief scene between two people having a dialogue in any location you wish. (You may use the short script in Appendix C if you wish.) Plan the coverage shots for three separate versions: one with simple shots, one with complex shots, and one with developing shots. Edit the footage from each shoot separately. Which cuts together best and why? After comparing each separate sequence, take all of the footage from all three shoots and cut a new combined sequence. Do you find it easier to edit a sequence with all three shot categories represented? Yes or no, and why?

Chapter Two – Quiz Yourself

1. Name as many of the basic shot types as you can remember.

2. When and why might you add an extreme long shot to your edited sequence?

3. What information can a close-up convey to the audience?

4. How might an extreme close-up provide important detailed information to the viewing audience, and in what ways (editorially speaking) might it keep information from then?

5. How can a dialogue scene two-shot possibly cause continuity of performance and continuity of action concerns for an editor?

6. Why would the American version of the MLS be called a "cowboy?"

7. Subjective question: what might the audience "feel" when a big close-up or choker of the film's villain is shown on the screen?

8. Can a drone's hovering camera be used to record a simple shot?

9. How does a "zolly" shot affect the audience and in what possible scenarios might it be used in a motion media piece?

10. Can you have a panning and tilting camera lens movement in a developing shot?

Chapter Three
Understanding the Audio Material

- Production Audio Sources
- Post-Production Audio Sources
- Audio Terms that You May Encounter

Sound

The creative use of sound, in any motion media production, is extremely important. Auditory stimuli easily affect humans on physiological, psychological, and emotional levels. Filmmakers and video producers have known this to be true for quite some time. "Silent" films were never intended to be silent. It was only technological limitations which kept the film projections mute. Whether it was a single piano or a large orchestra, music was arranged to accompany the screenings. This was done to ensure an aural component to the experience. The ability to manipulate the audience in additional sensory pathways grew in importance and has really exploded in today's cinema. Entire books are written on the subject of sound editing in movies, television programs, commercials, and web videos. Major awards are even presented to people who do it well. The following topics will provide a brief introduction to sound-editing terms, techniques, and practices in order to get you started on your way.

To begin with, how you use sound while editing a video depends on the type of motion media production it is, its genre, its content, its purpose, the quality of the sound assets, how it will ultimately be shown to the audience, etc. Suffice it to say that there are many, many factors that can lead to many different kinds of decisions about how an editor handles audio. One aspect that should be upheld across almost all types of video editing, however, is that special care should be given to the building and mixing of the sound tracks. This is true of very simplistic music videos with only two tracks, all of the way up to blockbuster action movies with 62 tracks or more.

Although an ambitious, resourceful, or experimental film production may draw from over 100 years' worth of archived sound recordings in various media (which have differing sound reproduction technologies associated with them), most will keep to the standard types of sound sources made available today: digital media files.

The following sections will help us to answer the question: what types of audio sources might an editor encounter during post-production?

Sounds Gathered During Production

No matter the motion media piece being produced, there are, typically, sound elements that get recorded. The camera department personnel work on getting the most usable moving pictures and the sound department personnel work on recording the most usable audio. The following categories represent the major types of sounds gathered during the production phase of filmmaking.

Dialogue

Dialogue encompasses what the on-screen talent says out loud (often based on scripted lines) – and is seen and recorded doing so by the cameras and microphones. Generically applied, dialogue can also refer to any intelligible vocal sounds made by persons seen uttering those sounds. A **monologue** may be a very long, typically uninterrupted speech made by a character in a fictional narrative film, but it may also refer to a lone host addressing the camera in non-fiction programming (such as in a game show, cooking show, talk show, etc.).

Room Tone/Natural Sound (NATS)/Ambience

Although there are differences of opinion around which term applies to which description, these three terms basically refer to a recording that captures the "sound" of the environment where video was recorded. Every place where the production team record picture and sound assets has its own unique "soundscape" that exists in the background – pretty much always there, but not necessarily noted on the conscious level by any listener. A city street, a business office, a hospital emergency room, a farmer's field, the cabin of a lobster boat: all of these locations have a relatively constant "buzz" of sounds going on within and around them all of the time. Dialogue happens over them and despite them. In controlled environments (especially with narrative filmmaking) when a crowd scene is recorded, the crowd are typically silent in the background and only instructed to make sounds (often called "walla") when asked to do so by the production team.

Room tone is traditionally done as a special recording of the filming environment immediately after the scene or interview has completed, but before any of the talent or crew leave the location. Everything is left just as it was (film lights on, windows closed, and, with inexpensive digital video cameras, the camera also running) and the **sound record-ist** (or **sound mixer**) voice slates and records at least 30 seconds of the room's tone while everyone holds the work and no one speaks.

Room tone, **natural sound** (**NATS**), and **ambience** audio clips can be used during the edit to even out the background sounds of dialogue tracks recorded in those spaces but at different times during different takes. If additional talent voice looping (also known as ADR – see later in this section) is required for the program, then these clean, studio-recorded audio tracks can be mixed with the original tone or ambience of the locations and edited in as though they were recorded on set with the other actual dialogue clips.

Wild Sounds

Although not part of the synchronous sound created while video cameras and digital audio recorders are rolling simultaneously on set during production, wild sounds are, typically, the responsibility of the sound department. A sound mixer (and maybe the **boom operator**) will go around the location where the scenes, interviews, or **B-roll** were visually recorded and capture the audio of specific *things*. He or she can record the sound of the sliding doors at a storefront, a particular refrigeration unit, the beeping of a cross-walk signal, birds in the trees, etc. These types of sounds fall between ambience and spot sound effects and can be used during the edit to help to fill in the sound bed and enhance the "reality" of the location seen on screen.

Soundtracks (Musical)

Usually thought of as music elements placed into the audio tracks during post-production, if the movie or real-life event being recorded has an actual music performance (a concert, an art gallery opening with musical performance, a live band at a bar, etc.), then these are part of the production video and audio as well. They are sometimes called "source music." They can be edited straight into the sequence's audio tracks as diegetic sounds or as an element in the non-fiction program's audio bed.

Sounds Gathered During Post-Production

Descriptors like "full," "rich," "engrossing," and "powerful" are often applied to a film's well-populated and well-mixed sound tracks. As the editing of the motion media piece is happening, the editor (or a variety of specially skilled **sound designers** and editors) gathers together additional audio files that will help to enhance the overall sound experience of the viewing audience. The following list typifies many of the kinds of sounds that are found or made up during the post-production process itself. They serve to augment (and sometimes replace) those audio elements recorded during production and generate a new "reality" for the motion picture story.

Narration/Voice-Over

Often, non-fiction (and occasionally fiction) programs require a voice-only track. These lines of monologue are typically recorded in a sound booth or other quiet, controlled studio environment with very good microphones. The narration is usually scripted and is written by the producers, et al. after the rough cut of the show is edited together – filling holes in the story, providing data dumps or time jump explanations required for program clarity and flow.

Automated Dialogue Replacement (ADR)/Looping

There are times when the recordings of production audio of the talent's dialogue may be of poor quality or otherwise unacceptable. In these cases, it can be very beneficial to have the talent return to the studio and re-record fresh, clear, or differently intoned lines of dialogue. These new audio clips are then hand synced into the sequence taking the place of the discarded production tracks. The clean audio from automated dialgue replacement (ADR) is mixed over the ambience or room tone in order to make the new material match with the soundscape of the overall scene.

Ambience/Tonal Tracks

These audio tracks may be lifted from the production audio of background ambience or room tone, but there are entire collections of pre-created ambience audio files available in libraries. Ambience does not have to sound exactly like an airport or a high school gymnasium during a basketball game. It can sound more like a general mood-setting track. Tonal tracks fall into this category. An eerie cave where the evil monster might be dwelling may not have a specific ambience, but it can have a deep, bassy, and echoey tonal quality to it (almost musical but not quite). These tracks are less about lending "reality" to a filmed location and more about generating an emotional and psychological response within the audience. These tones can elicit visceral reactions and have profound effects when mixed into horror and sci-fi films and some video game audio tracks as well.

Sound Effects (SFX)/Spot Effects

Typically, a sound effect is added to the sound mix to enhance the reality of the sound that a filmed object is supposedly making. Often, the microphones on a set are placed to just record very clean, clear, and present talent voice performance. Although certain actions and interactions with other objects may be occurring, the sound just does not get picked up by the mics very well. Sound effects are selected and hand synced into the sequence by the editor or sound editor.

There can be a lot of creativity involved with sound gathering and sound effects editing. Although numerous collections of sound effects exist online (and on CDs, if you remember what those are), it can be fun to customize your own. A doorknob turning can sound like a doorknob turning, but what does a magical wand that pulses out fireballs sound like? Combining known sounds with other, unrelated sounds can generate new sounds that conjure the feeling or essence of these oftentimes fictional things that make noises in our films. Non-fiction programming (especially for kids' shows or more fanciful, lighter fare) will employ sound effects like "swooshes," "boings," and other sounds that are not meant to sound "real" but are there to augment the audio tracks and generate a playful, fun mood.

Foley Effects

A particular kind of spot effect is the Foley effect, named after the Hollywood film legend Jack Foley, who popularized the technique. Special performers, Foley artists, precisely reproduce the movements of actors (with props and sound-making gizmos, etc.) while they watch the movie projected on a screen in a special sound-recording studio. Footsteps, leather jacket creaks, fabric rustling during a tussle, and brushing crumbs off a tablecloth can all be reproduced by these artists with the aid of numerous and often strange implements. These carefully performed and recorded sounds are hand synced into the sequence where the associated, on-screen physical actions occur in the narrative.

Soundtracks (Music)

Similar to the same item listed above, these audio files are typically popular music tracks of well-known songs that play in the movie or show. These songs customarily only appear for a brief period in the motion picture (a fraction of their full three minutes-plus duration), but will be heard fully, as a collection of songs and music, on the movie soundtrack sold separately online and in shops.

Sounds Gathered During Post-Production

Stings/Stingers

Stings (or stingers) are very short pieces of music, often only a few seconds in length, that are placed in the mix to draw attention to certain dramatic, shocking, or comic moments. These are mostly used in television programming and have become a bit of a cliché or an inside joke to some media producers. Stings are also often found at the end of scenes or acts and signal the coming transition to commercials or new material (sometimes called a "bumper").

Score

A score is original music composed specifically for the program being edited. Computer technologies and music production apps have allowed amateur musicians and composers the opportunity to score their own short web videos. Iconic motion picture scores (typically orchestral) conjure up vivid memories of our favorite scenes in so many movies. Humans are quickly moved along emotionally charged levels of story interaction by the use of music that fits the tone of the scenes. Epic battles, tense action, and romantic engagements are enhanced and enlivened by the sweeping strings, blaring horns, or resonating kettledrums. Customized scores are an excellent way to engage and manipulate the audience's emotions and imagination.

Audio Terms that You May Encounter

Sync Sound

This refers to synchronous sound sources: audio information, typically recorded on set during production, that can be attributed to some source in the visible, on-screen environment.

The term "sync" (short for "synchronized" or "synchronous") has been used in filmmaking for a very long time. It usually refers to the synchronization between the picture track of the film and the sound track(s). If there is a mismatch in the sync, then the actor's mouth moves to say words but the words are not heard on the audio track at the same time. They are out of sync. Achieving and maintaining sync is a very important aspect of editing film and video.

Emulsion film motion pictures are shot with a camera that only captures the pictures on a strip of light-sensitive flexible plastic. A separate device is required to record the audio (now chiefly on digital recorders). This process is sometimes called **dual-system recording**. These separate elements of picture and sound are eventually captured onto the computer and "married" together or "synched up" for the editing process. That is why we use the **slate** clapsticks to mark the sync point for the film image and the audio recording at the beginning of each take (head slate) – or, occasionally, at the end of a video clip after the main action has been recorded, as in a documentary or news event (tail slate) (Figure 3.1). Although video cameras have the capacity to capture both the picture and audio data into media files (or on tape), many video-originated productions choose to record dual system as well – for quality control over all production audio elements and for keeping camera and sound departments unencumbered by crossing responsibilities.

It should be noted that productions sometimes record motion imagery with no additional sound recording. The video camera will still capture the head slate information, but the camera assistant or "clapper" does not actually close the slate's clapsticks. In fact, three fingers are placed between the slate sticks (kind of looking like an "M") so that an editor can tell from the beginning that no corresponding audio track for this scene and take number was recorded. The shorthand reference for this kind of video-only clip is **MOS**. This acronym has many possible (and debated) origins and meanings, but the film industry unanimously uses it to mean a shot recorded without sync sound. (See our Glossary to learn more about MOS.)

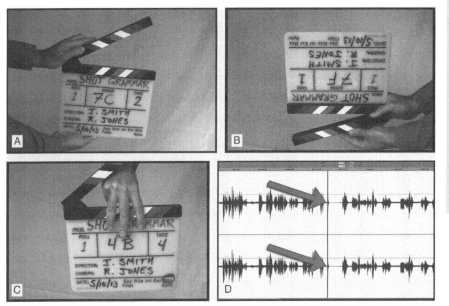

FIGURE 3.1 A slate is used primarily during motion media production when two separate devices record picture and sound information. A – a traditional head slate; B – a tail slate; C – an MOS head slate (where audio is not recorded); D – audio waveform "spike" showing where slate sticks clap together.

Audio Terms that You May Encounter

Once all of the dual-system files are on the editing computer, the editor or assistant will have to sync them. There will be one frame of video that shows the clapsticks fully closed (making contact) and there will be one "frame" of audio that has the sound of those sticks closing. The editor matches the picture "clap" frame with the audio "clap" frame and joins the clips together (sometimes forming a new reference master clip that contains the picture and all sync sound tracks). From that point forward, the sync picture/sound master clip can be edited, together, anywhere in the timeline.

Unfortunately for the editor, there are occasions when the production team either forget to head slate a take, frame the shot poorly and do not record the two sides of the "sticks" actually closing, or feel that slating is an unnecessary waste of time (which it never is) and do not do it all. If no clap slate has been used, then the editor must search through the video source clip for a unique "event" that shows something happening (like a hand clap, sneeze, door slam, etc.) and then listen to the corresponding audio clip to hear that same something. This picture/sound event will become the sync point for these media files. If no such picture/sound event is present in the video source clip, then the editor must hand sync the audio tracks to the picture track – a very time-consuming and rarely precisely effective method of syncing up production material.

Although video cameras do record both picture and sound tracks, these elements are captured into your editing computer as separate media files. These media files have references to one another and remain in sync for playback and editing. The software usually unites them by their **timecode** associations, but it is still your responsibility to keep them in sync while you edit. Depending on your software settings, trimming only one side of an edit with the video track selected but not its corresponding audio tracks will cause this loss of sync. The mismatch becomes the exact number of frames that you remove from or add to the video but do not also simultaneously remove from or add to the audio. You've changed time for one element but not both. To fix a sync shift like this, that exact number of frames could be removed from or added to the audio tracks only at that cut point in your sequence. Depending on your editing software, this exact number of "out-of-sync" frames may be noted in the timeline around the clips that have lost sync.

It should be noted, that just like with blurry images, audiences very much dislike out-of-sync videos. As the editor, it will be in your best interest to ensure proper sync for all audio elements in your edited program.

Diegetic Sounds

Sometimes referred to as "actual" or "literal" sounds, **diegetic** sounds are generated by persons, objects, or environments that exist within the world depicted in the story. The word is derived from the Greek word "diegesis," which means "narration" or a "recited story." Sound generators (anything that makes or causes sounds to occur) that live within the "reality" of the film space create diegetic sound. Whether these things are seen on screen or exist off screen does not matter because they are still within the diegesis or story world.

This does not mean, however, that the actual sound of the said persons, objects, or environments comes directly from production audio sources (such as ambience or wild sound tracks). Any applicable source may be placed on the audio track to fill in for the "real" sound of these sound generators. As such, it is important to give these sounds the tone quality, presence, and perspective that match the size, number, and proximity of the items that are supposed to be generating these sounds – in order to establish a relatable "reality" within the audience's experience.

From our list, thus far, sources such as dialogue, soundtrack (music from within the recorded experience), natural sound, and Foley sound effects may be considered diegetic.

Non-Diegetic Sounds

Also called "non-literal" or "commentary" sounds, **non-diegetic** sounds are sounds placed in your sequence's audio tracks that cannot be attributed to any source found as an element within the film's "reality." In other words, nothing in the film space is causing these sounds to occur, and no one in the film space can hear them. Non-diegetic sounds are typically used for dramatic purposes and are designed to emotionally and psychologically manipulate the audience.

Musical score/orchestration, soundtrack music (not emanating from a source in the film world), certain ambience and tonal tracks, and certain "non-realistic" sound effects may fall into the non-diegetic category. Voice-over narration is also sometimes placed within this grouping depending on whose thoughts are being voiced and what narrative technique is being used.

Audio Terms that You May Encounter

Sound Design

Every motion media piece should have some significant level of attention paid to the audio tracks that play back with the images. A 15-second web video or a three-hour epic motion picture can both benefit from having richly layered, genre-appropriate, "reality"-enhancing, emotion-inducing audio clips in their sequences. Sound design is employed in both fiction and non-fiction filmmaking and television programming.

Sound design is often associated with narrative film post-production, where a sound designer or a sound effects editor gather sounds together and through creative combinations, filtering and mixing, generate sounds that enhance the "reality" of the images and actions on screen. These augmented sounds can also reflect the thoughts and emotions being experienced by the characters and therefore allow for the audience to more deeply relate to the story. Spot effects, Foley effects, ambience, tonal tracks, etc. are all elements that combine together to form the auditory experience.

Sound Motifs

A sound motif is a musical "sting" or particular sound effect that is purposely associated with a particular character, object, or environment. Its use and reoccurrence in a single film or across a series of videos will signal (to the audience) the presence of that entity or location. It may be considered part of the sound design for the show. An obvious example is the breathy, echoey "Ja-ay-son Ah-ah-ah" announcing the arrival of Jason in the *Friday the 13th* franchise.

Chapter Three – Final Thoughts: Sound as Emotional and Physiological Manipulation

Picture and sound tracks work together to create a multi-sensory, motion media experience for the audience. Neglecting either could cause a disconnect. Sound, because it can be felt as well as heard, is a fantastic tool for manipulating the emotions of the viewer and can add to the visceral "reality" of very unreal cinematic content (think of the "thump" you feel in your chest when the T-rex stomps on the ground). Scores and popular song soundtracks can act as sense-memory stimulators and elicit genuine feelings like fright, sadness, and happiness. Do not underestimate the significance that richly layered audio tracks can have in your edited motion media pieces.

Related Material Found in Chapter Eight – Working Practices

#3, 22, 38, 39, 40, 45, 46, 47, 48, 49, 50, 51, 52, 53, 54, 55

Chapter Three – Review

1. Most audio files used today in post-production are digital computer files. Although a century of other sound sources may be accessed, these need to be digitized in order to use them in a computer-based video- or audio-editing application.

2. Dialogue is essentially a generic term for any lines from a script spoken by a performer who appears on screen. A monologue is any lengthy chunk of spoken words coming from one subject where no other subject contributes.

3. Natural sound is the actual sound of the location where video footage is recorded. Room tone is specifically recorded for use in mixing a scene's dialogue tracks.

4. Wild sounds are non-synchronous sounds recorded by the production audio team either on set or around the location where principal photography occurs. These may be layered into the audio mix to help to create the scene's "reality."

5. Soundtracks or source music are typically songs or music played at an actual event by an actual group of musicians.

6. Narration or voice-over is typically recorded cleanly in a controlled audio studio environment during post-production.

7. Automated dialogue replacement (ADR) or looping is done during post-production when the production sync-sound source tracks are compromised or a change in dialogue is needed. The actor listens to the previous performance and repeats the new, clean lines of dialogue in a controlled audio studio environment.

8. Ambience or tonal tracks are constructed sounds of spaces or semi-musical tones that play out under a scene to add to its emotional power.

9. Sound effects or spot effects are non-sync sounds (often taken from a sound library) that are layered into a sequence's audio tracks to augment the "reality" of spaces, objects, and actions (both seen and unseen) within the film world.

10. Foley effects are generated and recorded by artists who perform particular actions in a special recording studio as the movie plays for them on a screen. These performers re-enact the movements of actors and make the sounds that the production microphones could not pick up.

11. Soundtracks in post-production are excerpts from popular songs that get edited into a sequence to help to move it along and sometimes to help to get the feeling of the scene across to the audience in a familiar way.

12. Stings (or stingers) are very short musical or tonal audio pieces (just a few seconds) that signify scene ends or stress a particular action or dramatic moment.

13. Scores are original (often orchestral) music pieces composed specifically for that unique motion media piece. The pace of the music quickens and slows to match the actions seen up on the screen, emotionally connecting the audience with the show.

14. Synchronous sound or dual-system recording is used to keep the picture separate from the carefully recorded audio elements of a production. Editors must maintain sync during post-production so that mouths move in time with the words heard on the audio tracks.

15. Diegetic sounds come from elements within the film space.

16. Non-diegetic sounds are not supposed to be made by physical elements in the film space and they cannot be heard by occupants of that world.

17. Sound design is the process of gathering, creating, mixing, and editing sounds together to help to generate a sense of "reality" for the particular soundscape of a motion media piece.

18. Sound motifs can be creatively used in the audio mix to signify particular characters or events, "tipping off" the audience that someone is about to appear or something is about to happen.

Chapter Three – Exercises

1. Using a digital audio recorder (of decent quality if you have access; otherwise, the one built into your phone will be good enough), find at least five distinct locations and record the ambience/room tone of those spaces. (A mix of interiors and exteriors will be best, and be sure to voice slate the beginning of each recording so you know the place, date, and time.) Open the files in your preferred video- or audio-editing application and listen to each space. Note anything that seems interesting or useful and also listen for anything that might pose a problem. Headphones will help with this.

2. Using the files recorded in Exercise 1, boost the audio levels (gain control) on each ambience clip and listen to what that decibel level change does to the overall "background" sound.

3. Record a quick scene of a friend or family member doing a common, daily activity. Edit these simple shots together and augment or enhance the audio of each action by layering in and mixing appropriately some selected sound effects (or Foley effects you make yourself). Sound effects libraries may be available from actual lending libraries at your school or in your city, there are some free sources online, and there are some purchasable downloads as well. Your editing application may actually have some sound effects libraries pre-installed. To keep this interesting, make at least two versions of this mini-sequence: one that sounds "realistic" and one that sounds "over the top."

4. Record your own or acquire a short dialogue scene from a friend, etc. and edit the sequence together using the different kinds of audio files that are mentioned in this chapter.

Chapter Three – Quiz Yourself

1. In what ways can a performer's delivery of dialogue affect the audience?

2. Why would an audio recordist wish to record wild sounds at a large factory where video B-roll for a documentary is being shot?

3. Why is it helpful to keep all performers, crew, and machines running when the room tone is recorded for a particular location?

4. Why might narration for a non-fiction cable show about car restoration be scripted and recorded when the editing process is almost finished?

5. A scene from a fictional narrative film took place at an active bus station and all of the dialogue audio was heavily corrupted by excessive background noises. What might the post-production audio team be able to do to help to fix this problem?

6. How is sound considered a multi-sensory influence on the viewing audience's film experience in the large theaters?

7. Why should a Foley artist recreate the footsteps of a character running down a school hallway when an editor could hand cut each step individually from a sound effects library clip?

8. What purpose does the clap slate serve during post-production?

9. True or false: all video-editing software applications always keep the video clip data and the audio clip data "married" together (in sync) in the sequence, and the editor has no option to ever split them apart for creative purposes.

10. What is it called when a recurring character or action in a show or movie receives a special audio treatment that only occurs within the sound tracks when that character is about to appear or that event is about to happen?

Chapter Four
Assessing the Footage: Selecting the Best Shots for the Job

- Criteria for Shot Assessment
- Selecting the Best Shots

You should feel comfortable now identifying the various types of shots and sounds that may be used to create a motion media production. With these committed to memory, it will be that much easier to organize them when you acquire and review the material to be edited. Be forewarned, however, that not every shot type may be used to generate coverage for a particular scene. For example, it may not make much sense to look for an XLS in footage from a dialogue scene shot in an airplane cockpit – unless the production team provide you with an establishing shot of the plane in the sky or a POV shot from the cockpit down to the ground level.

Once you have the material organized, it will be helpful to review each shot for its technical and aesthetic qualities. Certain criteria work for some motion picture genres, but not all movies, shows, commercials, or music videos can be held up to one master checklist of good or bad visual and auditory aspects. What might never be allowed as acceptable in one program type may be entirely encouraged in another. So, as an editor, you will have to make your own judgment calls depending on the type of project you are editing and what the end goals of that project are set to be.

Criteria for Shot Assessment

Beyond judging whether your shots fall into the categories of simple, complex, and developing, you should be assessing them for their quality. The listing that follows, although certainly not exhaustive, should provide plenty of criteria upon which you might base an analysis of the material you will be editing. Again, the type of video you are editing will often come with its own style, traditions, and sense of what is acceptable and what is not, but you should at least be aware of these potential "gotchas."

- Focus
- Framing and Composition
- Exposure and Color Balance
- Screen Direction
- The 180-Degree Rule/Axis of Action
- The 30-Degree Rule

- Matching Angles
- Matching Eye-Line
- Continuity of Action
- Performance
- Continuity of Dialogue/Spoken Words
- Audio Quality

Focus

One of the chief issues that you may encounter as an editor is incorrect focus during a shot. Nothing can ruin a good performance like bad focus. It is the camera department's job to ensure good focus on shots, and, for the most part, they will. However, it only takes one false move or late start with the focus pull to turn a potentially good take into a bad one. With scripted fictional narrative filmmaking, the production team will often shoot multiple takes of a line reading or an action to ensure that they have the focus correct, so you should not have to worry too much with that kind of material. Unscripted projects, such as documentaries, corporate interview videos, or live news, often only allow one chance at good focus while the action happens in front of the camera. A soft-focus talking-head interview could render that entire interview unusable.

Why is soft-focus or blurry imagery so bad? It is the one technical factor in film or video that cannot be corrected during post-production. Unlike exposure, color balance, or even minor compositional framing changes, there is no fix for soft-focus footage. It becomes a problem because the viewing audience are intolerant of blurry images. As humans, our visual system is set to always see things in sharp focus (unless, of course, you require glasses or other corrective lenses to properly focus the light in your eyes). When we watch a moving image that has soft focus, we become distracted and uncomfortable as our eyes try to focus on the image that cannot resolve. It is unnatural for us to see things as being blurry.

When a filmmaker purposefully causes things to go blurry in a shot, it should have a thematic meaning or direct narrative connection. There usually is a subjective motivation for the blur (the POV of a drugged or injured character, for instance). If this does happen, placing some object within the frame in good focus should quickly follow the blurry moments or the editor should cut to a different in-focus shot within a reasonable time. So, unless a music video project is knowingly experimenting with radical focus shifts, you should avoid using blurry takes when you edit. If there are some well-focused moments in an otherwise blurry clip, mark those regions and salvage them for possible later use.

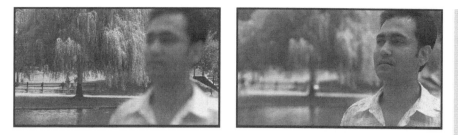

FIGURE 4.1   Audiences may forgive many things about an image, but they do not tolerate blurry pictures. Use the shots that have the best focus.

Framing and Composition

Living at the cusp between a technical issue and an aesthetic issue is the framing of a shot. It can be considered technical in the sense that sometimes the format of the recording device (film or video camera) may be a different size than the frame of the final deliverable product. This is especially true today if a documentary project will contain older MiniDV or 16mm film archival footage, which have a traditional aspect ratio of **4:3** for **standard definition (SD)**. Finishing the mixed-aspect-ratio video for widescreen **16:9 high definition (HD** or even **UHD)** may call for some framing adjustments in post-production.

As an editor, you may be called upon to **reformat** the video frame (scale it, "letterbox" it, cut it down to a smaller size as a **picture-in-picture (PIP)** or **split-screen** element, etc.). These days, with Cinema4K or UHDTV, you may have to perform what is called a **pan and scan,** where you take a large-resolution camera original format and extract a smaller frame size (like traditional HD) from it while simultaneously panning left and right to maintain some semblance of good composition in the new, smaller image. If you are mixing much older SD material into an HD project, you may choose to "pillar-box" the 4:3 picture inside the 16:9 frame size (Figure 4.2). No substantial frame aspect ratio changes are needed if working between traditional HD and UHD as they are both 16:9 in shape.

Aesthetic criteria for framing and composition have fewer immediate fixes. You will have to watch complex and developing shots for good focus, but also for good framing and proper composition. If an elaborate camera move bumps, jumps, sways, or in some way misses its mark while covering the talent or action, then you should not consider using that particular take, or at least not that particular portion of that take. Again, normally during production, there are quality controls for reviewing each shot, and if the filmmakers do not get it right, they usually perform the shot again, so you should have at least one good choice for your edit, but not always. That is where creative cutting comes into play.

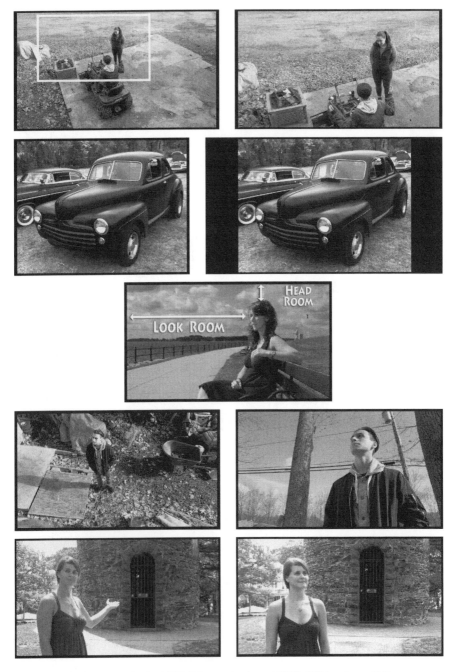

FIGURE 4.2 A–B – an example of an HDTV 16:9 extraction from a UHDTV 16:9 hi-res image; C–D – an example of a 4:3 "pillar box" inside a 16:9 frame; E – an example of a frame with good headroom, look room, and a visible horizon line; F–G – high and low angles on a subject; H–I – examples of subjective and objective shooting styles. (Photo credits: A, B, F, G – Anthony Martel)

Of course, you will also wish to gauge the qualitative attributes of a shot. Is there appropriate headroom? Is there appropriate look room? Is the horizon line parallel to the top and bottom edges of the frame (if it should be)? Do you think the eye-line works? Is the vertical **camera angle** too high or too low? Is the horizontal camera angle too subjective or too objective? Does it work with the type of project you are editing? Very few of these other aesthetic qualities of the shots can be fixed by the editor (short of using some software effects to resize or rotate an image) so it might be best to place them aside and use any other better takes if you have them.

Exposure and Color Balance

With the availability of powerful yet relatively inexpensive video-editing software, issues with the **exposure** and **color balance** of the images are no longer that difficult to fix. Of course, you would prefer that all shots were originally recorded with good exposure and had the proper "look" for the color palette of the project's visual design. If these shots exist in the master footage, then you really should start by selecting those first. But, if good performances or other visual material are present on shots that have exposure issues (the overall image is too bright or too dark) or color temperature shifts (the image looks overly blue or overly orange, etc.), then keep those shots for use and have yourself or a video colorist attend to their corrections with the software tools available. Even the

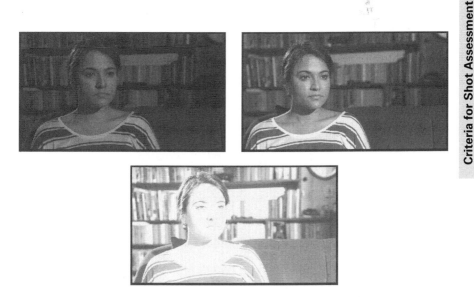

FIGURE 4.3   Select the well-exposed shots. If you have to edit using dark, light, or color-challenged shots, most video-editing software comes with some built-in exposure- and color-correcting tools to help.

most rudimentary video-editing software has some controls for altering image quality for **luminance** (brightness and contrast) and **chrominance** (**hue** and **saturation**).

Audiences do not like it if someone has green skin when there is no reason in the story for that character to have green skin. Additionally, consider your own editing needs. How would it look to cut back and forth from a dark shot to a very bright shot if these separately recorded images are a part of the same scene, the same physical film space? Our eyes and our brains could be missing valuable information as we try to adjust between and rationalize the extremes of dark and light. For everyone's sake, either correct the exposure and color issues or do not use the footage in the final project, if at all possible.

Screen Direction

This is mostly an issue with scripted fictional narrative media, but it comes up in other genres as well. Subject movement out of the frame of one shot and into the frame of the next shot must maintain consistent screen direction. To clarify, frame left is screen left and frame right is screen right when watching the images. The diegetic film space itself, the world in which the characters live and move, must be considered as real space; therefore it must comply to the same rules of left, right, up, down, near, far, etc.

If Shot A shows a character exiting frame left, then, when you cut to Shot B, the same character should be entering from frame right. The character's direction of movement

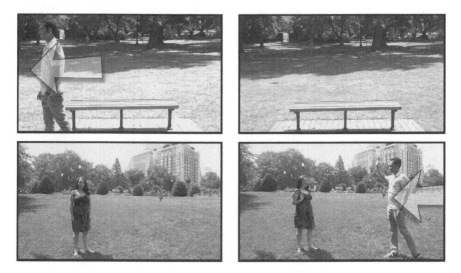

FIGURE 4.4 Maintaining screen direction of subject movement between shots helps to orient the action and reinforces the viewer's understanding of the film space.

within the film space should be consistent: right to left and right to left again (Figure 4.4). Done incorrectly, this could cause a momentary confusion in the viewer. As an example, if you show a character exiting frame left in Shot A, then show the same character entering from frame left in Shot B, it will appear as though the character has simply turned around and is magically re-entering a different location. This can also appear as a **jump cut**. Some schools of thought say "anything goes" in today's motion media world of movies, television, and web videos. They are counting on the viewing public's sophistication in understanding cinematic language. This may be, but you can never go wrong with maintaining proper screen direction – allowing for deviations if the genre calls for it.

The 180-Degree Rule/Axis of Action

Continuing the logic of our **screen direction** discussion, you must also analyze the footage to make sure that the production team respected the **axis of action** or the **imaginary line** while they were recording coverage for the various scenes. As you may know, the **180-degree rule** is established from the first camera set-up covering the action of a scene. This framing is usually a wide shot showing the subjects and their environment. An imaginary line, following the direction of the subject's **sight line**, cuts across the set or location and defines what is frame left and what is frame right. Each successive medium or close-up shot of the talent within the scene should be set up with the camera on the same side of this **line of action.** If this axis of action has not been respected, then, to the viewing audience, the spatial relationships of the talent will be flipped left to right or right to left. Traditionally, screen direction is maintained by shooting all of the coverage from the one, initial, side of this line.

If you consider one of the alternative names for this practice, the 180-degree rule, it might help to clarify what is going on. When the camera crew record the wide shot for a two-person dialogue scene, they have established the physical locations of each subject and the direction of their lines of attention or sight lines. The imaginary line, established by talent sight lines, bisects an imaginary circle around the talent and makes a 180-degree arc within which the camera should move for recording more set-ups. If the camera were to move across this line to shoot an individual's close-up, that character, once edited into the scene, will appear to be turning and facing the opposite direction. This will look incorrect to the audience because the shot will break from the established screen direction for this scene. As a result, you really should be careful if you are looking to edit in a shot that has **crossed the line** (Figure 4.5).

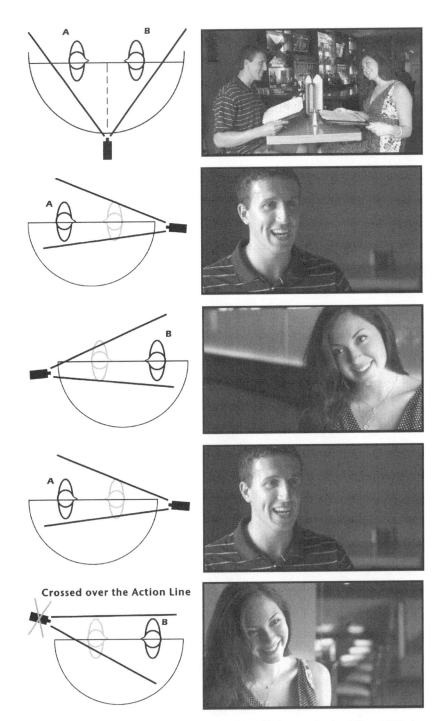

FIGURE 4.5 Coverage shots that cross the line may not be usable because they break the established screen direction for the scene. The two characters end up looking off screen in the same direction rather than looking back and forth at one another across the open film space between them.

Many filmmakers today are rather relaxed with this "rule." A free-form approach to talent and camera movement, plus the sophistication of the viewing audience, allow for some switches within the scene coverage. Although you can never go wrong in using the traditional action line guide, use the shots that fit the editing style of the scene or program and go for the strongest performances.

The 30-Degree Rule

Based around the concept of the 180-degree rule, the **30-degree rule** calls for the camera crew to move the camera around the 180-degree arc by at least 30 degrees before they set up for a new coverage shot of the talent. The reason is simple. If two images of one person (a medium long shot and a medium shot) are shot from two locations around the 180-degree arc and the physical distance between camera set-ups is less than 30 degrees, then the two shots, when cut together by the editor, will look too similar on the screen and cause a "jump" in the mind of the viewer (Figure 4.6).

This is one example of how a jump cut can occur. Without sufficient movement around the shooting arc, the viewpoint that the camera offers is too similar to the previous one and the subject will occupy nearly the same frame space. If you have to edit these two

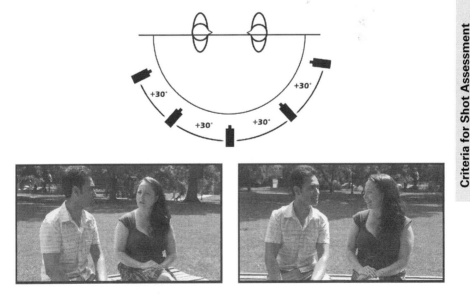

FIGURE 4.6 It is best to edit coverage shots whose individual angles on action are greater than 30 degrees apart along the 180-degree arc. If the camera angles covering the action are too similar, as in this example, the audience will perceive the edit as a type of jump cut. Images also containing very different subject sizes on screen would work best at the edit point.

Criteria for Shot Assessment

similar shots together, the imagery will appear to suffer an immediate jump in space and possibly in time. The angles of coverage and the shot type must be different enough to allow a believable alteration in viewpoints across the cut.

As the editor, you cannot control where the camera was placed for the close-up coverage, but you do have control over what two shots you juxtapose together at a cut point (provided there are more than two angles of coverage). Make sure that the two shots are sufficiently different enough in their horizontal **angle on action** so they do not appear to jump while viewing them across the edit. It would be best if the two shots at the cut point also had different focal lengths or obviously different subject sizes within their frames – further reducing the likelihood of a jump cut.

Matching Angles

When shooting dialogue scenes, the production team will most often shoot what are called **matching angles**: coverage of each character in each shot type where the angle on the person, her or his size in the frame, the lighting scheme, and the focus on the faces are all consistent with one another. One person's close-up will look very similar to the other person's close-up, but they will be on opposite sides of the frame. The compositions of the matching shots mirror one another.

Traditional master scene filmmaking technique has historically called for an "outside-in" construction of a scene's progression from beginning to end. Although not adhered to as much these days, it is a tried-and-true technique that will work for almost any motion picture. As an editor, you might assemble a traditional scene something like this:

- establishing shot – a very wide shot showing the location where the scene is to take place; may be an exterior even if the scene takes place on an interior set;
- wide shot – showing the characters and their placement in the film space;
- closer two-shot – bringing the two characters together in a tighter framing;
- over-the-shoulder (OTS) shot of the first character;
- answering OTS shot of the other character;
- medium close-up of the first character;
- answering medium close-up of the second character.

Cutting back and forth between matching coverage shots (OTS, MS, CU, etc.) will be easily accepted by the viewing audience because the images, although of two different people on opposite sides of the screen, "answer" one another and look like they belong

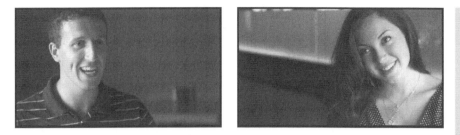

FIGURE 4.7 Use matching angles of shot types when editing coverage for a scene involving more than one person. When cutting back and forth between these close-ups, the audience sense the balance and the equality within the scene.

together – mirroring one another. In other words, the visual aspects of these images match, but in reverse.

Matching Eye-Line

Eye-line (sight line) is an imaginary line that connects a subject's eyes to whatever object holds his or her attention within the film world. If two people are speaking with one another, the other person's face or eyes are often the object of interest, so the eye-line would **trace** from Character A's eyes to Character B's face/eyes. It could be a person looking at a clock, or a dog, or a work of art, etc. Getting the audience to trace the eye-line from a character in a close framing to an object of interest not in the same frame can be tricky.

When you cut away from the shot of the person looking off screen to the shot of his or her object of interest, the eye-line must match (Figure 4.8). The audience must be able to trace the imaginary line from the subject's eyes, *across the cut point,* and to the object contained within the new shot. If this line does not flow correctly, then the audience will feel like something is just not right. As an editor, you cannot really fix eye-line mistakes;

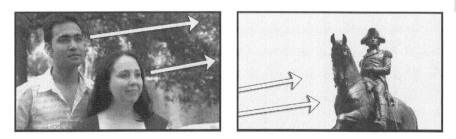

FIGURE 4.8 The eye-line or imaginary lines of attention should match across the cut point between two shots.

Criteria for Shot Assessment

you will just have to find some other way to cut around the issue (see the sections on the use of **inserts** and **cutaway** shots later in the book).

Continuity of Action

We discuss this in detail throughout the book, but it is a topic that frustrates many editors. The action performed by or around the talent in one shot should match, relatively exactly, the same performed action as seen in a different framing, angle and/or focal length within the same scene's coverage. This is called an **action edit** or **continuity edit**. Humans are very good at determining fluidity of motion. When things do not flow – when supposedly continuous actions do not match across a cut point – it is easily noticed (Figure 4.9).

Your job will be to finesse these action cuts as best as possible. Unless there is an obvious glitch in one entire shot, you may not be able to tell that actions will not match until after the footage review stage. Save all of the good takes and see which ones eventually cut best with one another. Trimming just a frame or two from the tail of one shot or from the head of the next might be enough to smooth over minor errors in continuity of action, but anything major will need to be addressed by other, more creative editing options – perhaps a simple cutaway or a customized effect – that fit the style of the project.

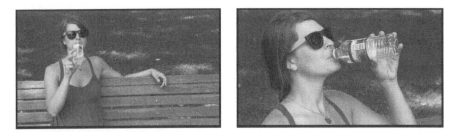

FIGURE 4.9   Watch out for continuity of action issues within the shots you are considering for the edit. Here, the water bottle jumps hands across the cut point.

Performance

The performance that an actor delivers on the film set is certainly an issue that the editor has absolutely no control over; it is decided between the actor and the director during production. You cannot fix bad acting or bad direction of good actors during post-production. You can, however, hide it or mask it through creative editing. As the editor, you set the pacing of the scene and the order and timing of line delivery, and, through the juxtaposition of clips of varying performances, you can alter the tone, mood, or perceived behavior of a character. You decide which performance works best in the edited story.

Sometimes, there simply is nothing else to cut to and there are no "better" takes to use. Cut in what you think works best for the overall scene, grin and bear it, and move on. If the talent's performance is actually very strong but his or her ability to match his or her **business** (holding a glass or cigar, brushing his or her hair, etc.) is what makes a certain take less appealing, be ready to cut in the best performance and let the discontinuity of the little business stand as it is. You will find that strong performances do what they are supposed to do: engross the audience and involve them more deeply in the story. A minor continuity glitch will most likely not even be noticed when actors are delivering a great performance to the engaged audience.

Continuity of Dialogue/Spoken Words

Be aware of actor line delivery when reviewing the footage. Does the talent say different words from take to take and shot to shot? Is there a different timbre in the voice or a modified rate of delivery? Directors will often encourage actors to try different emotions, tactics, and approaches to what and how the character is speaking and behaving. These variations can be a goldmine if they all work together in the scene. If they cannot be joined together, then the editor will be faced with some challenges. Laying in different audio from alternative takes may alleviate some of these issues, but sometimes things just will not match. As with most audio issues, there may be a way around them for a fix, so keep the footage for later use. Ultimately, you and the director may decide that going with the best performance is better than sticking with action or dialogue continuity within a scene.

Be aware that similar issues may be uncovered while editing documentary or other nonfiction motion media products as well. A person being interviewed may alter his or her speaking style in pace, volume, or intonation, etc. while answering just one question or addressing one aspect of the topic being discussed. An editor often has to condense an individual's response for time or clarity of message, and if the pace, volume, or tone do not match between and among words, then the audio portion of the edit will be compromised or unable to be achieved as desired. Similar issues may be found in the monologue or narration of "hosts" who do a lot of direct-to-camera addressing in their performances – likewise with stand-up news journalists in the field.

Criteria for Shot Assessment

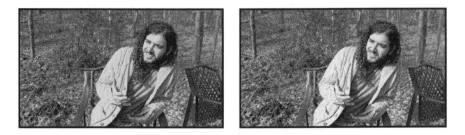

"What do you want?"   "What do you want from me?"

FIGURE 4.10 Lines of dialogue that stray from the script may come from inspired performances and even create a better story. Inconsistencies in speech from an interviewee may cause an editorial headache on a documentary show. (Photo credit: Zach Benard)

Audio Quality

Any sound sources, whether from a digital recorder, computer media files, or even HD videotape, must be of good quality in order to be used in the final audio mix. This holds especially true for any of the synchronous sound recordings from the production footage.

Some obvious issues to listen for:

- **Levels** – The volume should be adequate: not too quiet and not too loud (over-modulated) (Figure 4.11). Although the industry has a suggested range (mixing between −10db and −20db), each project will call for individual treatments – based on what is loud and what is soft for that particular content, the purpose of the video, and the intended means of exhibition.

  Pretty much all software has a means for increasing or lowering the audio levels of master clips, clip segments, and overall sequences. These are sometimes referred to as "gain control." Keep in mind that if you are given very quiet production/sync audio files, boosting their levels will not only raise the volume of the important spoken words you want to hear, but all other background sounds, including "white noise," that you do not want to hear.

- **Presence** – Does the audio recording match the image size? If it is a CU of a human subject talking, do the words sound like they are up close to the camera or far away? If it is a long shot with the talent further away from the camera, does the audio represent the correct distance perspective? Microphone placement during a scene may or may not have been done ideally for the images recorded. Equalization effects might be able to help in situations like this.

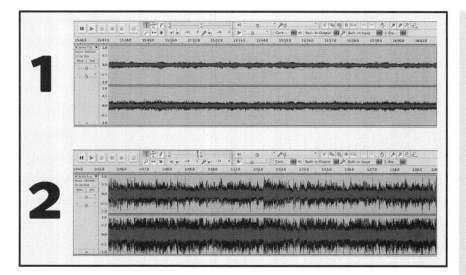

FIGURE 4.11   Choose material with the best audio first. Example 1 shows an audio clip that was recorded with very low levels. The sound energy waveform is a thin strip and the playback is quiet. Example 2 shows an audio clip with very high energy levels. The overall sound levels are loud. There may be ways to do simple fixes with audio-"sweetening" software to even out these two clips to proper levels.

- **Hiss** – Is there any background (electronic) "hiss" or buzzing, etc., in the audio signal? Audio filters or effects in your software may be able to "dial out" this particular issue.

- **Overlap** – Do the actors speak over each other's lines of dialogue? You cannot isolate an individual's line delivery if many subjects are speaking all at once. In the ideal scenario, each take of character dialogue recorded during production was done clean with no overlap so you, as the editor, may purposefully construct an overlapping moment of dialogue in post-production.

- **Ambience pollution** – This is unwanted sounds from the recording environment such as jet engines overhead, air conditioner motors, traffic, radios or music, footsteps, nearby conversations, etc.

- **Room tone** – Did the production sound recordist provide the editor with at least 30 seconds of room tone for each location/set that appears in the project? As you should recall, room tone is a special "ambience" or "wild" recording (typically meaning that no image was captured at the same time as the sound was recorded) that simply documents the sound of the physical space where all of the action for that particular scene took place. Editors use it to smooth out the audio bed, especially around dialogue cutting or ADR use.

Criteria for Shot Assessment

- **Does audio exist?** – Some technical issues (batteries, cabling, switches not switched, etc.) can result in no audio being recorded while the picture is recorded. You may find that the corresponding audio for a picture track you have was simply never recorded. If the production team were particularly lax with performing proper head slates at the beginnings of each shot, then you might have a purposeful MOS shot or it might be a technical glitch. Have fun figuring it out!

- **Rights** – It is easy to grab a portion of your favorite pop song and lay it in under your picture tracks, but if you do not own the rights (which is doubtful) or you do not acquire the right of use (which can be rather difficult and expensive), then you most likely cannot use that piece of music in your video.

  Creative artists, producers, music publishing companies, etc. are very strict about rights of use, so be careful what you select and edit into your sequence. Fair use for educational or artistic repurposing rights walk a blurry line, so it might be best to seek out friends with bands or local groups who may be open to granting you the rights of use of their songs. Explaining this to clients might be challenging, but they will thank you for it in the end. "Rights-free" music tracks are also available for download from many sources on the internet. The adventurous among you might actually try to compose your own – which is doable with many free apps and relatively inexpensive music creation software titles.

Unlike bad focus, there are some tricks that can be done to improve the sound quality of the audio. Video- and audio-editing software applications usually have simple controls for managing the easy stuff like levels and panning. Special audio filters or effects also exist to handle the more challenging audio signal manipulations (e.g., pitch shifting, time compression, reverb, equalization, hum removal, etc.). If the audio is really bad and cannot be salvaged by tweaking with the audio software, then you still have the option of replacing it entirely with new, cleanly recorded dialogue audio files that will match the picture exactly. Some refer to this as looping or automated dialogue replacement (ADR). An audio engineer is more likely to do this re-recording work with the acting talent, but the editor would most likely edit the ADR audio tracks into the timeline. Of course, on small projects you would have to do all of this yourself. So if the pictures are good, but the audio is bad, the media may still be usable – depending on the project, time, and availability of the talent – for post-production dubbing.

Be Familiar with All of the Footage

Reviewing and assessing the footage for quality issues and gauging usability at the very beginning of the editing process actually serve a two-fold purpose. Obviously, this will help you to "pull the selects" or set aside your best shots for use in the **assembly edit**. It also forces you to become familiar with all of the footage shot for the project. This is exceedingly important because it will be your job to know what options you have during the cutting process. Although not as popular today, capturing from a tape source into your computer allows you to experience the tapes in real time and to get your first familiarity with the material. If you are working with digital media files copied from a camera's hard drive or memory card, you will still have to watch all of the footage to assess quality and usability once it is available on your editing system. Plan for this extra time.

For scripted fictional narrative stories, the script initially guides your approach and the footage may match up for the most part. Use the best material you have when you follow the script's framework. As the editor, though, you are often given the ability to rework scene order and restructure the story a bit differently than what the script called for originally. You are paid for your storytelling abilities, not just as an assembly monkey. If you are working with documentary, news, or even reality TV footage, you will have to be rather familiar with everything that is shown (the coverage of events or the B-roll) and with everything that is said (interviews, narration tracks, etc.). Adding comments to your clips, embedding markers with script lines, or having a timecode transcript of interviews can all be helpful. The extreme importance of solid project and media file organization cannot be stressed enough here. You never know which piece of footage will turn a good edit into a great edit. As you begin to frame the story during the edit, the footage itself helps to give it form, direction, influence, etc. An editor familiar with all of his or her building blocks can construct a better project.

Chapter Four – Final Thoughts: So How Does All of This Help You?

The job of the editor goes well beyond just slapping together a few pictures and sounds with a song and a title or two. The editor is the person at the end of the creativity chain who takes all of the available material (all of the production footage, graphics, music, etc.) and puts it together in such a way that it makes sense, tells a story, gives information, and/ or entertains a particular audience. An editor is a storyteller who also has to possess technical knowledge, not just of the editing tools he or she uses to conduct the edit, but also of film language: the grammar of the shots and the quality of the sounds.

This chapter has presented you with a review of the simple criteria upon which you can base your judgments of "good" or "no good" where the footage is concerned. Knowing what not to use in your edited piece is almost as important as knowing what to put in it. Understanding film language and having the ability to scan picture and sound clips for compromising quality issues are important first steps in becoming a good editor.

Related Material Found in Chapter Eight – Working Practices

#10, 11, 12, 13, 15, 16, 23, 25, 27, 28, 29, 31, 32, 35, 58, 60

Chapter Four – Review

1. An editor should, ideally, watch and listen to all of the master source clips for a project so that she or he may determine which ones are qualitatively, technically, and aesthetically appropriate for use in the given program being made.

2. Soft-focus shots are pretty much unusable unless the inherent blurriness is part of a subjective POV shot or is quickly racked to some object in focus.

3. It can be helpful to an editor if the production footage exhibits solid composition and framing, and appropriate headroom and look room.

4. Shots that contain appropriate exposure and color balance will require less grading during the finishing stage of post-production and will therefore have a greater chance of maintaining good image quality throughout the process.

5. Shots that respect the screen direction of subject and object movement across and out of the frame will keep the imaginary physical space of the film world geographically true for the audience.

6. The action line on any given film set establishes the 180-degree arc in which a camera may traditionally be set up to cover the angles on action.

7. Jumping the line causes a reversal in a character's eye-line and flips the film world's references for left and right.

8. Shots coming from the same scene's coverage should be at least 30 degrees divergent from one another in their angles on action and have a different focal length or image magnification in order to edit together without a jump cut.

9. Audiences have come to expect matching angles from images that cover traditional dialogue scenes. The back-and-forth dialogue of Character A and Character B is seen from similarly framed, angled, lighted, and focused shots.

10. When the production team create a shot of a character looking out of the frame at some object of interest, the **reveal** shot of that object should be framed and angled such that it appears to be viewed by the character doing the looking, although not typically a literal POV. The eye-line of attention must match across the edit.

11. Continuity of action should exist between the two coverage shots that the editor chooses to juxtapose in the sequence. The cut on action will appear smoother to the viewer if movements, speed, direction, etc. are very similar if not the same.

12. Continuity of performance helps an editor to join two shots that cover a single character speaking, emoting, or reacting during dialogue. Differences in the tone, rate of delivery, or "business" may compromise the edit.

13. Audio sources may have numerous issues, so careful attention must be given them for volume, perspective/proximity, background noises, clicks/pops/scratches, etc. A private edit suite with good audio monitors (speakers) or a pair of good-quality, noise-canceling headphones will help to pick up on the anomalies.

Chapter Four – Exercises

1. Carefully watch and listen to your favorite show and see how many (if any) issues pop up that relate to the criteria discussed in this chapter. Even the most polished programs will suffer, in some ways, from a compromised edit or an audio glitch that will most likely go unnoticed by the average viewer. Practice sharpening your observational skills by purposefully looking for mismatched angles, weak compositions, action line jumps, jump cuts, poor audio dubbing, etc.

2. Record your own or acquire from a friend a short dialogue scene, assess the master clip footage, and edit it together as best as you can. Which problems that you detected in the master clip footage also appear to be problems in the edited piece? Which problems have been "fixed" by your clever editing and how did you do it?

3. Take the scene from Exercise 2 and strip away the dialogue tracks. Gain access to the same actors (if possible) and use your own version of automated dialogue replacement to record new versions of the scene's lines of dialogue. Edit these new audio tracks into your timeline and see how closely you can hand sync the mouth movement and the new dialogue audio clips.

Chapter Four – Quiz Yourself

1. When might it be a good thing to use a blurry shot in a story?
2. You are presented with footage for half of an entire scene that is accidentally amber-toned. The performances are strong but the color does not match the footage from the other half of this scene. Is it totally unusable or might there be something you can do to it or with it in your sequence? If so, what?
3. True or false: trimming just a few frames from the tail or head of clips at a continuous action edit may smooth out the illusion of movement across the cut, provided the subject performed the actions in a very similar fashion in each shot.
4. How might you handle adding historic 4:3 SD archive footage into a widescreen 16:9 HD documentary project?
5. Taking a traditional approach to covering a dialogue scene, why is it important to keep the camera within the initially established 180-degree arc of the action line's imaginary circle?
6. How might overlapping dialogue from multiple characters in coverage shots cause issues for an editor's choices while assembling the scene?
7. What does "ADR" stand for and how is it used to fix audio problems for a motion media project?
8. When might you have to reformat visual sources (change their shape or aspect ratio) during your editing of a project involving historical or archival media footage?
9. You have been asked to sync video and audio source master clips. You encounter a video-only clip whose head slate shows the fingers of the "clapper" (2nd Assistant Camera) between the clapsticks preventing them from closing and the letters "MOS" are written clearly on the slate as well. What does all of this mean to you, the editor, and how will it help you to find the matching sync audio file for that video-only master clip?
10. In the world of video editing, to what do the terms "luminance" and "chrominance" refer?

Chapter Five

When to Cut and Why: Factors that Lead to Making an Edit

- Information
- Motivation
- Shot Composition
- Camera Angle
- Continuity
- Sound

Editing a motion picture is more than just assembling a bunch of shots one after the other. The editor is tasked with creatively arranging various picture and sound elements so that the audience who view the finished piece will be moved, entertained, informed, or even inspired. This last statement really highlights a fundamental aspect of any motion media production (whether it is a feature film, a commercial, a situation comedy, a corporate video, etc.). The main purpose behind almost any edited project is for it to be shown to an audience. As an editor, you are challenged with crafting an experience that will affect a viewer in some way – hopefully in a way the producers of the project intend.

The material for the project was written with an audience in mind, the footage was recorded with an audience in mind, and you must edit it together with an audience in mind. And this is not just any audience, but the specific audience that the project is targeting. The same people who would watch a documentary about late nineteenth-century North American textile mills may not care to see a movie about the pranks at a college fraternity. Understanding audience expectations and their degree of involvement in the program will be an excellent skill to develop during your editing career. Anticipating the needs of the viewer will go a long way toward aiding your approach to editing the material.

Of course, different genres of motion pictures, television/episodic programming, and web videos, etc. may all require different editorial approaches. The unique content, exhibition avenues, and specific target audiences will necessitate the use of different editing styles, techniques, effects, etc. As you may be just starting out on your filmmaking journey and your editing career path, you should be watching as many of these motion media products as possible. You will begin to see how they are each treated, the common approaches taken, the presence or lack of certain shared aspects or elements, etc. Really watching and getting a feel for the work of other editors is a great way to help to train your brain. Over time, you will most likely develop a solid interest and rather strong skill set in just one of the programming formats (commercials, documentaries, feature films, news, etc.) and you may spend the majority of your editing career in that genre.

But before we get lost in such specifics about the future job you might have, let us return to the goal of our book, which is to discuss the basic grammar of the edit. Although it is true that different editing jobs will call for different editing techniques, it is also true that there are some attributes common to most styles of editing. These common attributes are the elements that your viewing audience (including yourself) have been trained to expect and comprehend when watching a motion picture. People are rarely conscious of these elements, but, through viewing film and television imagery over their lifetime, they subconsciously know how to "read" certain edits and they can easily decipher meaning in the flow of images across the screen. Just as the basic shot types have meaning in the language of film, how an editor strings those shots together in the motion picture also has meaning to the viewer. There is grammar in the edits.

In the previous chapters, we have outlined the stages of the editing process, reviewed the basic shot types of film language, listed source sound files, and examined criteria that will help an editor to assess the best and most usable qualities of the production material. We now need to focus more on the decision-making processes involved with assembling the picture and sound tracks. What factors or elements compel an editor to want to make an edit in the first place? Why cut from one shot to another very particular shot at that very precise moment in time?

The following list is meant to serve as a jumping-off point. These criteria are some of the major reasons for considering a cut when dealing with most material, but, as with many things in motion media production, other factors not mentioned here might come into play. However, using this list will put you in very good shape when editing decisions need to be made.

- Information
- Motivation
- Shot Composition
- Camera Angle
- Continuity
- Sound

Information

A new shot should always present some new information to the viewer. In a motion picture, this may primarily be visual information (a new character entering a scene, a different location shown, an event whose meaning is not quite known yet, etc.), but it may also be aural (voice-over narration, the clatter of horse hooves, a speech, etc.). A smart editor will ask herself or himself several questions regarding the "showing" of the story: What *would* the audience like to see next? What *should* the audience see next? What *can't* the audience see next? What do *I want* the audience to see next?

One of the many tasks set up for the editor is to engage the audience both emotionally (to make them laugh, cry, scream in fright, etc.) and mentally (to make them think, guess, anticipate, etc.). Asking the above questions can generate clever and inspired ways of showing the same story. In a mystery, you may purposefully show misleading information, and in a romantic melodrama, you may show the audience information that the characters do not yet know. Regardless of the kind of information presented, the fact that it is there to engage the audience, get them involved, and get them thinking helps to keep them interested in the story. When audience members are thinking and feeling, they are not paying attention to the physical act of the edit, and this engagement helps to keep the motion media pieces running strong and smooth regardless of the genre, content, or storytelling style. It also means that the editor has done his or her job well.

It must be understood that this element of new information is basic to all editing choices. Whenever one shot has exhausted its information content, it may be time to cut to another shot. As you construct a scene in a narrative film or a segment within non-fiction programming, is there new information in the next shot to be added to your sequence? Is there a better choice? Is there another shot, perhaps, from the same scene or from some other source, that does provide new information and fits into the story to make it flow? No matter how beautiful, cool, or expensive a shot may be, if it does not add new information to the progression of the story, then it may not belong in the final edit. Keep in mind, however, that some shots may not possess observable, "physical" information, but they may provide significant tonal value to the scene or the overall mood of the story. These kinds of shots add a different type of "sensory" information to the audience experience.

Information

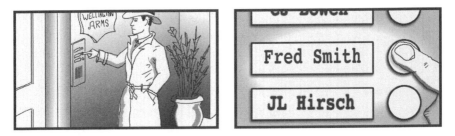

FIGURE 5.1 Each shot presented to the audience should provide new information about the story to keep them engaged and attentive. The MLS of this cartoon detective cuts to the CU of the nameplate and door buzzer. We learn where, who, and why just in these two juxtaposed images.

Motivation

The new shot that you cut to should provide new information, but what about the shot that you are cutting away from? What is the reason to leave that shot? When is a good time to leave the current shot? There should always be a motivation for making a transition away from a shot. This motivation can be visual, aural, or temporal.

PICTURE – In picture terms, the motivating element is often some kind of movement by a subject or an object in the current shot. It could be as big as a car jumping over a river, or as simple as a slight wink of an eye. What if you are shown a close-up of a young woman reading a book? During the shot, she glances to her left as if looking at something off screen. Editing logic would hold that you might then want to cut away from her close-up and cut to the shot that reveals the object of her interest – what she might be looking at in the film space. The motivation to cut away comes from the movement of the actor's eyes and the desire that this action initiates in the viewer to see what it is that the character is seeing.

A cut to the next shot, of a wolf in Grandma's clothing, provides the audience with new information. It may show them what the woman is looking at, and, in this case, it may keep them wondering. Is this wolf character in her reality – actually across the room? Is it simply an unrelated daydream? Is it a **flashback** based on an entry in the journal that she is reading? Or could the wolf character shot be a representation of her imagining what the content of the novel she is reading actually looks like (Figure 5.2)? The story, genre, concept, and purpose of this motion media piece will help the audience to understand the broader meaning behind why these two video clips are united, but the important thing to remember is that the outgoing clip content (woman, book, eye movement) provides simple yet ample motivation to cut to the incoming clip of the Grandma-wolf.

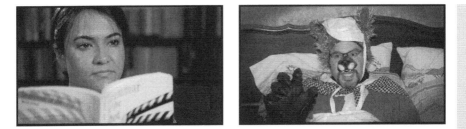

FIGURE 5.2   The picture content and subtle character movement of the woman directing her eyes away from the book and onto some unseen object provide the motivation for the editor to cut to the reveal shot.

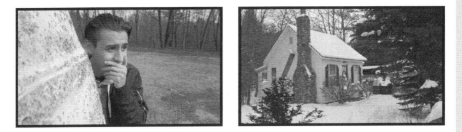

FIGURE 5.3   The picture content and subtle character movement of this horrified young man looking off screen at some unseen object motivate the cut to a new shot. It is obvious that the snow-covered cabin is not the object seen by the man. The reveal shot has been denied or at least delayed. (Photo credit: A – Anthony Martel)

Another tactic might be that you choose to *not* show the audience what the character is looking at off screen, but, instead, you cut to some other scene altogether for entirely different information and story progression. Not fulfilling the audience's curiosity keeps then wondering, guessing, and in suspense as to what the person was looking at and what happened to that person after we cut away (Figure 5.3). This approach, of delayed gratification, can work in drama, horror, and comedy – and just about any genre, provided you eventually return to that initial character and show something that is the "logical" result of what he was looking at earlier in the narrative. The audience will be pleased that you closed the loop on that particular plot point by finally showing them the object of interest. Either delaying revealing this information for too long or never answering that question can be a gamble.

SOUND – If you wish to use sound as a motivating element, then you would need to address the editing of both picture and sound tracks more precisely near that transition. The sound that motivates the cut could be generated by something visible in the shot currently on the screen. As a simple example, a medium long shot shows a stoic farmer standing in his kitchen. A teakettle, visible on the stove in this wider shot, begins to whistle. The whistle on the audio track of the MLS can motivate an informational

Motivation

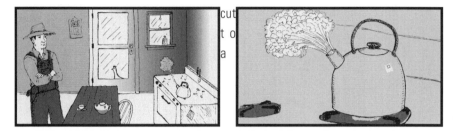

FIGURE 5.4 The sound of the teakettle whistling in the wide shot is ample reason to cut to the close-up shot of the kettle steaming away on the stovetop. As a visual metaphor, the boiling kettle can represent the undercurrent of anger being experienced by the frustrated farmer.

detailed close-up of the teakettle on the stovetop. Steam shoots up from the spout and the whistling seems louder (Figure 5.4). It should be noted that because the close-up shot actually magnifies the visual size and importance of the teakettle, it could be appropriate to raise the level or volume of the whistle in your audio track as well. This lets the sound produced by that object match the size of the visual object on screen and reflects the "perspective" or proximity of the close-up shot.

Now imagine that this story of the stoic farmer and the teakettle gets a bit more involved. Let's say that this farmer has just found out that if he doesn't pay his substantial back taxes, a railroad development company is going to take control over his ranch and evict him. The same simple cut to the steaming teakettle can take on symbolic meaning: it acts as a **visual metaphor** for the farmer's frustration and anger boiling just under the surface of his stoic façade. This is an example of a **concept edit**, discussed in more detail in Chapter Six.

A third and more advanced way of using audio as a transition motivator becomes rather complex in its design. An editor may create what is called a **sound bridge**. A sound, seemingly generated by something not seen or known to the audience, begins underneath Shot A. It motivates the transition into Shot B, where the origin of the strange sound is revealed. To modify our teakettle example slightly, let us say that we are seeing the same frustrated farmer in the kitchen with the teakettle in the MLS. The audience see the steam rise out of the kettle spout and begin to hear what they may interpret as the kettle whistling. This motivates the cut to a new shot of an old-time steam engine train's whistle blowing.

The sound of the train whistle, laid under the picture track of the kitchen MLS, acts as a motivator to leave that shot – even though the audience may not have initially caught

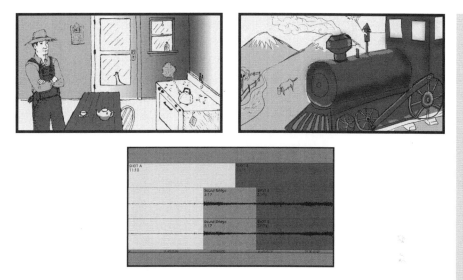

FIGURE 5.5 The incoming audio track for Shot B (the train whistle) starts playing underneath the outgoing video track of Shot A with the farmer and teakettle apparently whistling. The audience believe the train whistle is the kettle until we cut to the shot of the train. This is an example of a sound bridge – or sound leading picture.

on that the sound of the "teakettle" is, in fact, the sound of a train whistle. The incoming audio, starting earlier than the picture track edit, acts as a bridge leading the viewer into the new location and the new information of Shot B. The audience follow the unexpected transition because the new image of the train whistling gives them information to process and provides them with an unexpected surprise. They quickly figure out that the harsh whistle sound represents the farmer's building anger toward the manipulative railroad company (Figure 5.5). As you will learn later, this type of sound bridge edit is often referred to as a **J-cut**.

TIME – An editing choice may often come down to the timing. Feeling when to transition from one clip to another may be motivated by the overall pace of the project combined with the rhythm of each particular scene or segment of the video.

If your project is a fictional narrative film, then the pace of a scene – the duration of each shot on the screen – has a lot to do with the energy of the content, emotion, and purpose of the scene. Does your story involve a dramatic bank robbery gone wrong? Is there a tango-like argument between coworkers that shows unexpected romantic tension? Is there a somber scene where a parent must pack up the belongings of her deceased child? Of course, non-fiction programs also require an attention to timing and pacing. A segment for a kids' show highlighting young teen skateboarders may have a frenetic pace to the

Motivation

edits as opposed to the slower changeover of clips found in a documentary about elderly victims of predatory mortgage lending practices.

The motion picture example of the bank robbery may benefit from quick cutting of different and perhaps odd or canted angles on the scene indicating the confusion, fear, and unpredictable danger brought on by the disruptive and violent act. Both the participants in the scene and the audience are equally disoriented.

The flirtatious argument between unlikely romantic partners may emulate the rhythm of a tango where you cut back and forth and back and forth in equal time, as each character tries to outdo the other. Perhaps the rhythm quickens, as their argument escalates and the shots get tighter and closer until the characters are united in an "intimate" profile two-shot. Are they about to kiss? Then you choose to cut back out to a wide shot that lasts longer on screen to show them regain their composure and walk away in separate directions, having resisted their unanticipated romantic urges.

The grieving parent may be shown in wide shots of very long duration to indicate how still time is now that her child is gone and how isolated she feels – lost in this new world, sad and alone. Perhaps the few transitions in the scene are **elliptical** in nature (moving forward in time), showing the mother in different stages of grief while handling different objects in her child's room, as the lighting from the window changes to show the passage of time. Here, "film time" – different from real time – is absolutely under the control of the editor.

The pacing of your overall motion media piece can be much like a traditional roller coaster. There could be slow scenes, moderately fast scenes, and fast scenes combined together at different moments of the story's progression. As on a coaster, in order to go fast, you must first go slow: a long, slow ride up the first big hill, then a fast race down, then some little bumps, then a big hill with an unexpected turn, then racing down again and finally a few minor bumps and it's all over before you know it. If it's all too slow, it may feel like you are not going anywhere and become uninteresting. If it's all too fast, it may just become an annoying sensory overload without any breaks. Again, the pacing decisions can be motivated by genre, content, and intent, but varying the pace appropriately can give the audience a more engaging ride.

Shot Composition

Traditionally, the film editor could not significantly alter the composition of visual elements in the footage that he or she was given to edit. The relatively high resolution of

35mm film negative did allow for a certain amount of blow-up or frame enlargement. Standard-definition NTSC video (720 × 486) fell apart rather quickly when you tried to scale the frame. HD (1920 × 1080), being of higher resolution, allows for some blow-up and re-composition. It is only now, with high-end digital video imagers that can achieve an effective 4K, 5K, or 8K image resolution, that more substantial and sometimes requisite reframing can be done. However, none of these scaling options for the frame can significantly reposition subjects or objects within the depth (3D space) of the film space of the shots; that was the job of the director and director of photography during production.

The editor *can* certainly choose which two shots get joined together at a transition. Provided the correct composition is in the visual material, the editor can help to make the viewing of these images more engaging for the audience.

The easiest or most straightforward option for an editor can be to simply edit in all of the footage from one, long, beautifully composed shot – be it simple, complex, or developing. The beautiful, well-balanced shot was designed by the filmmakers to be a showpiece: it looks great and plays well once cut into the sequence. The audience are given the time to appreciate the shot for what it is as it unfolds in its entirety. Everybody is happy. However, do not be afraid to cut into this showpiece if the pacing, story, or characterizations can benefit from an added visual interruption.

Another simple technique is to take two basic but properly composed shots and transition them one after the other. A two-person dialogue presents the perfect scenario to demonstrate this. Your scene starts with a wide shot of two people sitting across the table from one another having a discussion. As Character A speaks, you cut to a close-up of Character A. He is sitting frame left with his look room opening across to frame right. Audiences have grown to expect that you will cut over to Character B listening in a matching close-up. She is sitting over on frame right with her look room opening across to frame left (Figure 5.6).

Using the alternating placement of characters frame left and frame right generates interest in the audience and causes them to stay engaged with the progression of the motion picture. As you cut from CU to CU, the audience get to experience eye-line match *and* eye trace across the screen and across the edit.

When the viewers are watching Character A speak over on frame left, their attention is over on frame left. They are aware, however, that Character A's attention is actually across the screen over on frame right. When the cut to Character B comes, the audience trace Character A's eye-line across the empty screen and rest upon the new face of

Shot Composition

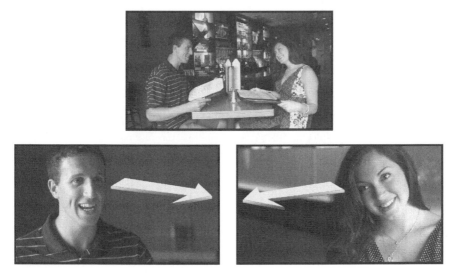

FIGURE 5.6 Simple, traditional compositions like these engage the viewers by asking them to trace the matching eye-line across the empty look room on screen.

Character B over on frame right. The compositional placement of Character B should be in such a screen location as to match the eye-line from Character A, so the audience are rewarded for following the eye trace across the screen and across the edit.

Like a tennis ball bouncing back and forth across the court, the eyes of the viewing audience will travel back and forth across the screen seeking the new information from each character as you cut from one shot composition to the other. You want to engage the audience's eye trace without making them search too hard for the next bit of information. Subtle searches around the screen's compositional elements will keep the viewing experience interesting, and more elaborate searches can make it more surprising. Complex and multi-layered shot compositions can look great on screen, but be aware of how you cut into and out of them. Think of how the audience will locate the new, important visual information within the more complex arrangements of on-screen elements. The more time required to find the new area of interest, the more likely they may get frustrated and momentarily pull themselves out of the viewing experience.

Camera Angle

In Chapter Four, we discussed how to review your footage and watch for shots that may have been taken from two positions on set less than 30 degrees apart around the

180-degree arc of the action line. This is one of the key elements of a shot that will help you to determine if it should be cut next to another shot from the same coverage. There has to be reasonable difference in the camera angle on action for two shots to be "comfortably" edited together.

When the coverage is planned for a scene, certain camera placements or camera angles are considered to be the most advantageous, and they are the shots eventually recorded by the filmmakers. Due to factors of time and money, only certain shot types from certain angles will be recorded and the production team try to fit the most information into the fewest, but best-looking, shots that they can. But an editor will never know from where around the 180-degree arc the camera was placed to record the actions of the scene until he or she reviews the footage. The editor can only do his or her best to place shots of differing horizontal angles (greater than 30 degrees apart) next to one another in the edit – particularly with dialogue scenes covered in the traditional master scene method.

The reason for this is simple. If two shots are recorded with similar framing from two, almost identical angles on action, then their resulting images will look too similar to one another, even though they are slightly different. This similarity will register with the viewer as he or she watches the program and it may appear to the eye as if there is a glitch or a jump in the image at the cut point.

The expression jump cut is used frequently in the analysis of editing for motion pictures. In this case, as in most, it simply refers to the fact that while watching the motion images,

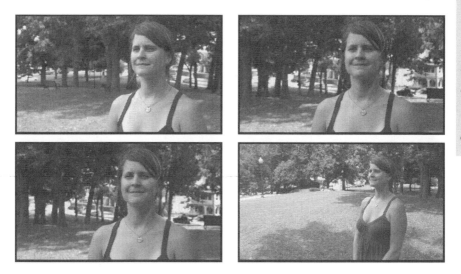

Camera Angle

FIGURE 5.7   Editing together two shots from similar camera angles will cause a jump at the cut point. Differing camera angles and framing will help to prevent the jump cut in the mind of the viewer.

the viewer perceives a jump, a glitch, or an extremely brief interruption or alteration to the pictures being shown. In our current example of these clean single shots with angles on action that are too close, we will find that the images of Shot A and Shot B are too similar in their appearance (Figure 5.7).

The audience will not see these shots as providing sufficiently different views of the same information. In their eyes, the image will merely jump, which they will consciously notice, and as a result it will pull them out of the viewing experience, which is something that the editor should try to prevent if such a treatment is not part of the project's established visual style. Jump cuts have become popularized in recent times via music videos, film trailers, and with certain feature film directors, but that does not mean that they are always excusable. To learn more about the purposeful usage of jump cuts in filmmaking, you should research the French New Wave director, Jean-Luc Godard.

Continuity

In traditional editing methodologies, providing smooth, seamless continuity across transitions is a very important element to keeping edits unnoticed by the viewer. This is called continuity editing or invisible editing. Unlike the purposeful use of jump cuts skipping across time chunks, the story of a traditionally paced, continuity-style edit is supposed to move forward, uninterrupted, where the shots of differing magnification (LS, MS, CU, etc.) flow from one to the next as if presenting continuous events. Experimental films, and the French New Wave movement of the early 1960s, established that visual continuity was not absolutely required. Today, many filmmakers disregard the strictness of continuity concerns in favor of best performance editing. Jump cuts, time shifts, and repeated and alternate action and line delivery have become part of an accepted style of editing and storytelling. Starting with the traditional continuity style, however, is a good way to learn the basic approach to visual story editing.

Once again, editors are not responsible for the quality of the footage that they are given, but they are responsible for assembling that material into the best motion media piece possible. If the production team and subjects have not provided visual material with compositional or performance-based continuity, it will be the editor's job to make up for that deficiency in some way in the editing. And to make matters more interesting, there are actually several different forms of continuity that need to be addressed at various points throughout the editing process. Let us take a look.

Continuity of Content

Actions performed by the on-camera talent should ideally match from one shot to the next. Because actors are obliged to perform the same actions take after take, for each shot covered in the scene, you hope that the overlapping actions are consistent. This is not necessarily always the case. The continuity of content should be watched for but may not be so easily fixed.

As an example, if the family dog is sitting in a chair during the wide shot of a dinner table scene, then the dog should also be seen in the tighter shots used to show the remainder of the scene. If the dog had been taken off set and there are no other shots with the dog sitting at the table with the family, then, as the editor, you get to make a choice. Do you begin the family dinner scene without the wide establishing shot that shows the dog? Perhaps you start the scene on a close-up of the character speaking the first line. Perhaps you start with a close-up of a plate of food, then move out to a two- or three-shot. Additionally, you have the option of showing the dog in the wide shot and then laying in the sound effect of the dog walking away on the hardwood or tiled flooring while you show the tighter shots of the family without the dog at the table. Perhaps you cut in a shot of the dog lying on the floor in a different part of the house. Regardless of your approach, you are searching for a solution to a continuity problem.

If a man picks up a telephone in an MLS using his right hand, then the telephone should still be in his right hand when you cut to an MCU of him speaking on the phone. If, for whatever reason, the production team have not provided any MCU shots of the man with the phone in his right hand, but only in his left, then you could **cut away** to some other shot after the MLS and before the phone-in-left-hand MCU. This will give the audience enough of a break from continuous action so that they can either forget which hand the phone was in, or believe that the man had time to transfer the telephone from his right hand to his left while he was off screen. In this case, the cutaway is any brief shot that will provide the appropriate distraction and time filler to allow the audience to make the leap in logic of object continuity adjustment (Figure 5.8).

So either the footage already contains the proper material to edit with the correct continuity of content, or the editor must create some means of hiding, masking, or "explaining" the visual incongruity. If the audience can be "tricked" into seeing something else, or if the performance presented is sufficiently strong, then the questionable content will most likely be overlooked. No matter the approach taken, the editor is like a sleight-of-hand magician purposefully distracting the eyes of the audience to cover the glitch in the picture.

Continuity

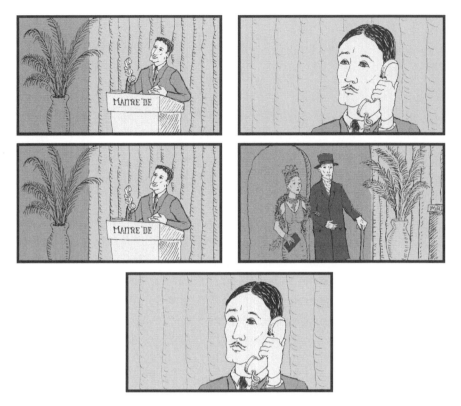

FIGURE 5.8   Using a cutaway shot may provide the needed break from inconsistent content so that the audience do not consciously notice the discontinuity of the telephone switching in the man's hands.

Continuity of Movement

Screen direction is the movement of subjects or objects toward the edges of the frame. This should be maintained as you transition from one shot to the next, if that following shot still covers the same movement of the same subjects or objects. The rules of three-dimensional space (left, right, up, down, near, far) still apply inside the fictional, pretend space of the film world. The production team should have respected the scene's screen direction and the 180-degree rule during the shooting of coverage. If they did not, and the new shot that you would like to use continues your talent's movement contrary to the established screen direction, then you may have to insert a neutral shot that will continue the narrative and still provide a visual break from the discontinuity of movement. This other inserted shot, of whatever material you have that fits the narrative flow, will offer the audience a visual break that allows the character time to reverse his direction in the third shot continuing the previous action (Figure 5.9).

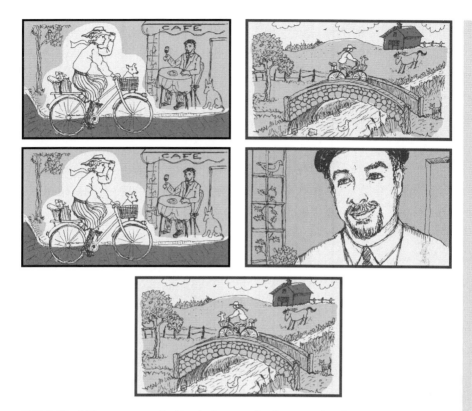

FIGURE 5.9   Subject movements should maintain screen direction across the edit point. If you wish to cut together two shots that reverse screen direction, then it may be advisable to use an insert shot to break the audience's attention on the direction of movement.

Continuity of Position

The film space itself has direction and also a sense of place. Subjects or objects within the shot occupy a certain space within the film world as well. It is important for the editor to string together shots where that subject or object placement is maintained continuously. If an actor is shown frame right in the first shot, then he should be somewhere on frame right in any subsequent shots during that scene. Of course, if the actor physically moves during the shot to a different location within the film space, then it is logical to show him on a new side of the frame. A moving camera may also cause the orientation of subjects to shift during a shot. Cutting together two shots that cause the subject or object to jump from one side of the screen to the other will distract the viewer and the illusion of "invisible" editing will be broken (Figure 5.10).

Continuity

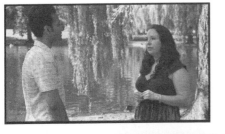

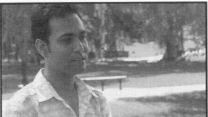

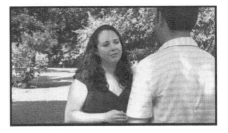

FIGURE 5.10 The physical position of subjects and objects within the film space and the shot composition should stay consistent across edit points. This woman appears to jump from screen right to screen left after the cut to the other character.

Sound

The continuity of sound and its perspective is of critical importance to an edited motion picture. If the scene depicts action that is happening in the same place and at the same moments in time, then the sound should continue with relative consistency from one shot to the next. If there is an airplane in the sky in the first shot, and it can be seen and heard by the viewer, then the sound of that airplane should carry over across the transition into the next shot from that scene. Even if the airplane were not physically seen in the next shot of this sequence, the sound of it would still be audible to the characters and therefore it should still be audible to the audience. An abrupt end to the airplane sound at the cut point would stand out, so the editor would need to add it back in underneath the picture and sound tracks of the second shot – although it should probably have its levels lowered in the mix.

Sound levels for voices and subjects and objects should be mixed consistent with their proximity to the main area of action and with their narrative importance throughout an edited scene. Changes in object distances from camera, either through shot choices or talent movements within the film space, should also be accounted for through raising or lowering volume and panning levels in the audio mix for those shots. The increase or drop-off of perspective, proximity, and presence should be appropriately represented.

Additionally, all spaces have a background noise level. It may be soft, deep, high, or loud, depending on the environment depicted on screen. As we saw in Chapter Three, this ever-present layer of sound is commonly called ambience, but it may also be referred to as **atmosphere** or natural sound (NATS for short). It is responsible for creating a bed of consistent audio tone over which the dialogue and other more prominent sound effects etc. are placed. This extra, uninterrupted sound bed is either lifted from the production audio recordings (sometimes called room tone), or generated by an editor or sound designer from other sources. This ambience track adds a mood or feeling and generates a layer of believability to the location of the scene for the audience. Its presence should be regulated in the mix so that it is minimized under dialogue, etc., but may become more prominent when it does not compete with other, more important sounds.

Chapter Five – Final Thoughts: Is There a Right or Wrong Reason for a Cut?

Yes and no. As with anything that involves a craft, there are the technical methods and reasons for doing things certain ways, but then there are the aesthetic or creative reasons for doing other things in other ways. How you make an edit and why you make an edit are two different aspects of the process, but they are always interrelated. You can edit a project as you see fit, but in the end, it will be the viewing audience who decide whether your choices were right or wrong. Did the edits work or not? Did the audience notice them or not? As long as you have reasons why you made each edit, you are on the right path. Keeping the various elements mentioned in this chapter in mind and anticipating what your audience would appreciate will keep you thinking about why you choose to edit picture and sound elements when you do.

Related Material Found in Chapter Eight – Working Practices

#9, 12, 14, 15, 16, 21, 22, 23, 25, 27, 28, 31, 32, 33, 35, 36, 43, 48, 51

Chapter Five – Review

1. Know your audience and remember that you are really editing a story for them to experience.
2. Each shot you transition into should provide the viewer with new information, or define a tone or mood that progresses the story of the project.
3. Each transition you create should be motivated by some visual or aural element within the shot you are leaving.
4. The timing of the shots in each scene and the overall pacing of the entire motion picture should reflect the energy of the content, mood, and emotional levels of the characters and the development of the story.
5. Juxtaposing appropriately dissimilar shot compositions across the transition leads the viewers' eyes around the frame as they seek new visual information, and therefore keeps them engaged.
6. Present differing camera angles and shot types to the viewers within a given scene or sequence so that they will not experience a temporal or spatial jump cut – unless that is a deliberate visual style in your project.
7. Ensure, as best as possible, that your transitions conform to the appropriate continuity of content, movement, position, and sound if you are going for the "invisible" editing style.

Chapter Five – Exercises

1. Watch a scene or section from any motion media project. Get a feeling for the frequency of shot transitions and see whether it remains relatively constant or if it increases or decreases at particular moments. Does the frequency change with changes in the emotional content of the program?
2. Using the same scene or section, determine what factor(s) led to the edits occurring when they do. Is it information, motivation, composition, camera angle, continuity, or a combination of several? Is it something entirely separate from these factors?

3. Edit together a brief sequence (maybe ten clips) of any source video that you have available. It helps if the material is of all different subject matter. When you edit it together, take notes on what object or portion of the screen you look at just after each cut point. Show this same sequence to a friend or classmate and have him or her tell you the first thing he or she looks at after each cut. Screen the sequence several more times to other individuals and record their objects of interest or the areas of the frame that they look at. Compare what you, the editor, chose to look at in each new clip with the responses of your selected viewers. Do they match? Is there a trend? Are they all different? What might these results mean?

4. Create a quick scenario where a sound bridge across the cut could be applied. You only need two shots: the end of one segment, A, and the beginning of the next segment, B. Cut two versions of the transition: one with a straight cut from A to B, and one with the same straight cut but with your bridging sound clip across the cut underneath both the end of A and the start of B. Play the two versions back to back. Which do you prefer? Which do others prefer?

Chapter Five – Quiz Yourself

1. You are given five shots: 1. a WS of a high school cafeteria; 2. an ECU of a mobile phone text message saying, "Duck!"; 3. as MS of a boy being hit by a volley of green peas; 4. a CU of the same boy looking off screen at something; 5. an MLS of the same boy seated at his table taking his phone out to look at it. In what order would you edit these five clips and what factors play into your decisions?

2. What significance does the shot composition have when you cut from one shot to the next? How can these compositions engage the audience?

3. How can a mismatch in screen direction or screen position from two different coverage shots challenge an editor cutting a dialogue scene?

4. The background sound of an environment or location within a film has several names. List as many of the names as you remember.

5. How can the pacing of a motion picture be like an amusement park ride?

6. What is a "visual metaphor" and how can it be used in motion media pieces, both fiction and non-fiction?

7. How could a cutaway shot help to join together two other shots that display performance or action discontinuities?

8. What was at least one trait popularized by films made under the French New Wave movement of the early 1960s?

9. True or false: pacing is not a significant aspect of editing videos or a major concern for editors fine cutting a sequence.

10. Create two fiction film scenarios: one where a simple, visible action motivates a cut to a new shot, and one where a sound element within the scene motivates a cut to a new shot.

Chapter Six
Transitions and Edit Categories

- The Cut
- The Dissolve
- The Wipe
- The Fade
- The Action Edit
- The Screen Position Edit
- The Form Edit
- The Concept Edit
- The Combined Edit

Now that you are familiar with basic shot types, sound assets, and some factors that lead to selecting useful clips and making a solid edit, we should really shed some light on the most common types of transitions that you will use at those edit points. We will be discussing the cut, the dissolve, the wipe, and the fade. Each one of these four transitions carries with it its own meaning when viewed within a motion media project. Audiences understand these transitions and have certain expectations around their traditional use. We will break down each one and analyze how they play into the six elements of information, motivation, composition, camera angle, continuity, and sound.

Transition and Edit Terms

Before we start examining each picture track transition, we should establish a few terms and discuss how video-editing software applications think about them. As you may know, your video master clips (or full-duration video source files) live as references inside a bin or folder within your video-editing project. You typically mark an IN and an OUT to demarcate your usable footage from that master clip and you edit that shorter duration (IN to OUT region) into your sequence. We will call this first clip in your timeline Shot A. The start frame of this shorter video clip (A) is called the **head frame**. The end frame of this clip is referred to as the **tail frame**. So the beginning of any clip (master or otherwise) is called the head, and the end is called the tail.

Now let's edit another short clip into your timeline. You find a different source master clip, mark the IN/OUT, and edit this new, short clip (B) into your sequence (Figure 6.1).

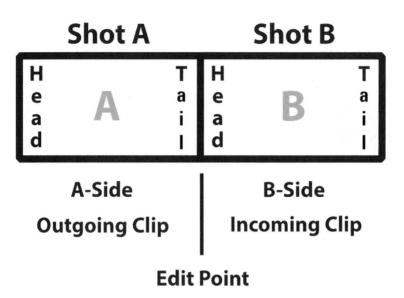

FIGURE 6.1   A straight cut joins the head of Shot B with the tail of Shot A. In video-editing software timeline windows, sequences progress in time and information from left to right. Shot A is the outgoing shot on the A-side of the cut point and Shot B is the incoming shot on the B-side of the cut point.

So now, the head frame of Shot B is edited (joined, spliced, etc.) onto the tail frame of Shot A. This type of edit is a straight cut. This cut is the transition between Shot A and Shot B. Shot A is considered the **outgoing clip**: its information is ending at the cut. Shot B is considered the **incoming clip**: its information is just beginning at the cut. It may seem overly simplistic, but any frames to the left of the cut point live on the **A-side** of the edit, and any frames to the right live on the **B-side**.

As a technical note, all transitions except for the cut and some fades require that extra frames of media be available from the outgoing shot and the incoming shot so that they may overlap and create the transition effect. To help to explain how dissolves and wipes are formed, we will have to revisit the master clips for our Shot A and Shot B. The unused frames of your master clips still exist, and are hidden from view awaiting use in the bin or folder. These unused frames are called **handles**. Any frames of the master clip prior to your clip segment's IN mark are called the **head handle** and any frames coming after the OUT mark are called the **tail handle** (Figure 6.2).

In order for a dissolve or wipe to occur at the cut point between Shot A and Shot B, you must apply the effect. But in order for the effect to work, there must be more frames of video in the original master clip's tail handle that come after the last visible tail frame of Shot A in the sequence. The same will hold true for Shot B. Its first visible frame after the cut, or the head frame of that clip segment, must have video frames that precede it

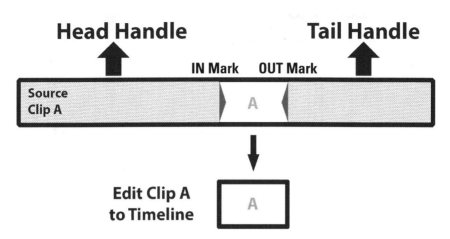

Head Handle

Tail Handle

IN Mark **OUT Mark**

Source
Clip A

A

**Edit Clip A
to Timeline**

A

FIGURE 6.2 Here, the IN/OUT portion of the master clip is going to edit down into the timeline sequence. What remains unused in the master clip content are the head and tail handles.

in its master clip's head handle. These extra frames of video (and maybe audio) that are accessed from the unused master clip's handles are borrowed by the editing software to make the dissolving or wiping transition effect visible in your sequence (Figure 6.3). If your original media source does not have these extra frames in the "hidden" handles, then you will not be able to create that transition effect of that duration with that positioning across the cut. The required extra media is simply nonexistent.

As an example, if you are editing a 1080p/30fps video sequence and you wish to add a default one-second, centered-on-cut dissolve at an edit point in your timeline, then the

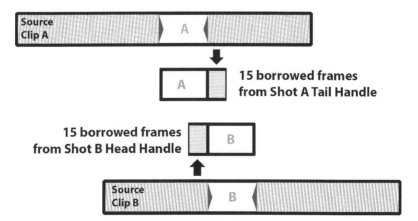

Source
Clip A

A

**15 borrowed frames
from Shot A Tail Handle**

A

**15 borrowed frames
from Shot B Head Handle**

B

Source
Clip B

B

Transition and Edit Terms

FIGURE 6.3 Video-editing applications must borrow frames from the related master clips' head and tail handles in order to visually display the dissolve or wipe transition effect.

software will "borrow" 15 frames from the tail handle of Shot A (for after the cut) and 15 frames from the head handle of Shot B (for just prior to the cut). In total, 30 frames of outgoing and incoming video will be dissolved across the edit point. Those 30 extra frames, 15 from each side's master clip, that were once hidden in the handles when the transition was a straight cut, are now visible inside the transition effect.

The Four Major Categories of Transition Types

The Cut

The cut is the most frequently used transition in any kind of motion media product. It can be defined as an instantaneous change from one image to another. If you are working in the continuity style of "invisible" editing, then the viewing audience should not consciously notice the cut transition. When it is made at the correct moment, following as many of the positive edit elements as possible, it will seem transparent within the flow of space, time, and action. Creatively, however, cuts do not have to be invisible. A hard and abrupt jump from one screen image to another can represent the mood of your story perfectly. Hidden or not, straight cuts instantly change picture or sound (or both) for the audience experiencing the video.

As a brief reminder, the term "cut" stems from the very beginnings of emulsion film motion picture production. The actual strip of flexible plastic that contained the images in individual frames was physically cut, either with scissors or with a guillotine-type razor blade splicer. Joining two shorter strips of film together, with either tape or glue, was the easiest, fastest, and cheapest way to make a transition. Hence, it was used a great deal. The people who cut filmstrips were called cutters before they were called editors. The expression still holds today even though most people who carry out film and video editing use computer software. In fact, several video-editing apps use a "razor" tool to make "cuts" or "edits" in the virtual media clips in the timeline. An editor can still be called a cutter and the act of editing a film can still be called cutting. Over the 100 years since the origins of cinema, the cut has not changed at all.

The cut is most often used where:

- the action is continuous;
- there needs to be a sudden change for visual or aural "impact;"
- there is a change in information or location.

It is possible to make good cuts and not-so-good cuts. If you consider all six of the following elements when you are making the cut, you are much more likely to help yourself to make a good edit (Figure 6.4).

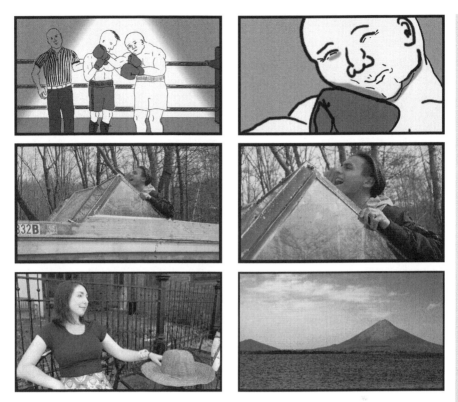

FIGURE 6.4 A–B – a cut can unite two shots that represent continuous action; C–D – a cut can punch in along the same lens axis to lead the viewer into a closer shot of the subject; E–F – a cut can end a sequence and lead the viewer into a new location. (Photo credits: C & D – Anthony Martel)

1. **Information** – Ideally, every shot in a motion media piece should offer some form of new information. When the shot currently playing on screen, Shot A, has exhausted all of its visual and aural information, the editor needs to cut to Shot B to provide the audience with something new to see or hear. Depending on the genre, content, and purpose of the video being edited, the new shot that is cut to may be an establishing view of a location, a close-up detail of machinery, a clip highlighting the sound of rain falling or a baby crying, etc.

2. **Motivation** – There should always be a reason to make the cut. There may be a physical action or visual element within a video clip that motivates the editor to cut to the next shot. It might also be a sound element on the audio tracks that motivates the cut to the next clip. Something within Shot A leads to the need to display Shot B.

   For example, a character, seen in a medium shot, suddenly whips his head around and stares, wide-eyed, off screen – CUT TO – the monster emerging

The Four Major Categories of Transition Types

from the forest. Shot B, of the monster, is called a reveal. The action within Shot A and the expression of the talent engages the audience and compels them to want to know what is being seen. The editor obliges and reveals the monster clip after the cut. In non-fiction programming, you may be watching a talking-head interview where the subject is speaking about her training for an extreme sport – CUT TO – the athlete, at dawn, running up some rugged hill terrain. The content of her words motivates the cut.

The nature of the program being edited and the content of the footage help to determine why and when a motivated cut can occur. An editor may simply determine that pacing, alone, is a good enough reason to motivate the cut. The timing of shots, clip durations, and frequency of cuts play an important role in motivating edits. These durations of time are generally not marked down in seconds or frames but take on more of a "gut feeling" unit of time known as a **beat**. They create the rhythm of the scene and add to the overall pacing of the entire story. Rather than a visible or auditory cause, the motivation for the cut's timing could be based on this intangible yet somehow instinctually knowable beat or feeling that it is now time to cut to something different.

3. **Composition** – If the frames of the two shots at the cut point are too similar in their compositions, even though they may be of totally different subject matter, it can appear as a visual jump cut to the audience. If visual objects on the incoming frames of Shot B appear in similar places on screen as objects that had been on screen in Shot A, the glitch may cause the audience a moment of confusion.

   Of course, the compositions may be similar enough to create what is known as a **form edit** or **graphic edit** where the shapes, forms, colors, and/or contrasts of each shot at the cut point are matched on purpose (see more on this later in this chapter). Traditionally, the start frames of Shot B should present a different composition from the end frames of Shot A.

   Using differences in composition at cut points forces the audience to immediately engage their eyes and brains and search for the new visual information in the new shot. As long as they are not confused by an overly busy composition in the new shot, they do not even notice the actual cut as they get engrossed in experiencing the visual elements of the new images on the screen.

4. **Camera Angle** – During the editing of a fictional narrative scene, each successive shot cut into a sequence should show a different camera angle

from the previous shot. A clean single or an over-the-shoulder shot recorded somewhere else along the 180-degree arc could immediately follow a medium long shot of two people talking in profile. Focal length changes, in addition to the changes in the horizontal angle on action, will be most effective.

There are rare occasions where a filmmaker wishes to cut together two coverage shots of the same subject along the exact same lens axis. This editorial practice is often referred to as a **punch-in**. It is also called a **cut-in** or an **axial edit**. To create this scenario, the production team must have recorded two coverage shots, say an MLS and an MCU of a stationary subject, without altering the horizontal angle on action – either by physically moving the camera between shots, or with a change in focal length. Punching in can be very dramatic or comedic in its use. Space and time are cut out and the viewer is immediately transported up to or away from the subject (along the same line of view or axis). The lack of significant difference in the angle on action between the two coverage shots does cause a jump cut, but it is done for visual storytelling purposes.

5. **Continuity** – The continuous movement or action should be both evident and well matched in the two shots to be cut together. The cut is instantaneous, so the fluid movement should be maintained across the cut. Viewers are extremely attuned to discontinuities in action across cuts and these differences of speed or object placement are easily detected and disliked.

6. **Sound** – There should ideally be some form of sound continuity or sound development across the cut point. If a cut happens within footage from the same scene and location, then the ambience should carry over across the cut. Audio levels should match the visuals' perspective on the screen for each shot at the cut point. Editing dialogue scenes can be especially tricky because of the precision required in finding that moment to cut just prior to or just after a word or syllable. The levels, intensity, and pacing of the word flow across the cut should also match.

If you cut dramatically from one location or time to another, then immediate differences in sound type and volume can be useful to highlight the shift in space, time, or feeling. These are sometimes called **smash cuts** (and could also apply to abrupt visual changes at the cut, such as a very dark image cutting to a very bright one). Otherwise, a gradual shift might be preferred where **L-cuts** or J-cuts help to smooth over the changes in sound at the audio transitions. (See Chapter Seven for additional information on L-cuts and J-cuts.)

The Four Major Categories of Transition Types

In a perfect world, you should give consideration to each of the above elements, but that may not always be achievable. Your goal should be to watch for these elements in all of your footage, train your eyes and ears to pick up on them, and use them as appropriate during your editing process. You should always use cuts when creating your assembly edit (what some people call the **slop edit** due to how quickly you are able to just slop the selected coverage shots together). The cut is the default edit tool of editing software and it is the fastest way to work. When trimmed as necessary, each cut in your final sequence should be unnoticed by anyone who watches the show if you are using an "invisible" continuity style of editing. Straight cuts are widely accepted when they work and wildly distracting when they do not (did somebody say jump cuts?). Develop your editing skill set around solid cuts and you will never go wrong. Play too much with the grammar of the cut and you may run into too many visual problems with your work.

The Dissolve

This is the second most common transition used in motion pictures, and, unlike most straight cuts, it attracts attention to itself on purpose. A dissolve is described as a gradual and momentary blending together of the ending picture frames of Shot A with the beginning picture frames of Shot B. This is traditionally achieved via a superimposition of both shots with a simultaneous downward and upward ramping of opacity (visibility) over a particular period of time. As the end of Shot A "dissolves" away, the beginning of Shot B emerges onto the screen underneath it at the same time. You get to briefly see the images overlapping.

A dissolve may also be referred to as a "lap dissolve," a "lap," and sometimes a video "mix." The standard default duration of dissolves in editing software is one second, but this can be easily changed to the length required by the given variables at that particular dissolving point in the story – provided you have those extra available frames in the master clip, called handles.

The dissolve is most often used where:

- there is a change in time;
- there is a change in location;
- time or actions need to be slowed down or condensed;
- there is a somber or emotionally quiet component to the subject in the story;
- there is a strong visual relationship between the outgoing and the incoming images.

A good dissolve may be achieved when the following elements are considered at the point of transition:

1. **Information** – Much like a straight cut, the new shot should contain new information for the viewer to digest. Whether the dissolve is condensing time over a long, continuous event, changing time periods or locations, or joining disparate concepts through matching imagery, the second shot into which you are dissolving should offer something new to both the viewer and the story of the motion media piece.

2. **Motivation** – As with all transitions, there should be a precise motivating action or narrative need to apply a dissolve. This could be moving backward or forward through time, or into or out of states of consciousness. The visual content, story, and genre of the video project play a large role in determining the motivation for the use of the dissolve. Because dissolves happen across certain durations, they are usually associated with slowing the rhythm of a scene.

3. **Composition** – The two shots dissolving together should each have compositions that overlap easily and avoid a visual "mess" – particularly at the midpoint when both images are, typically, at 50% opacity. You may dissolve opposing compositional frames (in Figure 6.5, Shot A has its subject frame left while Shot B has its subject frame right) to unify the images in one momentary yet well-balanced blended frame.

   You may also create a **match dissolve** where the compositions of the two shots are very similar but they have different subject matter. Consider the following example of a scene that involves a man who is a werewolf. As he begins to twitch and snarl, you cut to an XCU of his bloodshot eyeball with pupil dilating rapidly, then dissolve to a CU of the full moon. The two round objects, the pupil and the moon, match in composition and shape as the dissolve momentarily joins these images for the audience. Their visual union underscores their thematic connection as well (see the form edit section later in this chapter).

4. **Camera Angle** – Whether you are working on a short narrative film or a non-fiction program, you will generally dissolve between two shots that present differing camera angles on the action, either from coverage within the same scene or from two adjacent segments in the story. It is as if the audience are able to "move about" the film space and observe different actions or locations from a variety of camera angles at different times.

The Four Major Categories of Transition Types

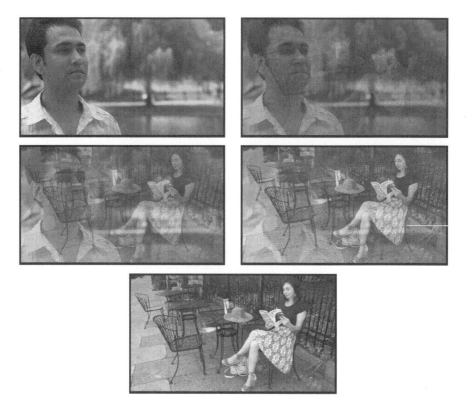

FIGURE 6.5 Frames that represent a dissolve from one shot to another. The man is thinking of his long-lost love.

Sometimes you may need to collapse time for one long, continuous event recorded from the same angle. Consider the following example of a bank robber who is "trapped" in his hideout waiting for his partner to arrive. The scene encompasses time from late afternoon to late evening with appropriate lighting changes throughout. It is all shot from only one stationary camera angle: backed into the corner of the small room facing outward. To compress time and quickly show the escalating agitation of the man, the editor dissolves between short portions of footage. From daylight through drawn shades to dim desk lamp, the audience get to watch the character move around the room, sit down, lie down, check his phone, peek out the window, etc. – all over elapsed film time via these multiple, slow dissolves.

5. **Sound** – It is customary to also mix together the audio tracks of the two shots being dissolved in what is often called an audio **cross-fade**. As the picture for Shot A is dissolving away gradually under the incoming image of Shot B, the audio tracks for Shot A are also fading down (growing quieter) while the audio

tracks for Shot B are fading up (growing louder). As discussed in Chapter Five, sound bridges (audio tracks spanning across the cut point) may require long, slow audio dissolves to properly blend the incoming audio element.

6. **Time** – An important element in the efficacy of the dissolve is its duration, or how long it lingers on screen. One second is usually the default duration for dissolves in video-editing software, but a dissolve can last for as long as there is visual material in each shot involved in the transition (also known as the handle). In general, the dissolve should last as long as is required for its purpose in the motion picture. A quick dissolve of just a few overlapping frames, sometimes referred to as a **soft cut**, might be preferable to an instantaneous straight cut – but beware that this can imitate a jump cut. A long dissolve can be on screen for several seconds and may, along the midpoint of this longer duration, appear more like a superimposition of the two shots rather than a dissolve. If the story calls for such a visual treatment of these two images uniting for this longer period, then so be it.

The dissolve allows the editor to play with time differently than the straight cut. If you are editing a story that involves a flashback, you could dissolve from the last shot of the present time to the first shot of the events from the past. The audience are softly escorted through story time with the blending of these images and scenes. The dissolve is also often used to create a **montage** of many different images of events over time. For example, a full day at an amusement park can be condensed down into ten different shots that dissolve from one to the next. The final sequence lasts only 30 seconds of screen time. Usually, such special treatments of visual material are planned by the filmmakers from the outset of the project, but editors should feel free to experiment with dissolving time if they find certain scenes to be too long.

It is important to note that dissolves can also slow down time and manipulate the emotions of the audience when accompanied by **slow-motion** imagery. This technique is often used in motion media commercial advertising of products, as a means of trying to make them seem sexy, alluring, or grandiose. In fiction filmmaking, you often see this treatment of slowing down fast action to reveal the true efforts, emotions, and pain of the subjects, such as in a boxing movie or in battle scenes. A romantic or maybe an emotionally sad sequence can also use dissolves rather effectively to slow down events and give the audience time to view and digest the meaning of the material. The gradual transition from image to image softens the experience. It is said that the dissolve is the "tear jerker" transition. Dissolves allow the viewer time to think and feel, and are associated with more languid, somber, dreamy, or "thoughtful" emotional responses to the visual story elements.

The Four Major Categories of Transition Types

As a technical aside, you should be aware that most video-editing software applications must "borrow" frames from the full source clip in order to generate the dissolve of the requested duration at the cut point in the sequence. Sometimes, the "hidden" frames of the handle (the tail of Shot A and the head of Shot B) reveal visual or aural information that is not desired. A clap slate is in the shot, or you hear the director call out, "Action" (Figure 6.6). There are methods present in the software to address this, such as trimming

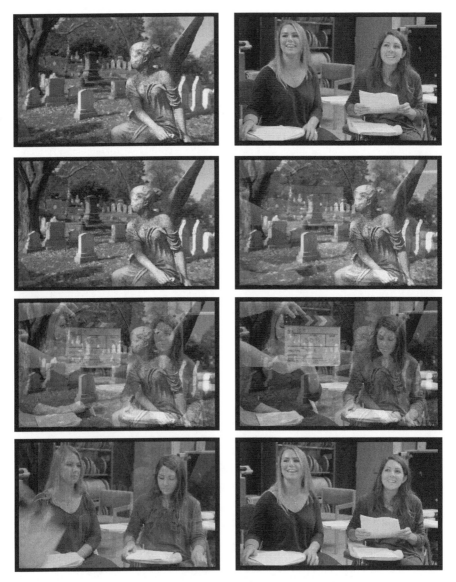

FIGURE 6.6 The two shots work well as a straight cut, but when a dissolve is added, the clap slate is revealed in the frames borrowed from Shot B's head handle.

the transition point earlier or later, altering the dissolve duration, or adding a **freeze frame** for just a few frames at the transition. It should be noted that all transition types, except the cut, require the use of these handle frames, and the presence of unwanted picture and sound elements should be closely monitored.

Dissolves can be used in any time-based motion media piece such as fictional narrative movies, television shows, music videos, documentaries, animated cartoons, how-to and wedding videos, etc.There was a time when you would have been hard pressed to find dissolves in the daily news, but even factual reporting has incorporated the "manipulative" transition – an indication of how the rules of visual grammar are changing with our never-ending 24-hour mobile access to motion media.

The Wipe

The wipe may be thought of as a cross between a cut and a dissolve. It happens across time like a dissolve but it tends to be performed very quickly. You get to see both images on the screen at once, as in a dissolve, but there is usually no superimposition involved. Wipes are meant to be noticed by the audience and often appear as shapes, or with other graphic elements associated with them. Wipes can zigzag, iris, or spiral, and move diagonally, horizontally, or vertically across the screen, replacing the previous shot with a new shot.

The wipe is most often used where:

- there is a change in time;
- there is a change in location;
- there is *no* strong visual relationship between the outgoing and the incoming images;
- projects call for more visually graphical and engaging treatments at transitions;
- there is an ending to a scene, act, or program (as an "iris out to black" in silent cinema).

A good wipe, often a highly stylized transition effect, does not always demand consideration of the standard elements that lead to good edits.

1. **Information** – Certainly, the shot wiping onto the screen will provide the viewing audience with new information, but it need not be related to the

The Four Major Categories of Transition Types

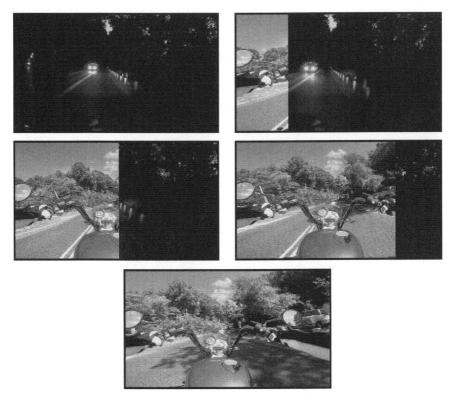

FIGURE 6.7 The wipe literally wipes one image off the screen and replaces it with a new one. Wipes may be used as fast and fun transitions from any shot to any other shot.

existing shot that is being wiped off. It is also possible to use a graphic (like a team logo) or large-font text to wipe across the screen. This additional visual wiping element provides even more information to the viewer – and can often "mask" the otherwise awkward wiping motion as the shots transition on screen.

2. **Motivation** – The simple need for an editor to leave one location or one segment of a program can be enough motivation for the use of a wipe. The movement of an object in the outgoing shot may also provide motivation for a certain shape, timing, or direction for a wipe effect. Sometimes, if you have no purposeful way of getting from one place, time, or topic to another, you can use a creative wipe to "entertain" the audience across the duration of the transition and lead them to a totally new place, time, or topic.

Within the grammar of editing transitions, the wipe is the most fanciful way of moving around time and space. If the motivation for the edit transition is to quicken the pace, then fast wipes are a fun and stylized way to achieve this speed of changing the visual elements of the motion picture.

3. **Composition** – With careful planning, a clever filmmaker may conceive of strong vertical or horizontal movements within the shot composition, and a clever editor will turn these visual elements into what are called **natural wipes** (see Chapter Eight). Objects found within the action of the outgoing picture frames (such as doorways, wall corners, or a bus passing across the foreground) appear to push, pull, or in some way wipe across the screen. This allows for a cut or a wipe to the next incoming shot.

   Because there will be portions of two different shots on screen, it can be beneficial to have the compositions match, mirror, or balance one another in some way during the wiping process. You may also find that the style or shape of the wiping element is an interesting graphical composition in itself, and the shots just ending and just beginning around the wipe do not require any special visual connection.

4. **Camera Angle** – Much like the freedom offered by the images' compositions around the wipe, there is no real need to adhere to the differing camera angle rules here. The wipe serves to literally wipe the slate clean from the previous shot and introduce new visual content; camera angles are beside the point, although you should still feel free to creatively explore your options.

5. **Sound** – Depending on the type or style of wipe you choose to use, sound can be treated as a straight cut, an L-cut, a J-cut, or a cross-fade at the transition. Sound may lead the wiping shot or follow after it. You have a great deal of freedom in playing with how the audio behaves during the wipe. Depending on the type of program being edited, it is often appropriate to give the wipe action its own sound effect, such as a **swoosh**.

6. **Time** – Just as dissolves happen across time, wipes need to have durations as well. Fast wipes can transition quickly from one shot to the next when the tempo of the edited piece necessitates moving the story along rapidly. If the edited show calls for slower, more lingering wipes, then they could last for a second or more, although this may get tedious for a viewer. Fast and fun is generally the way to go.

The graphical wipe often acts as an energy enhancer, a fun distraction, or a visually stimulating way to bridge two disparate and otherwise not easily joined segments of a program. In classic Hollywood films of the 1930s, wipes were a fanciful, graphically

The Four Major Categories of Transition Types

pleasing way to transition from one place or time to another. In recent history, the *Star Wars* movies have used wipes rather effectively. They take the place of the more mundane dissolves and have more pep. Within today's motion media landscape, wipes can take on any shape or form and are appropriate to use in most genres, such as non-fiction pieces, comedy, fantasy, sci-fi, children's programming, and even "fluff" news segments. They are less common in dramatic, feature-length fiction filmmaking these days.

The Fade

If you have ever gone to the theater to see a stage play, you know that at the start of Act I, the house lights dim down, the curtain opens, and the stage lights fade up to reveal the setting and the actors. At the end of the scene, act, or play, the stage lights fade down to darkness. Motion pictures and some sequences from television programs also traditionally begin and end with a fade. If you have ever read a screenplay, you probably saw that the first line was FADE IN and the last line was FADE OUT. This is like the **fade up** and **fade down** lighting cue in the theater. The movie screen starts out entirely black and then the black gradually fades away to reveal a fully visible image signaling that the story has begun. As a fade-out, the frames of the images at the end of your show gradually fade into a fully opaque black screen signaling that the story has ended. Fades can take on any color in your video-editing software (with the default color usually being black), but most often you will see black and occasionally white used professionally.

The fade-in is most often used:

- at the beginning of a program;
- at the beginning of a chapter, scene, sequence, or act;
- where there is a change in time;
- where there is a change in location.

The fade-out is most often used:

- at the end of a program;
- at the end of a chapter, scene, sequence, or act;
- where there is a change in time;
- where there is a change in location.

For a fade to be most effective, the following elements should be considered:

1. **Motivation** – The fact that the motion picture is beginning motivates the use of a fade-in, and when you have reached the end of a segment or act, it is acceptable to fade out. That is motivation enough for the fade. A fade-out followed immediately by a fade-in at the cut point is often called a **dip to black** or **kissing black** and serves as a means of slowing the pacing between segments – like a long, slow blink of your eyes (Figure 6.8).

2. **Composition** – It can be very helpful in achieving a clean fade-in or fade-out to use shots that will either begin or end (or both) with a low-contrast image. Compositionally speaking, you would not wish to have prominent areas of dark and light within the frame, because as the opacity gradually fills in the image or takes it away toward black, the discrepancy between the heavy light and dark areas of the frame will create an imbalance in brightness and make the fading action appear uneven or poorly timed.

3. **Sound** – It is traditional to have the sound levels rise up under the brightening picture of the fade-in. The audio should also fade down as the picture exhibits the fade-to-black or fade-out at the end. If a fade-out from one scene lingers on the all-black screen, it is often acceptable to fade up the new audio of the yet-to-be-seen next segment before the fade-in occurs. This is an example of **sound leading picture**.

4. **Time** – Like the dissolve and the wipe, the fade requires an appropriate duration. Depending on the project, it could last anywhere from half a second to several seconds. Usually, you will just feel what the right amount of time is because staring at an all-black screen for too long, without any new information on the audio track, will feel off-putting. This is a good example of when you should listen to your gut and feel the appropriate beats to establish contextually appropriate timing.

   The default duration for fade effects in most video-editing software is one second. This is obviously a good starting point for the duration but you may wish to go longer depending on the purpose of the fade at that point in the motion media piece and the type or genre of show that you are editing. Typically, a fade does not require access to the master clip's handle frames, but is applied to and manipulates those frames already cut into the timeline at the tail or head of the selected shot.

Fade-ins and fade-outs have long been part of film language and standard tools of the editor when starting or ending any motion picture project. They act as transitions into and out of the dream-like state that is motion picture viewing.

The Four Major Categories of Transition Types

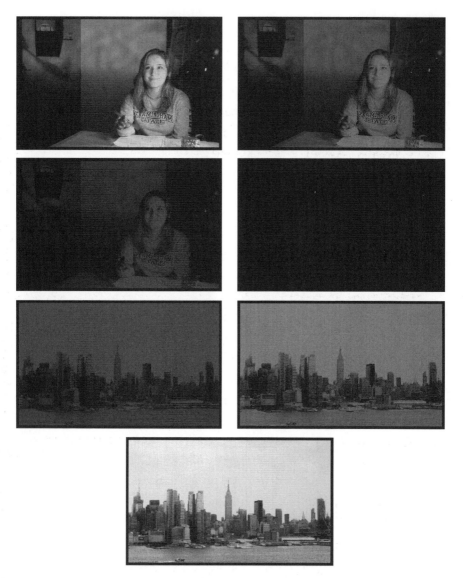

FIGURE 6.8 The fade-out ends one segment and leads the viewer to new visual material as it transitions through a fade-in at the head of the first shot in the next segment. (Photo credit: G – Mike Neilan)

The Five Major Categories of Edit Types

So far, we have explored three categories of shot types, 11 kinds of basic shots, six elements that help to make a good edit possible, and four major categories of transitions. Now, we are going to examine five categories of edit types that touch on most of the major kinds of edits that can be performed with most material. Granted, the type of project that you are editing will help you to decide which kinds of edits you will be able to execute. Certain genres call for certain editorial treatments, but most programs could be completed using one or more of these edit categories.

Our five categories for the different types of edit are:

- the action edit
- the screen position edit
- the form edit
- the concept edit
- the combined edit.

In Chapter Five, six elements were outlined, consideration of which helps to make edits stronger. The five categories listed above are all different types of edits; therefore, it would hold that consideration of the same six elements should also benefit each type of edit. Let us examine each one and provide some examples.

The Action Edit

The action edit is nearly always a straight cut. As its name implies, this category encompasses edits between shots that depict continuous action or movement of subjects or objects. As a result, this type of edit may also be called a **movement edit** or a continuity edit. A general action edit scenario could be: Shot A showing a subject performing an action – CUT TO – Shot B depicting a continuation of that action as seen from a different angle around the subject and with a different shot type. Movements appear to be smooth and continuous across the cut. Time is unbroken.

To demonstrate the action edit in a simple film narrative, let's say we see (in a long shot) a woman sitting at a cafe table pick up a book and open it. She lifts the book closer to her face to read it. Then there is a cut to a new shot. After the cut, we are shown the woman in close-up (seen from a different horizontal angle) holding the book so that we can see the title on the cover and watch her eyes scan the pages rapidly (Figure 6.9).

The long shot provides the audience with important information about the location, the subject, and the time of day, how the woman is dressed, and what her actions are like: slow, quick, normal, or abnormal. The new CU shot shows the book title and her eye movement indicates that she may be reading.

The Five Major Categories of Edit Types

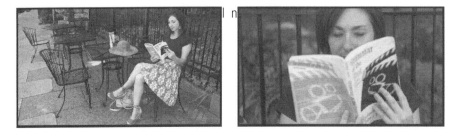

FIGURE 6.9 In this action edit, the lifting of the book up to the face motivates the cut. The book raise will begin in the wide shot. This movement motivates the cut to the close-up, which shows the action complete.

the long shot, the woman will pick the book up from the cafe table and raise it closer to her face. The action of lifting the book will be a good place to make the cut. The action is the motivator, using the raising of the book to initiate a cut into the closer shot that reveals the book's title and the woman's eyes.

Regarding the composition of the shots, we find the arrangements of subject, objects, and set dressing within the frame of the long shot create a strong diagonal exterior space. There are **foreground**, **middle ground**, and **background** layers. The close-up shot offers a centrally weighted frame with the details of the book taking up most of the space. Although framing the woman toward the right may have been more in line with her placement in the wider shot, the title of the book and the appearance of the woman's eyes are the most important things in this new shot. Their just-right-of-center framing is working better for the "showing" of narrative information in this case.

In the long shot, the camera angle is on a 3/4 profile of the woman's left cheek. In the close-up, the camera has moved around the arc and approaches her face with a more frontal framing. The change in shot type helps, and the difference between the horizontal camera angles of these two shots is more than adequate for the cut to appear natural.

The most important aspect of the action edit is the continuity, and the continuity of movement really should match at this cut point – hence the use of related terms "match cut" and "matching action." The coverage in the long shot of our current example does provide the action of the woman raising the book from the table and opening it in front of her face. The close-up repeats that same overlapping action of the book raising and opening, plus it continues along with the woman's eye movements across the pages.

As the editor of this action edit, you would be free to cut and match the movement of the book at any point during the action. It may be advised to show only the initial movements of the action in Shot A and then have the remaining action complete itself in Shot B. Furthermore, some suggest starting the second (continuing) shot three to five frames before the actual frame of "best match" for continuity. The theory is that those fractions of a second of screen action are "lost" as the viewer reorients her or his vision to the different locations of objects continuing the movement on the screen. Because you cut on action, the audience are less likely to perceive the edit, and merely register the presentation of new information about the book and about the woman's eyes.

Finally, because this is a street scene, the ambient sounds could be rather varied. There should probably be some sounds associated with the background of the location: perhaps a bus driving by or a car horn honking here and there, plus the chirping of birds, etc. You could even address the sound of the book being picked up or the pages turning by adding some Foley effects of these actions once you move into the close-up shot. The sound bed should match across the cut.

The action edit is quite common and can be used in very elaborate action hero chase scenes or in very quiet, slow-moving melodramas. As long as there is a continuous action or movement in the frame, the editor can use that to match the same action from another coverage shot from the scene. Some recommend a one-third/two-thirds approach, where you cut away from Shot A at a point where the action is one-third complete and cut into Shot B when the matching action has two-thirds remaining. In practice, you are free to cut anywhere along the action that makes the edit work. If you have adequately considered the six elements listed above, then the action edit should be smooth and unobtrusive, and allow an uninterrupted visual flow for the story unfolding on the screen.

The Screen Position Edit

The **screen position edit** is sometimes called a **directional edit** or a **placement edit** – "directional" because it helps to direct the viewer's eyes around the screen, and "placement" because it is the unique placement of subjects or objects in the two shots cut together that makes the viewer's eyes move around the frame. This type of edit can be a cut, a dissolve, or even a wipe, but it is usually a cut if there is no passage of time implied by the edit.

The way that the shots of a scene are originally conceived (through storyboards or script notes), composed, and recorded will help an editor to construct a screen position edit. Two shots in the coverage were designed to lead the audience's eyes around the screen. Usually, one strong visual element occupies one side of the frame and casts its attention, movement, or line toward the opposite side of the frame. Cutting to the new shot, the object of attention is usually shown on the opposite side, fulfilling the viewer's need to see something occupy that visual space. The goal is to engage the audience physically (eye movement around the screen image), mentally (seeking and finding new visual information about characters and the plot), and emotionally (what you draw their eye to in the new shot may be cute, horrific, breathtaking, etc.).

A basic example of a screen position edit is the traditional two-person dialogue scene shot with master scene technique. Beginning with a medium long shot, two people, in profile to camera, face one another and have a conversation. The standard coverage would call for solo medium shots and maybe medium close-ups of each of the two characters. When it is time to edit, you could go from the wider two-shot into the solo medium close-up shot of Character A, who is shown frame left. While speaking, his gaze is directed toward frame right. You cut to a medium close-up shot of Character B, who is shown frame right looking frame left (Figure 6.10).

The new, close-up shot of Character B yields new information for the audience, in the look on her face or in her eyes or in the words she chooses to say or not say. Any gesture by Character A, or even the line of dialogue being uttered, would be a motivator for the cut. The mirrored screen position satisfies the composition category. The audience had their eyes over on frame left for Character A and then had to move them across the screen at the cut point to observe Character B in the new shot. The camera angles around the shooting arc are significantly different. Continuity of dialogue delivery is achieved with the cut, which also means that the sound is continuous as well. Not every screen position edit will take into account all six of the edit elements, but this simple example does.

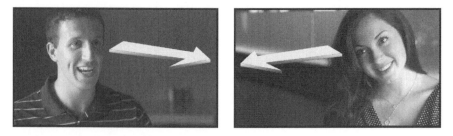

FIGURE 6.10 The screen position edit in its most basic form. One subject is frame left while the other occupies space over on frame right in the next shot. The eyes of the audience are directed across the screen at the edit point following the sight lines.

The Form Edit

The form edit is best described as a transition from a shot that has a pronounced shape, color, or dimensional composition, to another shot that has a similar shape, color, or dimensional composition. These types of edits are usually preconceived during the writing or pre-production phase because the visual elements that will match require the correct treatment of composition and, sometimes, screen direction. Rarely is the form edit just blind luck on the part of the editor but it can happen, so watch for the opportunity in the visual material. Form edits are sometimes called graphic edits.

If using sound as the motivation, the form edit can be a straight cut, but in most cases, the transition will be a dissolve. This is particularly true when there is a change of location and/or perhaps a change in time from one shot to the next. The term "match dissolve" is often used to describe this type of form edit. Our werewolf eye-pupil/full-moon dissolve mentioned earlier is a good example.

A simple scenario will serve to demonstrate a form edit. In a story about a man returning to his small rural village after finding success in the big city, we experience a series of close-up shots of a jet plane tire, a car tire, a bicycle tire, and a wagon wheel. The objects are also spinning counterclockwise as they travel over the ground. The four circular shapes are roughly the same size and occupy the center of the film frame in each shot. Essentially, they all match. As the editor, if your goal is to condense the man's travel time,

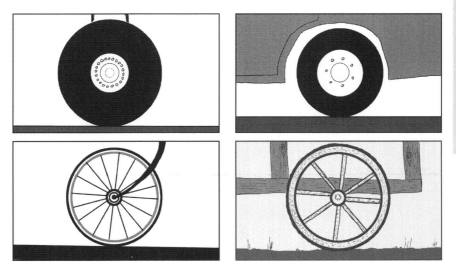

FIGURE 6.11   The form edit of the wheels dissolving into one another quickly takes the audience to new, and increasingly rural, locations.

you could dissolve from one wheel shot into the next until you end up with the close-up of the wagon wheel (Figure 6.11). You could then cut to a shot of the man sitting among some goats and dried corn stalks in the back of a mule-drawn wagon.

The audience will understand that the dissolve transitions are condensing time. The technological de-evolution of the wheel shapes will show the audience that the man is moving further into the rural area of his home village. The consistency of shape and composition helps to keep the viewer's eye trained on the center of the screen and allows the viewer the focus needed to comprehend the meaning. The sound elements will also change from very loud to rather quiet as they cross-fade into one another under the corresponding dissolving pictures, supporting the audience's sense of location change. Music under this mini-montage could also be appropriate.

Form edits are also often used in advertising and television commercials. It can be difficult to deliver your message concisely in 30 seconds, so most often advertisers try to show their message in easily understood graphical ways and with visual metaphors. Take, for instance, a public service announcement (PSA) for an anti-smoking campaign. The **spot** calls for a studio shot of several cigarette packs standing up on end in a field of endless white. One pack is the most prominent, standing up in front of all others. During the spot, this shot dissolves into a shot of headstones at a cemetery. Each cigarette pack was standing in the exact spot where a grave marker is now standing in the second shot (Figure 6.12).

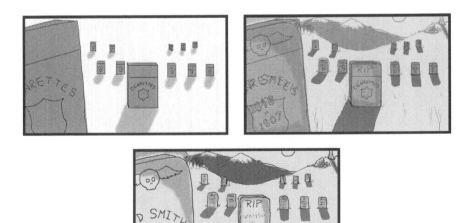

FIGURE 6.12 The form edit of the packs dissolving into the headstones generates a new meaning in the mind of the viewer.

The audience can draw a conclusion from this form edit: that smoking cigarettes may lead to an early death. Whatever the perceived message of this PSA, the use of the form edit (match dissolve) is what helps the audience to interpret meaning. The shapes are simple rectangles. The compositions match exactly. The juxtaposition of these "charged objects" and their "union" during the dissolve generates a rather clear meaning and also conveys the message smoothly and succinctly. Provided the duration of the dissolve for this form edit is long enough, and the audio tracks work together, the audience would be carried easily from one shot into the next thanks to the matching forms. This form edit may even work well as a straight cut, or a very quick series of back-and-forth cuts flickering on the screen very rapidly, generating a "lightning" flash effect.

The Concept Edit

The concept edit may stand alone as a purely mental suggestion. This type of edit is sometimes called a **dynamic edit**, an **idea edit**, an **intellectual edit**, or **intellectual montage**. The concept edit can take two shots of different content and, through the juxtaposition of these visual elements at one particular time in a story, can generate implied meaning not explicitly told in the story. This type of edit can cover changes in place, time, people, and even the story itself, and it can do so without any obvious visual break for the viewer.

Most often, the concept edit is planned by the filmmaker from an early stage of picture development. He or she already knows that the two separate shots, when joined together in the narrative at a certain point, will convey a mood, make some dramatic emphasis, or even create an abstract idea in the mind of the viewer. It is rare, but not impossible, for an editor to create a concept edit from footage that was not intended to form a concept edit. Be forewarned, though, that these types of edits can be tricky, and if the intended meaning is not clear to the viewer, then you may just contribute to an unwanted interruption of the flow of visual information and cause confusion.

The previous example of the cigarette packs and the gravestones is very much like a concept edit. The idea that smoking may be bad for you stems from the picture of the packs dissolving into the picture of the gravestones. Their blending on screen joins them together in the mind of the viewer – formulating the concept that smoking can lead to death.

Another example of a concept edit would be the following scenario. Two couples are out on a date and one woman announces to the group that she and her boyfriend are now engaged to be married. The male friend turns to the newly engaged man and

The Five Major Categories of Edit Types

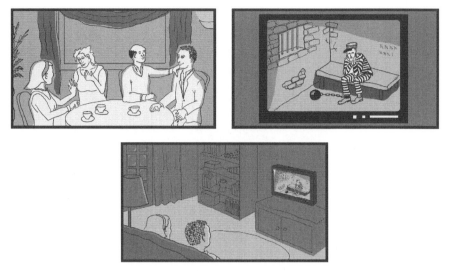

FIGURE 6.13   The concept edit conjures an idea in the mind of the viewer through the juxtaposition of seemingly unrelated shots. Does the newly engaged man feel that marriage may be like a prison sentence?

asks, "So how does it feel to be getting married?" – CUT TO – A close-up of a television screen; an old black-and-white prison movie is playing and the inmate wears shackles around his ankles – CUT TO – A wide shot of the engaged man and woman, sitting on a couch watching the movie (Figure 6.13).

Neither shot has anything to do with the other. The group shot of the couples at the restaurant is in no way connected to the close-up shot of the old prison movie. The insert shot of the prison movie is only contextually related to the third shot of the living room because that movie is playing on the TV in that physical space. The six elements need not be considered here, for it is not the elements in the shots that make the concept edit, but the effect of what happens in the viewer's mind when these shots are joined together at that time. Clearly, the engaged man is having some second thoughts about the concept of marriage.

Almost 100 years ago, filmmakers from Soviet Russia became entirely enamored of the power that editing possesses over an audience's reaction. They found that the juxtaposition of the clip content created a new meaning that the content alone could not necessarily bear out. Lev Kuleshov is famous for conducting a film-editing experiment where he took the same close-up clip of a man's expressionless face and intercut it with shots of a bowl of soup, an apparently dead child in a coffin, and an attractive woman reclining on a sofa. When he showed this mini-sequence of unrelated clips to audiences and asked them what they thought, the audiences overwhelmingly assigned different emotions to the actor's neutral facial expression: hunger, sadness, and desire. Thus was born the **Kuleshov effect** and the idea behind our concept edit is based partly on this psychological reaction within an audience when they view juxtaposed images (Figure 6.14).

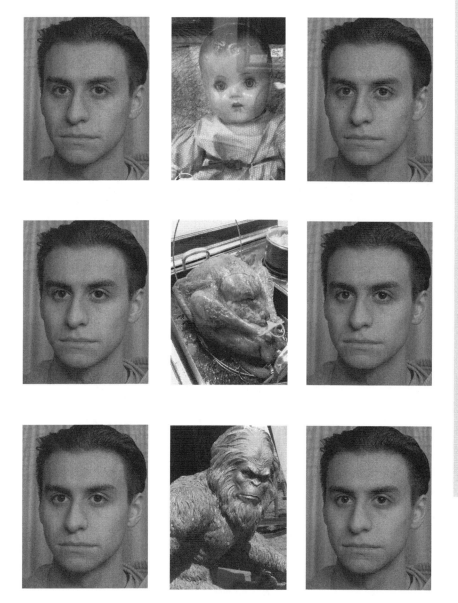

The Five Major Categories of Edit Types

FIGURE 6.14 Our version of the Kuleshov effect. When these images are edited in motion across time, the audience are likely to assign an emotional response to the otherwise neutral facial expression of the actor. The mere juxtaposition of the images generates a new concept in the mind of the viewer. (Photo credits: Anthony Martel)

The filmmaker Sergei Eisenstein helped to popularize the Soviet montage style of story showing. He favored discontinuous action and often juxtaposed disconnected imagery back to back to back in his sequences in order to get the audience to formulate new meanings and new feelings in their own minds. Intellectual montage explored this thought-inducing technique to the fullest. Some edits could generate clear and common reactions within the audience, but others may have been more open to interpretation or even too difficult or confusing to draw a real conclusion about the intended meaning. Some argued that this ambiguity was also part of the process and anything that made a viewer think was a good outcome. Today, common examples of the concept edit are not nearly as esoteric to decipher – for better or for worse.

The Combined Edit

The **combined edit** can be a difficult edit to come by in edited programming because it requires a good deal of pre-production planning on the part of the filmmaker. It would be rare that two unplanned shots could be cut into a combined edit by the editor alone. The combined edit combines two or more of the four other types of edits. One transition may contain an action edit combined with a screen position edit, and there may be a form edit and a concept edit all in one.

Consider a children's fantasy story where young brothers, dressed in their pajamas, are playing together just before bedtime. They are pretending to fight off some goblins with a flashlight and a pillow. One brother tosses the flashlight to the other – CUT TO – A sword landing in the hand of the second brother, now clad in battle armor, standing on a narrow ledge in a cave fighting off real goblins (Figure 6.15).

If planned well and shot properly, this scenario has many elements that will make it a good candidate for a combined edit. First, the action of tossing the flashlight across the

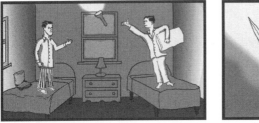 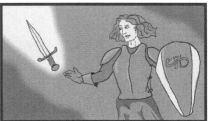

FIGURE 6.15 The combined edit takes on multiple attributes of several other edit categories. Action, screen position, form, and concept edit elements are present in this cut from the boy playing to the boy fantasizing about actual heroic deeds.

room makes this an action edit. Second, the screen position of the flashlight and sword is similar. Third, the forms of the two objects are similar: the flashlight and the handle of the sword. And lastly, the concept of the power of imagination may be gleaned from this edit. The boys at play actually transform into the heroes of their fantasy.

Chapter Six – Final Thoughts: Does Everything Always Apply?

The job of the editor is not to memorize the six elements to consider when creating an edit or the five types of edit categories as presented in this book, but to use the reasoning behind these concepts to inform his or her choices while making the edits. Knowing that cuts, dissolves, wipes, and fades are made in different ways, have different meanings, and can convey different experiences to the viewing audience is very important. Joining shots together at a certain time, in a certain way, for those certain reasons is really what your goal should be. Remember that the editor has an obligation to create an informative, engaging, and, hopefully, entertaining experience for the target audience. How you assemble the video and sound clips helps to guide the audience and manipulate them (in a good way). Knowing the grammar of the edit will help you to better execute the edit. This, and practice over time, will enable your skills to develop even more.

Related Material Found in Chapter Eight – Working Practices

#23, 24, 25, 26, 27, 28, 29, 30, 31, 34, 35, 37, 38, 39, 40, 41, 42

Chapter Six – Review

1. Straight cuts are great for continuous action, when there needs to be a sudden change for visual impact, and when there is a change in plot point or location.

2. Dissolves are used to help to change time or location, to draw out an emotion, or where there is a strong visual and/or thematic relationship between the outgoing and incoming imagery.

3. The wipe can be used to jump in time, to jump in location, to unite two totally unrelated shots simply to move the story along, or just because the project calls for a more upbeat, graphically engaging transition.

4. The fade-in begins a program, scene, or sequence. The fade-out ends a program, scene, or sequence. Fade-ins and fade-outs are also used often on audio clips for smooth entrance/exit.

5. Action edits join shots that cover continuous, uninterrupted action or movement.

6. Screen position edits, through well-planned shot composition, purposefully draw the audience's attention from one section of the screen to another at the cut point.

7. The form edit unites two shots with two similarly framed objects that have similar shapes or movements. This is usually executed with a dissolve to show the audience how the objects look alike.

8. The concept edit unites two seemingly unrelated visual shots at a certain point in the story and the result is an idea, concept, or relationship in the minds of the viewers. It hits them on an intellectual level and makes them think. It is based on Soviet montage theory.

9. The combined edit is still just a cut, a dissolve, or a wipe at one transition, but it combines elements of several of the edit types, often matching actions, positions, and forms, and generating ideas. These make for rather powerful storytelling moments.

Chapter Six – Exercises

1. Either record your own or acquire the media for a simple dialogue scene. Assemble it with straight cuts, fine-tune the rhythm through trimming the tails and heads of the shots, and watch your sequence. Then add dissolves at every cut point and watch the sequence again. How does it feel? Which way do you prefer and why? Have the dissolves caused any technical or aesthetic problems with the pacing, mood, or visual elements of the scene?

2. Create any kind of wipe across an edit point for any two video clips in a sequence. Copy and paste those same two clips again in this mini-sequence and keep the same wipe effect. On the second instance of the wipe, add some sort of swoosh or other sound effect so the timings and duration feel right. Watch both versions (without added sound effects and with). Which do you prefer and why?

3. Record a variety of shots (LS, MS, MCU, CU) of a friend juggling, bouncing a ball, or doing something that shows controlled and repeated subtle movements. Edit a brief sequence of these coverage shots with action edits, timing their continuity of action and movement as smoothly as possible. Practice using your trim tools at the cut points to really fine-tune the illusion of uninterrupted action.

4. Take the action edit sequence from Exercise 3 and add one-second dissolves to each cut. Is the illusion of continuity maintained? If not, can you tweak the head and tail timings of the clips to smooth it out? What happens if you replace all of these dissolves with some kind of wipe effect? Does it change the continuity of action? Does it alter the pacing or change the "energy" of the piece?

Chapter Six – Quiz Yourself

1. Name the four basic transitions discussed in this chapter. For what editorial purposes might you use each one in a sequence?

2. What is a "jump cut?" What can cause it? When might you choose to use one?

3. What is the key component required of footage for you to create a "punch-in"/"cut-in"/"axial edit?"

4. What are head and tail "handles" and when might you need to access them?

5. In order to create a "form" or "graphic" edit, what kinds of images are required?

6. What kind of edit unites two matching shapes or compositions from two different shots across the transition?

7. What kind of edit places two unrelated images in sequence, but generates an implied meaning, thought, or feeling in the mind of the viewer?

8. In video-editing jargon, what is a "beat?"

9. You have joined the head of Clip B to the tail of Clip A as part of a montage sequence in your assembly edit timeline. As a straight cut, everything looks great, but when you add a one-second dissolve centered on the cut, you suddenly see a few blip frames of the camera slate on screen. Why might this be happening and how might you be able to fix it?

10. What is a "flashback" and how might you creatively transition into that show segment and out of that show segment?

Chapter Seven
Editing Terms, Topics, and Techniques

- Timecode
- Montage
- Parallel Editing
- Multi-Camera Editing
- Composite Editing
- Rendering
- Chromakey
- Video Resolution
- Sound Editing
- Color Correction/Color Grading
- Importing Still Images
- Digital Workflow
- Technology vs. Creativity

These days, much is expected of a video editor. Depending on the job size, budget, and purpose, many editors are tasked with performing more than just straight cuts. The increased sophistication and capabilities of the editing software have, in some ways, coerced the editor into expanding her or his skill set. Graphics creation, motion effects, music selection, and audio mixing may all be part of the modern editor's responsibilities.

Having covered many topics regarding shot type, shot quality, transition types, and edit categories, you are in a good place to go out and start editing. No one source of information will be able to tell you everything about the art, craft, and job requirements of an editor, but, by now, you should have a solid grasp of basic approaches to thinking about how to handle general editorial decisions.

We address a lot of the *what*, *where*, and *why* questions. Information on *how* to edit can be found in many other sources. Each video-editing software application has its own unique "engines," media workflow, tool names and functions, etc. There are specific classes you may take, online training and tutorials to work through, many books to read with practice media, etc. in order to learn how to edit in those software titles. As this is an introductory book on the concepts and general practices behind editorial decisions, such precise technical information is well beyond our scope.

In this chapter, we will augment our list of topics by addressing some additional terms, concepts, and techniques. Learning from a book is an excellent way to start wrapping your brain around the editing process, but there is no replacement for on-the-job training. The fun and satisfaction are to be found in the editing process itself, so get ready to go to work.

Additional Editing Terms

Timecode

A film frame is the unique space of a single recorded image along perforations or between sprocket holes (depending on the gauge or size of the film strip). Emulsion film, being long strips of thin plastic, uses feet and frames to count lengths and/or durations and therefore time. Even though emulsion film acquisition and exhibition has decreased dramatically in recent years, we still refer to our video recordings as "footage." Videotapes, having no perforations, use a special track on the unbroken length of tape inside the plastic cassette that counts time according to an electronic pulse that notes the hours, minutes, seconds, and frames (appearing as HR:MN:SC:FR, where the example of the one hour and 37 second mark on a tape would read as 01:00:37:00). Digital media files have similar **meta-data** embedded inside the computer file that keeps track of a great deal of information including the hours, minutes, seconds, and frames, but does so digitally (Figure 7.1). This notation is called timecode.

The frame rate for a particular format is also involved in this counting scheme. Emulsion film recording and projection has a standardized frame rate of 24 frames per second (24fps). Old-school, twentieth-century standard-definition NTSC video in North America has a frame rate of roughly 30fps (29.97) while European PAL video has a 25fps rate. So for archival PAL projects on your editing software, you would be able to watch 25 separate frames in one second, and for NTSC SD projects, you would be able to see 30. Of course, these frames would go by your eye so quickly in one second that you really do not get to distinguish one frame from another. You would have to step through one frame at a time to see the 30 individual frames of that second of video.

01:00:37:00

Hours : Minutes : Seconds : Frames

or

1 Hour and 37 Seconds

FIGURE 7.1   The counting scheme of video is known as timecode. Digital video source files, videotapes, and edited sequences can each have unique time durations, but they share the same rate of time progression of hours, minutes, seconds, and frames.

Standard-definition NTSC and PAL broadcasting is all but gone, and with the advent of increasingly capable digital video cameras, additional frame rates are available for video production (and playback). The old interlaced fields of SD video frames were briefly used in high definition as well with 1080i (or 30fps, 1080-line, interlaced) video. Now, most cameras generate a progressively scanned stream of digital images, meaning that for each frame there is just one full image (just like emulsion film cameras have done for over 100 years). Without getting too technical, you may soon see more commonly used progressively (p) scanned image frame rates such as 24p, 25p, and 30p being phased out as newer high frame rates (HFR), such as 48p and 72p, are making headway in mainstream filmmaking. This means that editors will, increasingly, need to pay extra attention to how their video source material was recorded time-wise.

Timecode (TC) is the counting scheme, or the clock, that video-editing software uses to keep time for frame rate playback and for keeping sync. The picture information and the audio information (when they come from the same associated media files or tape source) will have the same matching timecode frame for frame. Depending on the recording camera and the medium (hard drive, memory card, or videotape), the timecode data may be set in different ways. Digital video recorders that generate media files typically begin each unique file with 00:00:00:00 and count up to its individual duration.

Additional Editing Terms

Videotapes typically have a continuous timecode across the entire tape (either pre-striped or laid down as the camera records each frame). Unique shots start and stop along the stream of continuous time. As such, you may encounter tape sources that have unique tape names or numbering schemes (the first physical tape has 01 hour TC and the second physical tape has 02 hour TC, or the first hour of shooting was assigned 01 hour TC by the production team and the second hour has 02 hour TC, etc).

Video-editing software keeps track of all TC references and shows this data in the bins and folders, in the playback windows, and in your sequence timeline. The project settings often dictate the counting scheme for your timecode on edited material and it is often best if they match frame rates, although most software can now mix and play back different frame rates in the same timeline; if not, they can certainly convert from one frame rate to another.

Montage

The term "montage" has several meanings when used in relation to motion picture editing. For the French, the word simply describes the act of assembling the film, which is the job of the editor. For many involved in Soviet silent cinema of the 1920s, it emerged as the montage theory of editing, which is a belief that two unrelated images can be edited together to generate a new thought, idea, or emotion in the mind of the viewer. An example of this concept edit was presented earlier in this book. A young couple announcing their wedding engagement in Shot A is then followed by an image of a prisoner with a ball and chain around his ankle in Shot B. A viewer might get the idea that the filmmakers are equating marriage with a prison term.

The more widely applied meaning of montage today refers to the **montage sequence**. This involves a series of quick clips, usually accompanied by music, that show a condensed version of actions, activities, or events over time. In a teen comedy, it could be a series of shots showing the friends getting ready for the prom; in an action movie, it could be a series of shots showing the elite fighting team going through tough training; in a romance, it could be a series of quick clips showing a young couple going out on multiple dates and falling more and more in love with one another. A montage sequence serves a very useful purpose by condensing important plot points and developments that might otherwise unfold across a day, several weeks, or even years, into a shorter, more manageable duration. The audience do not have to watch every aspect of these events to understand their results. Think of it like a highlight reel of important plot events that, if shown in their entirety, would take up way too much screen time.

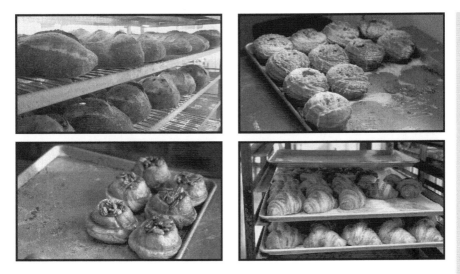

FIGURE 7.2   Montage sequences typically show a series of quick shots that are related to a larger scene, segment, or topic of a show or movie that condense time and provide a lot of visual information. They are often accompanied by fun and fast music.

Parallel Editing

Used primarily in fictional narrative filmmaking, **parallel editing** (also known as **cross-cutting**) calls for a special construction where two plot lines of the story's action are intercut with one another. In other words, a portion of one plot line is shown, then the sequence shifts over to showing the other plot line which, in the film world, is supposed to be happening simultaneously.

This technique proves especially effective during an action sequence – often a race against time. The pace of the sequence may also get more "frantic" as the two storylines unfold, building the suspense and getting closer to the dramatic climax. This can be achieved by making the shots in the sequence increasingly shorter and shorter. The frenetic energy of the cuts carries over to the audience, who are feeling the urgency of this pacing and the race against time.

Multi-Camera Editing

Most fictional narrative filmmaking is accomplished with just one camera. The shot types described earlier in this book are typically composed, lit, and blocked for the one camera that is used to record the coverage for that scene. It can take a significant time to accomplish all of the shots needed to edit the scene for the movie. There is another practice,

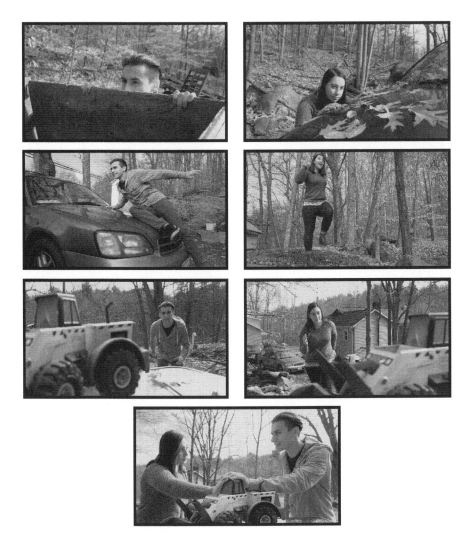

FIGURE 7.3 We cross-cut back and forth between the actions of two separate characters as they progress toward a common goal. This is an example of a type of parallel editing done within the same scene. (Photo credits: Anthony Martel)

however, where multiple cameras are used on set to shoot different angles of the same action, getting differing shots of coverage while the actors perform the action one time on one take. Camera 1 records one character's close-up and Camera 2 records the other character's close-up at the same time. Provided both performances are good, the production saves time and money shooting coverage in this manner. Using multiple cameras is very popular when recording studio-based situation comedies for television, soap operas, reality programming, news, talk shows, sporting and competition programming, live theater, musical concerts and, with certain directors, very "performance"-heavy scenes or stunt work in fictional narratives.

The beauty of multi-camera editing is that all of your source footage for each take from each camera matches. A cut at any point will have a corresponding matching frame from another camera angle to cut to in perfect sync. Certainly, all action should be seen from all coverage angles, but also the cameras may share or identical timecode, so at 00:24:17:00 (24 min. 17 sec.) a cut from one camera will have the next frame of image and time match for all cameras recording the event. Most professional video-editing software has a built-in process for matching up all of your camera source footage. As a result, you have the option of cutting to any camera angle at any point in time, much the same as a television studio director in the control room has the option of switching from Camera 1 to Camera 3 to Camera 2, etc. (Figure 7.4). Because the audio was also recorded as one unbroken track during the performance, all of the camera images should match up perfectly while playing over the one sync source of audio.

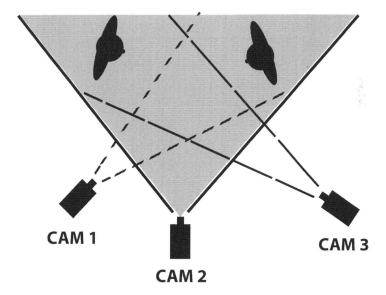

CAM 1   **CAM 3**

CAM 2

Additional Editing Terms

FIGURE 7.4   Recording scenes with multiple cameras is common in TV studio production, but is also becoming more prevalent in location shooting of other motion media genres. WS and CU shot coverage is completed during a single performance.

Composite Editing

Think of composite editing as multi-layer editing where more than one image is seen on screen at one time. This will necessitate the use of more than one video track in your timeline and the use of visual effects or filters on the clips on the upper tracks. Your video project, or sequence, will have a set frame size based on the image resolution of the video format that you are editing (see later in this chapter for more details). Most clips will have the same resolution or size, and if you stack one on top of the other, you will only see the top video track because it will block your view of anything underneath it. A visual effect or filter, such as a superimposition or a picture-in-picture (PIP), will be needed to treat the upper track so that the lower track will at least be partially visible.

Split-screen effects are created using this method. You could make two separate shots of people talking over the telephone fit into one screen by compositing the two clips on Video Track 1 (V1) and Video Track 2 (V2) of your timeline and applying some crop and reposition effects to each. A PIP inset is done in a similar fashion, whereby you reduce and reposition the video clip on V2 (Figure 7.5). This technique is used frequently on TV news broadcasts.

Each video track in use counts as another data stream that needs to be processed. The more compositing of video tracks you do in your sequence, the more difficulty the computer system will have playing back the multiple media files; this is especially true for high-definition media. Most straightforward fictional narrative motion pictures will not need very much composite editing, but any projects that could benefit from multiple images or composited elements will need this approach. Music videos, sci-fi or fantasy films, commercials, and even corporate promotional and wedding videos may call on split-screen effects, PIPs, or composited visual effects (VFX). A render (see next section) may be required in order for the more complex stack of video clips to play back in sync on your system. Otherwise, you may experience sluggish, stuttering playback or dropped frames.

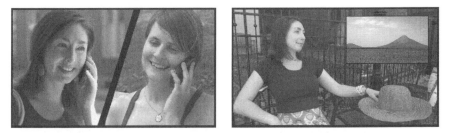

FIGURE 7.5 Composite edits are made out of multiple video layers. These examples show a split-screen phone conversation and a picture-in-picture over a background video track.

Rendering

Regardless of the video-editing software that you use, some video or audio elements in the timeline will eventually need to be rendered during an editing session. Rendering is the creation of new, simplified media files that are based on the merged result of numerous affected clip references in your timeline. Rendering will allow the system to play back complex effects or composites more easily. Typically, if you have created a complicated visual effects composite of six HD media streams (V1 up to V6), the system may have difficulty playing it in real time. The software is trying to heavily manipulate each pixel of each frame of each layer in the composite all at the same time. If you render the affected clips, the system creates a brand new single "merged" media file that shows the result of all effects in the composite.

These new and independent rendered media files do get referenced during playback of your sequence, but they have not deleted or replaced the original clip references that your system was struggling to play back. Those original clips still live in your bins. Be aware that rendered clips are, in essence, "physical" data and they do fill up space on your media drives. Also, if you make a change to any content in a rendered clip or effect composite, it "unrenders" or reverts back to the original complex media file references. Rendering times vary depending on the power of your computer system's processors and amount of RAM, the complexity of manipulation by the effects, and the complexity of original source media. Don't be surprised if it takes a while.

Chromakey

When you watch a meteorologist deliver the weather report in front of a large radar image showing swirling patterns of cloud movement, you are seeing the result of a **chromakey**. You may be more familiar with the terms "green screen" or "blue screen." These names refer to the same process, whereby a certain color (chroma) is "keyed out" or made invisible and removed from a video image. Post-production software is used to select that particular color (most often green or blue) and turn it invisible while the remaining pixel data in the image is untouched. This layer of "keyed" video becomes the foreground element (the weather person clip on V2) or the top layer in a composite. Then, some other video image (clouds on the radar clip on V1) is placed on the layer below to become the visible background of the new composited video image.

Although you could key out any color in your video clips, the colors green and blue are most often used because they are two colors whose range of hues are not normally

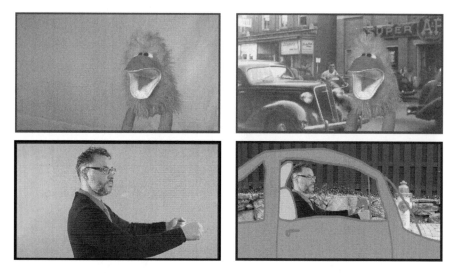

FIGURE 7.6 Most video-editing software applications have some form of chromakey effect. Here, a green sheet was keyed out to create the composite of the puppet over the old photograph background layer.

present in the skin or hair of human beings. Be advised that people with green or blue eyes will have their irises disappear if a similar green or blue color of chroma-screen was used during production. Another type of key, known as a luma-key, uses a low black video voltage (sometimes called "super black") to make this transparency. You may find this used on graphic elements where the super-black pixels can be turned invisible by your editing software while "normal" video black pixels remain unaffected. You could also create these still graphics with the **alpha channel** instead of creating super-black luma-keys.

Video Resolution

A video image is made up of a grid of tiny boxes each filled with particular brightness and color data. These tiny boxes are called **pixels**, which is shorthand for "picture elements." The more pixels of data you have in your image, the higher the resolution it will have. A high resolution means a greater ability to show more precise detail. High-definition (HD) video, in today's technology market, is a moderately high-resolution capture and playback format for digital motion imaging on television and the web. 4K and 8K video are growing these numbers exponentially.

Video resolution is customarily represented by two numbers (#A x #B). The first number describes the quantity of pixel units arranged horizontally in a single row across the screen's grid, left to right. The second number indicates the quantity of these rows stacked up from the bottom of the screen to the top (i.e., pixels in a vertical column). Full HDTV is represented by the resolution 1920 × 1080. This means that there are 1920 tiny pixel boxes arranged horizontally from the far left of the image to the far right of the image in a single row. Then there are 1080 rows stacked up from the bottom of the frame to the top. Simple math tells us that a total of 2,073,600 pixels are used to make up the entire image.

In comparison, old-school standard-definition digital video has an image resolution of 720 × 480 (North American NTSC-DV) and 720 x 576 (European PAL-DV), with an overall pixel count that is just a small fraction of that for HDTV. As a quick technical note, SD video uses rectangular, or non-square, pixels, while HD, graphics-editing software, and computer monitors all use square pixels for the creation and display of images.

Today, ultra-high-definition television uses a screen resolution of 3840 × 2160 (approximately four times the amount of image data as full HD). Soon, 8K UHDTVs will display even more information. When will more ever be enough?

More pixels may mean more detail, but it also means more data per frame to be analyzed, processed, and displayed by your video-editing computer system. Even a robust system can handle only so much information in the processing pipeline (hard drives, processor, RAM, graphics card), so editing with full-resolution video can slow things down. Most editing software allows you the option to convert your original files to a more compressed version. The pixel count will remain the same, but the amount of data represented in each pixel "region" is filtered and averaged down so that the system does not have to think as hard. For playback as streaming web videos, the compression may also involve converting to a lower frame resolution, so that the final video media file has a smaller overall size in megabytes. An accompanying loss of visual quality may also be detected in the smaller video file.

TABLE 7.1   The Aspect Ratio and Pixel Resolution of Video Formats

	SDTV (NTSC)	HDTV	Full HD	UHD	4K Cinema
ASPECT RATIO	4:3	16:9	16:9	16:9	1.9:1
PIXEL DIMENSIONS	720 x 486	1280 x 720	1920 x 1080	3840 x 2160	4096 x 2160

Additional Editing Terms

Additional Editing Topics

Sound Editing

Earlier, in Chapter Five, we discussed the teakettle whistle as a motivator for the edit. Beyond being a source of motivation, the audio track is a powerful component within the storytelling architecture. It can help to underscore the surface reality of the scene. Consider the following example from a headache relief medicine commercial. A woman is seen sitting in a noisy business office in a wide shot. There is a cut to her in an MCU. The audience would expect the noisy business office ambience to continue to be heard under the new MCU of the woman. If they are not presented with that continuity of audio, they could be pulled out of the viewing experience, wondering what happened to the sounds. The cut would draw attention to itself in a negative way.

What if the same scenario occurs, except that this time there is no office noise after the cut, only dreamy, ethereal music is heard? This new audio information seems to match the calm look on the woman's face as the medicine takes effect. This peaceful music is her internal soundtrack: it is representational. The audience are given new information about the internal mental or emotional state of this woman. Within all of the office craziness, the medicine is now helping her to stay calm and collected in a near-meditative state. The editor has used sound to draw positive attention to the transition through providing the audience, and the woman, with a break from the office noises (Figure 7.7).

Sounds can also make statements that go against the visuals being presented to the viewer. Consider the following example. You have an interior medium two-shot of a man telling his friend that he is "going to hunt for a job." The roar of a lion is heard on the audio track and a picture transition takes us to a wide shot of a crowded, bustling city street during commuter rush hour. Animal noises are mixed in the audio tracks along with

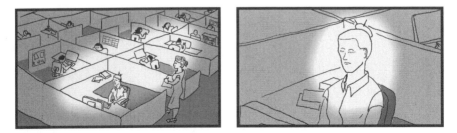

FIGURE 7.7 The noisy office sounds that caused the woman's headache drop away at the cut to the MCU and mix into ethereal music. This changeover on the audio track reflects her inner peace after she's taken the medicine.

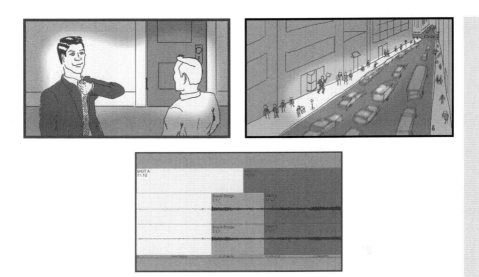

FIGURE 7.8   The lion's roar bridges Shot A to Shot B, which continues the animal sound metaphor. The third image shows what the clips of this sound bridge might look like in your sequence timeline.

the busy street ambience. The character from the previous shot, the job hunter, is now out in the wild on the hunt for a new job. If detected, the audience might normally wonder about the animal sounds playing while watching a busy city street, but because it follows the context of the job hunt, the otherwise out-of-context animal sounds actually become story-enhancing sounds (Figure 7.8). They underscore the metaphorical big-city "jungle" theme being explored in the story.

As with our train whistle example in Chapter Five, the lion's roar from the sound metaphor above presents another sound bridge. The roar takes us from one shot into another. In these examples, the sound of the next shot is heard before the picture of the next shot. We call this "sound leading picture." The opposite holds true as well. You may have the sound of Shot A carry on under the newly visible picture of Shot B. We call this **picture leading sound**. Perhaps you have a wide shot of a man dropping a bowling ball on his foot. As he yelps in surprise, you cut to an extreme long shot of treetops in the forest. As the sound of his yelp continues under the new picture of treetops, flocks of birds fly up and away as if startled into flight by the man's cry carried so far across the countryside (Figure 7.9).

The editing practice of having either picture or sound start early or end late is known as creating a **split edit**, an L-cut, a J-cut, or **lapping**. Picture and sound tracks are really separate media streams when they live inside your editing software. In most scenarios,

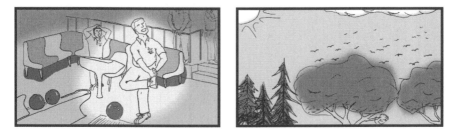

FIGURE 7.9 The yelp of the man bridges across the edit and laps under the split picture track.

they will play in sync and be placed in the timeline together. It is easy to see how you then might end and begin both picture and sound track(s) for two shots at the same moment in time. This is called a straight cut or a **butt-cut**.

Assembly edits, and maybe the rough cuts of your sequence, will most likely be all straight cuts. As soon as you start to finesse the edits in the fine cut, you may find that offsetting the cut point for the picture or the sound is advantageous, or sometimes necessary, especially during dialogue editing. You are making split edits for creative purposes. One track leads or follows the other (Figure 7.10). When done correctly, these split edits can make your transitions either very engaging or very smooth for the audience. When done incorrectly, they can put the brakes on pretty quickly.

In dialogue scenes, a J-cut will also provide aural motivation for the picture track to cut to the person speaking. Many believe that this practice emulates how we hear and see in our real lives. Picture yourself having a conversation with a friend in a cafeteria. You suddenly hear the voice of another friend who is coming to join you. You turn your head to see your other friend as she approaches the table where you are sitting. In this scenario, you hear your friend's voice (she is "off screen") before you see her approaching (the "cut" to her MLS). Record these actions with a camera and edit them, with the J-cut audio tracks, just like it happens in real life.

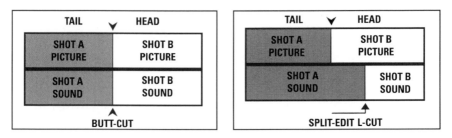

FIGURE 7.10 An example of a butt-cut becoming a split-edit L-cut.

Color Correction/Color Grading

A key component to the finishing phase of post-production, the color correction process allows for an editor (or a special technician known as a colorist) to tweak the brightness, contrast, and color of the final clips in the video sequence. The term "color correction" is usually applied to making major changes in the exposure range, contrast levels, and/or colors of an image that appear wrong on the screen or inappropriate for the story being shown (brightening an underexposed clip, removing too much blue near the windows on an interior shoot, or removing the green on a person's face from the bounce light in a midday, grassy exterior shoot). A color-neutral gray scale, good contrast, and scene-appropriate hues are the main goals. The term "color grading" (or "color timing") is also used during this phase, and refers to making creative alterations to the contrast and color values so that shots match or to manipulating the imagery so that a special "look" can be achieved (dark and moody; desaturated color palette; bright and super-saturated, cartoon-like colors, etc.).

Whether it is spot correction or overall project grading, the main goal of this process is to get the video to have the desired look. Both technical and aesthetic reasons can drive a post-production team to make these choices. It is much more complicated than this, but video cameras basically capture and record light information as electronic voltages based on the quantity of light energy obtained from the different wavelengths of the visible spectrum. If the film set is dark, then there isn't much energy (voltage or signal) present to record the scene and it may appear dark with weak color data. If the film set is very, very bright (there is a lot of energy and therefore voltage), the video image may appear too bright and washed out.

As an editor, you would most often hope that the production team have recorded images that represent the full spectrum of shadows, mid-tones, and highlights, and have adequate color saturation. When you have an appropriate amount of energy to manipulate, the color correction tools in your video-editing software can do more with the signal and yield the desired look of the project. When the original media file is either too dark or too bright, there is often not much that can be done to really improve the overall look of the image because the data that the correction tools need to manipulate was never captured in the encoded video file in the first place. Some very high-end video cameras can output sensor data at the equivalent of "camera RAW" (uncompressed image format) and software will have a greater chance of manipulating the imagery's tonal range and color data.

There are two main parts to the video signal: luminance and chrominance. The luminance refers to the light levels or the overall brightness and contrast of an image.

Additional Editing Topics

Gauged along the gray scale, an image with good contrast should have areas that are representative of dark shadows, mid-tones of gray, and bright highlights. A high-contrast image will have both very strong dark areas and bright areas but will have very few mid-tone gray elements between. A low-contrast image will have the reverse: mostly mid-tone gray with very few truly black or truly white areas in the frame. During color correction, it is traditional to first establish the black level of the video signal (the "set-up"), then the white level (the "gain"), and finally the gray mid-tones (the "gamma"). With your contrast levels set, you would then move on to making color (or hue) adjustments.

Keeping it simple, chrominance refers to color values, which are manipulated by different tools in the software. They allow you control over actual color or hue values from the color spectrum. They also allow you control over the voltage of a color, or its saturation level. Desaturating a video image (removing all color voltages) turns it black and white. Saturating an image (driving up the voltages or boosting the color "energy" signals) amplifies the color content and can make colors look unnaturally "thick" or "deep" like a candy apple red. The voltages, for both luminance and chrominance values, should not be over-driven or under-driven or they can compromise the quality of the video playback on electronic displays such as television and computer screens. There are devices called **video scopes** that help you to measure and analyze the video signal and to keep it within the "legal" zone.

Color correction provides you the opportunity to make bad video look better and to creatively "paint" a contrast and color "look" for your overall video project. You can work your way through your sequence doing shot-for-shot and scene-for-scene correction and grading. The flesh tones of your subjects should look appropriate for who or what they are, the color palette should look as you wish, and the shadows and bright areas should be where you want them. These changes are best achieved through the use of properly calibrated color monitors and digital, HD, or UHD luma and chroma scopes. These extra devices are usually very expensive, so if you are working on your own projects, you may have to make do with the built-in tools available in your video-editing or color-correcting software. If your edited program is ever going to air on television, then you would absolutely want to color correct your sequence, but any video project, even just for web distribution, can benefit from the tweaks of the color correction phase of post-production.

Importing Still Images

Common still photographic digital cameras are capable of recording very high-resolution still imagery. As an example, you may have a still photographic digital file that is approximately 3500 x 2300 pixels. Even if you are editing in a full HD 1920 x 1080 video project, the video resolution (and frame size) is much smaller than the still photo you want to add to your sequence. The still photo file, pixel for pixel, is larger than the active picture area of the full HD video and would have to be scaled down to fit. What if you have downloaded an image file from a website (like a JPEG) and you intend to add that file to your timeline? The web image is only 200 x 200 pixels — far smaller than the HD video frame. Scaling the tiny image up to fit closer to the HD picture frame will make it look terrible. Each video-editing application handles the import and still photo conversion process differently.

As a video editor, you may be asked to add such still photographic images to your project. You can use a photo-editing application to make cropped copies of the original photos so they take on the pixel dimension and frame size of your video project (i.e., a 1920 x 1080 cropped photo will import and fit into your full HD video sequence). Depending on your video-diting software, the imported file may come into your project as a reference to your full-resolution original photo and you can use a filter/effect to scale and reposition the larger photo so that it fits into your video frame area. Other applications can be set to import converted versions of the original file and force it to resize to fit within the video frame, either on the horizontal or vertical axis, depending on the dimensions of the original photo file. Very small photos (like 200 x 200) will not scale well (because expanding pixel data degrades image quality), and if you need to incorporate them, you should know that they will remain very small or look very bad.

Additionally, a still photo is only one frame, but it does not play as only one frame in the video sequence. That would be a meager blip of 1/30 of a second or so. The import process may create new media of a longer duration where that one still frame is replicated to play over and over and over again as multiple instances of the same frame. So, if you need three seconds of that imported still image in your sequence, you can edit a clip segment of three seconds into your sequence.

Most higher-end photo manipulation software will allow you to create multi-layered still images or masked (cut-out) images with the alpha channel. Much as video has the red, green, and blue color channels (RGB), still photographs may exist in that color space as well. The fourth channel, alpha, is like a transparency switch that makes all color data for that specific pixel turn off or go invisible. The chromakey that we explored earlier is like this. Be aware that a true alpha channel can only be saved in certain kinds of image files — .TIFF being one of the most universally popular. Often, the video-editing application needs to be made aware that the alpha channel is present so that when a masked image is imported, the background (or masked region with alpha) remains invisible, and the video elements on the track below in the sequence will be seen.

Digital Workflow

The power, flexibility, and relative convenience that editing software has brought to the world of visual media creation are undeniable. It is not all fun and games, however. There is a responsibility, often placed upon the editor's shoulders, to be organized and knowledgeable about file types, media assets, and the interoperability of various software applications. This creation, storage, and sharing of video and audio materials is generally referred to as workflow. It is increasingly rare for post-production workflows to incorporate **analog** source materials (like physical strips of motion picture film prints or analog videotape). Most independent software users and post-production facilities are now deep into the digital workflow, where all video and audio elements needed for a story are created, stored, used, and authored as digital files on computers.

Today's multiplicity of digital video cameras use many different encoders and file types to create their amazing high-resolution imagery. Not every version of digital video-editing software uses the same types of files and not everyone encodes, stores, or accesses these files in the same way. A modern editor, in addition to being a great storyteller, must also be knowledgeable about these file types, feel comfortable with general computer functions (on multiple operating systems), and understand media drives, cloud networking, etc.

A wise film production team will have plotted out and verified the file-type workflow through the post-production process before they record their first take. The user-assigned details can also make a huge difference in how smooth the workflow becomes. Naming conventions differ from place to place, but logic dictates that developing a sensible and concise method for naming projects, bins, sequences, clips, folders, graphics, source tapes, etc., is essential. With clarity in your naming and organization of your raw, digital materials, you are already well on your way to a more efficient digital workflow for the life of your editing project.

Technology vs. Creativity

Film editing has been around for over 100 years and videotape editing for about 50. Computer-aided or digital non-linear editing has its origins around 1990. So whether it was scissors and glue, videotape decks, or computers, the one thing that all of these techniques/tools have in common is that they are all a means of assembling a story of some kind — a story that needs to be experienced by an audience that will be informed, manipulated, and entertained by the content and style of the assembled motion media piece. The editors, over the years, have been the skilled craftspeople, technicians, and storytellers using these devices and techniques — to show those stories to those audiences. The tools that they have used have simply been a means to an end.

Today, in the digital age, the tools are different, but the skills of those who use them remain the same, or at least they should. Unfortunately, many people get lost in the nuances of the latest editing application and they separate the importance of their story-telling abilities from their knowledge of the software's functionality. Or worse, they get so caught up in learning the latest bell or whistle in a specific editing application that they forget their primary goal as storytellers. No one should confuse button-clicking abilities with solid editing skills.

There is a wide variety of video-editing software available on the market today. Several applications are of professional quality and are used by high-end, post-production facilities, television networks, movie studios, and the like. Many are geared for more in-home/consumer use and have fewer capabilities. Knowing how to use several of these applications will benefit the newbie editor. Knowing one is a great start, but knowing more about using several editing applications from the high end will expand your job prospects considerably. The important thing to remember is that no matter what tool you end up using to perform the actual edit, at that point in the filmmaking process, you are in control and you are the creative force behind the crafting of the story.

Chapter Seven – Final Thoughts: Old Techniques Done with New Technologies

Montage, parallel editing, and even composite effects shots have been around for over a century; the new tools that make these things happen and the ease of use of digital technologies have allowed so many different techniques to be used in so many different types of motion media pieces. Live action movies, TV shows, and web videos are all "time-based" motion pictures — as are animated cartoons. Even though we still have progressive (digital) frames, the use of timecode helps us to keep track of durations and sync in the construction of these time-based media pieces. Editors need to be knowledgeable on the oldest of motion picture editing techniques while always staying on top of the latest technological advancements and workflow that will help to show their stories tomorrow.

Related Material Found in Chapter Eight – Working Practices

#13, 56, 57, 58, 59, 60

Chapter Seven – Review

1. Timecode from original sources allows you to maintain sync between your picture and sound tracks within your edited sequence.

2. A montage sequence is a series of quick clips, usually accompanied by music, that shows a condensed version of story-related actions and events that would normally happen over a longer period of story time.

3. Parallel editing cuts two simultaneous storylines together so that concurrent action can be seen by the viewer at one time during the program. This is usually done for action sequences.

4. Multi-camera editing allows you to edit footage of the same event captured by several cameras all at the same time. It is useful for sports events, rock concerts, soap operas, dance sequences, and staged situation comedy television programs.

5. Composite editing refers to creating a stack of video sources in a sequence where the application of filters or effects allows you to see portions of all of the clips at once in one frame.

6. Depending on your video-editing software and hardware performance, you may need to render more complex HD video clips or composited visual effects segments in your timeline. The software generates new, easier-to-play, single-stream media files.

7. Chromakey effects remove a particular color value or shades of a hue (most often green or blue) from a video image and allow the transparency of that color region to show video elements on the lower video tracks of the timeline.

8. All video formats have a screen dimension referenced by its width in pixel units by its height in lines or rows of pixels. For instance, full HDTV has a 1920 x 1080 video resolution, but UHDTV has a 3840 x 2160 resolution.

9. Split edits, L-cuts, and J-cuts change the start time of the picture track or sync sound tracks for a clip in the timeline. If picture leads sound, then the audience see a cut to the next video clip while still listening to the audio from the previous outgoing clip. If sound leads picture (often referred to as a

sound bridge), then the audience hear the sounds of the next incoming shot underneath the video that they are still watching in the current clip.

10. Sound, whether matching the visual elements or contrary to them, is a great tool to enhance meaning in the story and to engage your audience on a different sensory level.

11. The goal of the color correction process or color-grading phase of post-production is to allow the editor to make all shots in the sequence look as they should for the needs of the program. Basic contrast and color balancing helps the images to look better, both technically and aesthetically. Special color treatments or "looks" may be added (e.g., a cold environment can be given a steely blue/gray color treatment; a hot desert may be made to look extra "warm" orange-amber).

12. Digital still images may be imported into your video-editing project, but be aware of the dimensions of the image versus the dimensions of your video project's format. Images from the web may be smaller, and images from digital still cameras may be larger, but few will exactly match the frame size of your video. Cropping, resizing, and repositioning may all be required.

13. Become familiar and comfortable with the workflow needed for managing digital media assets and the creation of computer-based video edits. Thinking ahead and knowing your end result can save you some big headaches.

14. As an editor, do not let the complexity of video-editing software get in the way of your good decision-making abilities and solid storytelling skills.

Chapter Seven – Exercises

1. Create a montage sequence. Record video of a school or family event or simply the "happenings" in your town. Review the footage and pull your favorite clips. Assemble a montage sequence and add a piece of music appropriate to the mood and pacing of the visual elements.

2. Practice parallel editing. Create a scenario where a person is inside a location searching for something important and another person is outside, making his or her way to that location to pick up that very same important item. Cut the coverage of each individual as separate mini-sequences and get a feel for how they play back to back. Now create a new sequence using parallel-editing (cross-cutting) techniques with straight cuts – nothing fancy. Watch this new sequence

for pacing. Does it generate tension and suspense? If not, how could you tweak the shot selection and the timing of the shots to make it more suspenseful?

3. Use a duplicate version of your final cross-cut sequence from Exercise 2 and see where you can create effective split edits or L-cuts on the audio tracks. Then color correct each clip in the sequence so that it has good contrast and a neutral or balanced color spectrum.

Chapter Seven – Quiz Yourself

1. What information is represented by the following timecode: 01:06:37:14?

2. Do you think a dissolve could be considered composite editing even though it may occur on a single video track? If so, why?

3. This may depend on your editing software, but can rendering an effect clip in your timeline generate new media on your media drive? If you change something about that rendered video clip, will it "unrender?" Will it delete that newly created rendered media file?

4. What are the two most common colors used for creating chromakey transparencies in video production?

5. What does it mean that full HDTV is 1920 x 1080?

6. Should you first address the contrast (blacks, whites, and grays) of a video image or the color values when grading the shots in your timeline?

7. True or false: most digital still images that you import will have the exact same frame dimensions as the video format in your editing project.

8. What is a PIP and when and why might you employ it in a video project?

9. How might the technique of cross-cutting help to show a story more dynamically?

10. True or false: "video scope" is just another term for an old TV set.

Chapter Eight
Working Practices

The working practices presented in this chapter are commonly accepted guidelines, or good tips, for you to think about while you are editing. Some offer specific techniques to follow, while others simply suggest some good habits that you may consider as you work. You may not encounter these precise scenarios on every job or in each motion media project, but you should be aware that they may come up. You will learn how to recognize them and you will find ways to address them appropriately. The working practices have been developed over time and have been found to work within many editing styles and within different genres. Each project should be viewed with fresh eyes and you will be left to judge whether or not these working practices apply to the piece that you are editing.

It should be noted that in today's highly visual media marketplace there are many venues where motion images are displayed. The variety of television programming, webisodes, commercials, short films, feature films, documentaries, promotional videos, broadcast news packages, etc. all require some degree of editing before they are experienced by the viewing public. As you advance in your editing career, you will learn what each of these program types requires for its individual editorial workflow and established styles, etc. Starting with the following section of working practices as a solid base, you will be in a good position to fine-tune and augment your own list of editing "dos" and "don'ts."

Finally, there will be cases where an editor has done everything right – the correct type of edit, the correct elements, etc. – so that in theory the cut or dissolve or wipe should work. But it does not. One of the skills of an editor is to analyze the material and find out why the awkward edit exists. Of course, it could be that an exact cause cannot be found, but it is still up to you to find a solution. Editing is not a perfect craft. There is always room for creativity and discovery, and that is part of the fun of the process.

1. Pay Careful Attention to Media and Project Organization

Reason

As much as editing is about creative, visual storytelling, the process relies heavily on efficiency and timeliness. Establishing good habits of project asset management and organization will help an editor to work more confidently through any project.

Solution

Known drive allocations, clear folder structures, and purposeful naming conventions across the board can go a long way in helping any person involved with the post-production workflow to stay on top of his or her project's materials. Solid organization is key – especially if more than one person has to share time working on the video piece.

Whenever possible, original source media files need to have a complete set of copies on another drive as back-up. Keep your functional set of source files in the same folder on the same drive throughout the edit. Give your project a name that will be short and clear to all who need to access it. It can be helpful to pre-create bins/folders inside your project for some of the most common assets: footage, sequence versions, music, SFX, titles, imported graphics, etc. Using a date as part of a name (for a bin or sequence) can help you to figure out what is old and what is most recent. Many editing software apps have the ability to color code files, sort and sift bin contents, or make duplicates of pointer or source files with different names.

Exception

No exceptions. Even the most simple or quick project should follow your same good habits of organization. Keep everything where it belongs and you will reduce your risks of headaches and lower your stress levels.

2. Learn and Use Keyboard Shortcuts

Reason

All video-editing applications have some keyboard shortcuts available and the professional-level software has many that can even be customized per user. Moving the mouse and clicking buttons and menus in the interface is a good way to first figure out how an application functions, but it is time consuming and not entirely elegant. Learning and using the available keyboard shortcuts that execute commands in the application will save time. Speed and efficiency are highly valued in post-production.

Solution

When you are first starting out, take note of the equivalent keyboard command each time you mouse-open a menu to select a function. Try new keyboard shortcuts every time you work in that particular software. Over time, you will remember what lives where and you will use the shortcuts more and more. Most applications will have a master list of keyboard commands in their Help menu. Some even come with a "cheat-sheet" PDF or printout that shows the icon for the command on each programmed key cap.

As several of the major video-editing applications can live on either a Windows or a Macintosh operating system, it would also be very wise for you to become familiar with some basic operating system keyboard shortcuts as well.

Exception

Certain functions in each video-editing application cannot be mapped to keyboard keystrokes, so they can only be selected by using the mouse cursor to click within the interface. Also, depending on your software, the layout of the interface buttons for simple and frequently used commands may make it easier sometimes to just click the mouse. The "Function" keys on certain small keyboard laptops can be a bit snarky at times as well and may have to be "freed" from operating system command mapping. Also be aware that some apps embed certain commands on the numeric keypad of full-size keyboards and, sometimes, such key equivalents are not present on laptop keyboards.

	Windows OS	Mac OS
SAVE	Ctrl+S	Cmd+S
UNDO	Ctrl+Z	Cmd+Z
NEW	Ctrl+N	Cmd+N

FIGURE 8.1 Using keyboard shortcuts within the editing application will greatly increase an editor's efficiency. Memorizing and using the most common operating system keyboard commands is also advisable.

2. Learn and Use Keyboard Shortcuts

3. Organize Your Timeline Tracks and Maintain Consistency Across Projects

Reason

You can potentially have many different types of video and audio sources that will need to find a home in your sequence. If you organize your video and audio tracks in the timeline so that they contain particular assets, you always know where to place things. Simplicity and clarity lead to efficiency and speed during the editing process.

Solution

Create an order to the track content. Perhaps V1 and V2 are reserved for production video, V3 is for keyed titles, and V4 is for keyed imported graphics. On the audio side, you may place sync audio production tracks on A1 and A2, voice-over narration on A3 and A4, ambient clips (NATS) on A5 and A6, music tracks on A7 through A10, SFX on A11 and A12, etc.

The order of video tracks does matter for image processing with special effects and keyed titles, etc. but audio tracks can live wherever you wish. The point is that you should figure out an orderly arrangement for media types that fit your workflow and your style. If you maintain this track organization across sequences and across editing jobs, then you will work more efficiently. Capability and speed are valuable skills for an editor to possess.

Exception

Even the most basic of video sequences will still default to production footage living on V1 and sync audio living on A1 and A2. That is an aspect of track media organization. Also be aware that certain post-production facilities use prescribed track orders of their own to maintain consistency across their edit suites and edited programming. It is always best to check with the producers or engineers to see how they want things set up when you are doing work in someone else's "house."

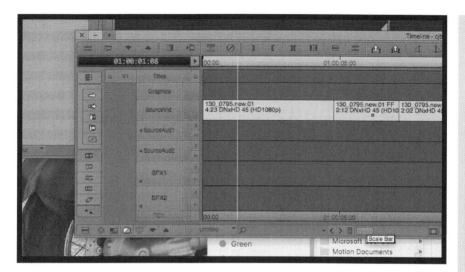

FIGURE 8.2   Some software allows for track panel renaming. This may help with sequence organization across projects.

4. Keep Your Rough Cut Long

Reason

No matter what kind of programming you are editing, this guideline applies. Keep your sequence longer in the first pass or two after the full construction of the assembly edit. Without knowing overall pacing or timing issues or scene-ordering issues, it will be hard to make final decisions about shot, scene, and sequence length. You will be better able to judge what can be removed after the entire assembly edit has been viewed a few times. If usable material is already missing from the rough cut, then you may be inadvertently ignoring a better creative opportunity.

Solution

From the outset, you should include everything from picture and sound tracks that you feel will help to properly show/tell the story. At that early stage of editing, you really do not know what will be useful or superfluous, so keep it all in. After a pass or two at the entire piece, you will get a much better feel for what works and what does not, what should stay and what should really go.

4. Keep Your Rough Cut Long

Often, you have much more material than the final **running time** of the program will allow (30-second commercial, 15-minute educational video, 30-minute situation comedy show, two-hour feature film, etc.). Some things that were initially included in your first versions of the edit will stand out as unnecessary. Other times, you will have to make hard choices that call for removing very good segments just to make the final running time cut-off. Regardless, you should always start with the most material and then pare it down – that is what editing is all about.

Exception

Some news packages have extremely short airtime and you will not be able to pad out the first cuts and then tweak. You will most likely have very little time to finesse and you will simply have just enough time to cut something together to get it to air in the right time slot.

Motion media pieces made for the web (YouTube, Hulu, vlogs, even Netflix and Amazon Prime originals) are not specifically limited to time slot durations (unlike shows that air on traditional commercial broadcast television). These projects can add more material if the quality of the show can bear it out – although many do keep to the traditional time slot durations because they are future-proofing their sale and playback by traditional television broadcasting networks.

5. Review Each Edit or Series of Edits as You Make Them

Reason

You will not know how the shot transition works if you do not watch it play back after you perform the edit. Without reviewing the edits in your sequence, with real-time playback and not scrubbing, you will not be able to appropriately judge any matching action, dialogue continuity, shot timing, overall scene pacing, etc.

Solution

After an edit or a series of edits in the assembly stage, you should move your playhead earlier in the timeline and watch across the shots and the cuts that you have just laid in. Watching every single edit may take up some time during this phase, but you need to gauge your progress frequently. During the rough and fine cut stages, you should review each trim and tweak as it is being worked on to know if you are getting the timing that is needed. After you complete an entire scene, it would be wise to sit back, watch it through from beginning to end, and note any moments that seem to require more attention.

Exception

Even projects that have a very fast turnaround time will require the editing and reviewing process.

6. Duplicate Your Sequence Before Making Major Changes

Reason

Moving ahead with your sequence construction is your main goal, but sometimes you can take one step forward just to take two steps back. Rather than keeping one version of your sequence that you constantly change around trying to get to your final edit, it is preferable to copy, duplicate, or iterate your sequence so you maintain an archive of your progress across time.

Solution

Each video-editing software application should have a way for an editor to make a copy of the sequence under construction in the project. Some apps copy while others duplicate, but your goal is to keep your current version as it is and make any new changes (especially significant changes) to a new version. Some editors append things like "_v1" or "_v16" to the name of the sequence to keep track of the chronology of versions. Others tag the date to the end of the name, etc. This way, if you (or the client) are displeased with the direction in which a particular section of the sequence is going, it is easy to open an older, archived version and replace parts in the newer version as needed.

Exception

If your sequence has a very brief turnaround time or it is just a fun project for yourself, this may not be necessary, but otherwise, duplicating/copying a sequence into versions can become a good habit to get into.

7. Seek Feedback While Editing Your Motion Picture

Reason

A project worked on for many hours, days, or sometimes months can become stale to you over time. The fresh eyes of other individuals may help you to see weaknesses that you could no longer objectively notice. Parts that you have grown fond of may not actually be suitable to the overall story. It may also be that you are having some difficulties with a certain scene's assembly or you are hitting a wall trying to find ways to bridge two disparate segments of the project.

Solution

It is strongly advisable for an editor to show his or her work to other people to get their feedback. Just because you, as an editor, think something really works does not mean that it will play the same way for others. Often, showing your work to other people will bring up points that need to be addressed, edits that do not quite work, or even places that are rather successful.

Listening to constructive feedback and suggestions from other people and creating your own solution to those potential problem areas is an essential skill that you will need to develop as an editor. You may feel that you have done everything right, but the opinions of others bear a certain weight as well — especially if they are paying you.

Exception

Unless you live alone in a cave somewhere, you should always make time to have other people review your edited piece. No one should work in a feedback vacuum.

8. Put Aside Your Edited Sequence for a While and Watch It Again with Fresh Eyes

Reason

When you are the editor of a feature film or any long-form documentary piece, etc., you become "married" to the movie. You live with it day in and day out, sometimes for weeks or months at a time. You are often listening to the same sections over and over and over again. You grow to anticipate the words and the pictures until they no longer really stand out in your mind but are part of the editing "wallpaper." It becomes very easy to blind yourself to edits that are not working or entire sections that may play better in another location within the sequence.

Solution

Time allowing, you would be wise to take a break from the editing process. A day or two away from the well-known material will help you to forget the exact pacing, the cut points, the lines of dialogue, etc. – perhaps not forget entirely, but you will be watching the piece with less anticipation. This respite should give you fresh eyes and ears to view and listen to your story. When you approach the same material with fresh senses, you may pick up on which edits are not working and which scenes within the piece may play better elsewhere.

Exception

Obviously, if you are involved with much shorter or more straightforward cutting jobs that have a quick turnaround time, then you will not have the luxury of taking a day or two away from the material to refresh your senses. You will hope that an overnight break will be enough time away for you to be more critical of your own work come morning.

9. Use Shots with Matching Headroom When Cutting a Dialogue Scene

Reason

Let us assume that the clean single MCU shots found in Figure 8.3 are part of an established two-person dialogue scene. To cut from a shot with correctly framed headroom to another shot with incorrectly framed headroom will look as if one of the subjects has suddenly altered her height.

To cut from one take of Character A with incorrectly framed headroom to a good shot of Character B and then back to another correct take of Character A will make it look as if A is bobbing up and down.

Solution

The incorrectly framed headroom shot is nearly impossible to correct. Video-editing software may have the ability to resize and reframe the footage, but enlarging video frames may cause image quality to degrade depending on the resolution of the original footage. If the poorly framed MCU of Character A is of high enough resolution (full HD or higher), you could enlarge it to a standard close-up and edit it with the well-framed MCU of Character B. Otherwise, some of the footage might be usable for cutaways, if it is not too badly framed. If there is not more than one take of this action or dialogue delivery, the entire shot might have to be rejected and replaced by another, even if the speaker is not seen to be speaking. An over-the-shoulder two-shot may be a solution – or stick to the wider two-shot as a safety.

Exception

The exception here is when the two shots being edited together both suffer from the same bad headroom framing. Obviously, if the headroom is completely wrong, the shots may

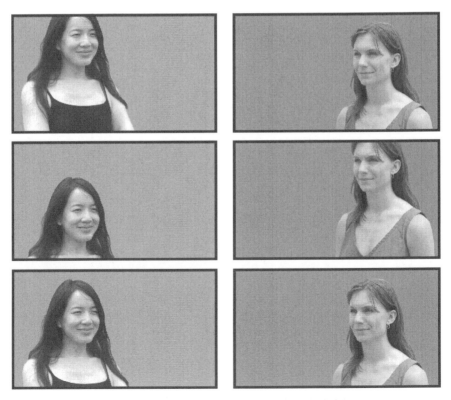

FIGURE 8.3 Beware of headroom issues when cutting "answering" coverage shots of a dialogue scene.

not look traditionally well framed, but because you may not be able to do much about it, throw caution to the wind and go for the shots with the best performance regardless of headroom. If the performance is engaging enough, most viewers may not even notice the differences in framing.

10. Avoid Shots Where Distracting Objects Are Too Near to the Subject's Head

Reason

This is a question of shot composition that has failed at the shooting stage. As an editor, you will not be able to change this questionably composed image. The presence of unwanted lines, shapes, objects, signs, etc. in the shot's background can be rather confusing or distracting to the viewer. It may also result in a humorous reaction not wanted by the filmmakers at that time. If offered such a shot, it is best not to use it if at all possible (Figure 8.4).

Solution

There really is no solution to this problem short of using some special effects like a picture-in-picture, a split screen, or some kind of mask, clone, or blur effect that either

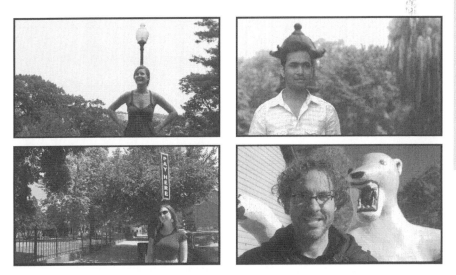

FIGURE 8.4   Poor shot composition is not the fault of the editor, but the choice to use any of these shots in the final edit does fall under her or his domain. Omit, use effects, or just go for it, but be aware of the possible consequences when the audience observe these oddly placed background objects.

crops or obscures the offending background object. Of course, if the filmmakers made such a composition intentionally for comedic reasons, then it would be appropriate for use.

Exception

You may be able to use this shot if it has a very shallow depth of field and the background (containing the offending object) is almost completely out of focus. The only other possible use is in a fast montage, where the shot is seen only for a very brief period of time.

---

11. Avoid Shots Where the Subject Gets Awkwardly Cut Off at the Edge of the Frame

Reason

This type of framing may be considered aesthetically unpleasing by many viewers, but that would not be your fault for you did not shoot the footage. Attempting to use closer shots (medium shots, medium close-ups) that have such framing will cause complications for the edit. When the partial face of a character is in one shot and then that same face needs to

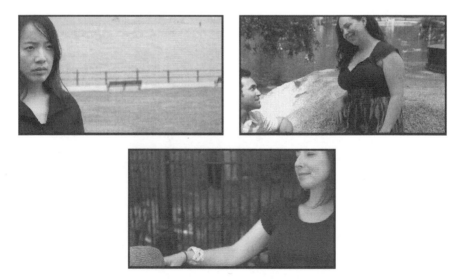

FIGURE 8.5 Compositions like these can make a smooth edit tricky. Try to avoid using footage that contains missing heads or where portions of faces are only partially visible.

be cut to for the next shot, it will cause a jump cut or potentially a continuity problem with action, line delivery, performance, or screen direction (Figure 8.5).

Solution

Sometimes the shot can be used, but it depends what comes before and what comes after. It also depends on the duration of the shot and the type of motion media project being edited.

Exception

These shots could be used in music videos, commercials, experimental films, and maybe in quick-cut action scenes, or where clips before and after do not cause a jump cut.

12. Cut Matched Shots in a Back-and-Forth Dialogue Scene

Reason

As you edit coverage from a traditional dialogue scene between two characters, you will most likely move in from a wide two-shot to tighter singles or over-the-shoulder shots. This allows the audience to get more familiar with the characters and their actions/reactions during the scene.

Established film grammar would suggest that the production team shot matching coverage of each character for this scene (this is not always the case, but let us assume that we have these assets within the footage that you are editing). It is possible that you may have been given a variety of shot types for each character (medium shot, medium close-up, close-up, over-the-shoulder shot, etc.). Matching shots, when recorded with similar focal lengths, at similar distances from the subject, and under similar lighting conditions, often yield similar frame composition, focus depths, etc. Audiences like to see two similar shots cut together as opposed to two mismatched shots within the same scene's back-and-forth dialogue. It creates a coherence and a flow to the visual imagery.

In Diagram A in Figure 8.6, two people are standing having a conversation. Cameras 1 and 2 are at a similar distance from each subject, Character A and Character B. Both of the

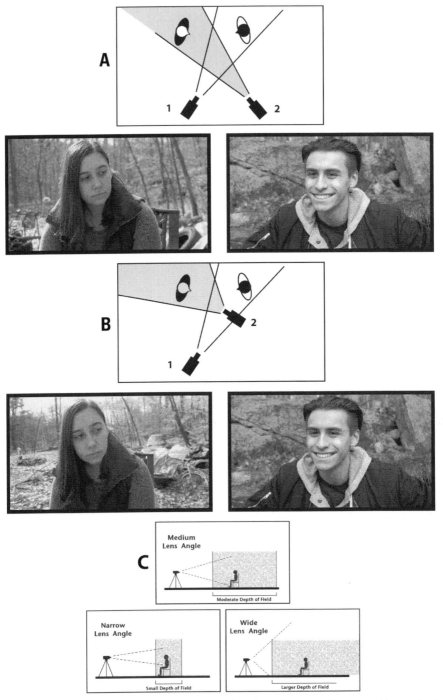

FIGURE 8.6 Diagram A – matching coverage generated by reciprocating camera placement and lens angle of view; Diagram B – mismatching coverage due to altered camera distance and focal length; Diagram C – the depth of field changes with focal length. (Photo credits: Anthony Martel)

shots are taken, for example, at a narrow lens angle (telephoto or long focal length) and both of the shots are framed as medium close-ups. When this is the case, the editor has subjects roughly the same size in the frame and backgrounds that are out of focus to the same extent. The audience get to focus their attention solely on the speaking characters.

In Diagram B, the position for Camera 2 has changed. The shot type should remain the same: a medium close-up. So at the new set-up for Camera 2, the lens angle will now have to be wider (shorter focal length). In this case, the background may be in focus and the perspective on the distant background may be altered. Consequently, the editor would be cutting from a medium close-up with an out-of-focus background to a medium close-up with an in-focus background revealing a wider field of view.

Solution

If a selection of good shots is available, then preference should be given to those with similarity in the quality of framing, focus, lighting, and perspective. If not, then see if you could cut away or insert some other shot in between to distract the audience from noticing the dissimilar shots.

Exception

The exception to this practice is where a wide angle must be used to show a subject moving from foreground to background or the other way around. Generally, with significant available light, the wider the lens angle used, the more the picture background is in focus. In other words, the depth of field is greater (Diagram C in Figure 8.6). Additionally, shots of unmatched visual qualities may have to be edited together in this scenario if those are the only takes made available to you.

---

13. Ensure that Subjects Talking on the Telephone Appear to Be Looking Across the Screen at One Another

Reason

Traditionally, film grammar indicates that the characters speaking over the telephone from two separate locations should be composed so that they look across the empty frame, and from opposite sides. This will generate the idea in the viewer's mind that they are addressing one another across the screen as you cut from one single shot to the next and back again (Figure 8.7). The subjects' look room, lines of attention, and screen placements, etc. all combine to engage the audience in the conversation.

Solution

Hope that the composition of the footage for this scene was done in such a fashion. Otherwise, edit whatever material you have because you cannot alter the subject's placement within the frame unless you use a flip effect and reverse the video image horizontally (provided there are no written words or numbers on the screen that would then appear backward). If both shots are framed correctly, you may even create a split-screen effect with this coverage and have both faces on screen at one time.

Exception

There may be good dramatic reasons to change this working practice. If one person is shot with his or her back directly toward the camera, then the direction of the other person may be changed if the footage allows it. Additionally, if the coverage of each individual shows him or her moving around with mobile phones, then this practice may not apply due to the constantly changing action line of each shot.

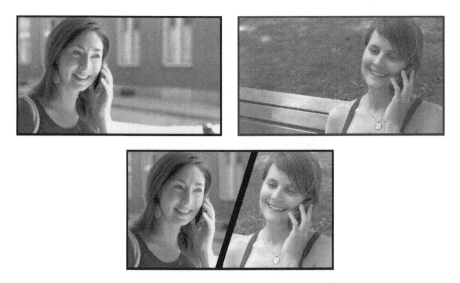

FIGURE 8.7 Static shots of a two-person telephone dialogue recorded in two separate locations should be treated as if the subjects occupied the same film space and were speaking to one another in person. Proper framing and look room should be present in the shots. Joining them together in a split screen can be easily achieved.

14. In a Three-Person Dialogue, Beware of Cutting from a Two-Shot to Another Two-Shot

Reason

If you have coverage of a three-person dialogue scene that contains several two-shots, then in all likelihood the central character will appear to jump from one side of the screen to the other (Figure 8.8). A shot taken from Camera Position 1 shows the center person (Character B) on the right-hand side of the screen with Character A on the left. If you now cut to another two-shot from Camera Position 2, then this shot will show Character B on the left-hand side of the screen, with Character C on the right-hand side. This is a screen placement jump cut for Character B and can disrupt the visual flow of the shots and confuse or annoy the audience.

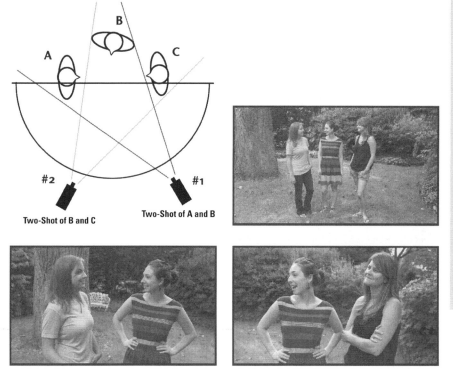

FIGURE 8.8 In this example, three people covered by two two-shots will result in a compositional jump for Character B from frame right to frame left at the cut point. Instead, use any other coverage to separate the connection of the troublesome two-shots.

Solution

Provided other coverage shots are available, cut to a single shot of a person instead. For example, cut from a two-shot of Characters A and B to a medium close-up of Character C. Or, conversely, cut from a medium close-up of Character A to a two-shot of Characters B and C.

You could also cut back out to a wide shot of the entire trio between both of the two-shots, provided there is appropriate continuity. If available and appropriate, you could also edit in a cutaway or insert shot before you return to Characters A, B, and C.

Exception

There are no exceptions to this practice unless the style of editing for this project accepts and encourages such visual jumps.

15. With a Single Subject, Try to Avoid Cutting to the Same Camera Angle

Reason

There is a strong chance that a jump cut would result if you edit two shots taken from an identical or extremely similar camera angle (see the six elements of the cut in Chapter Five). This relates directly to the traditional film shooting practice known as the 30-degree rule, whereby each coverage shot of the same subject or object in a scene should come from the same side of the axis of action and be at least 30 degrees different in camera placement along the 180-degree shooting arc.

In Example 1 of Figure 8.9, cutting from the medium shot at Camera Position A into a medium close-up at Camera Position B could present a problem in the form of a jump cut. Cutting from a medium close-up to a medium shot, however, is less of a problem.

Solution

It would be better to cut to a medium close-up from a different camera angle, provided one was actually recorded by the production team.

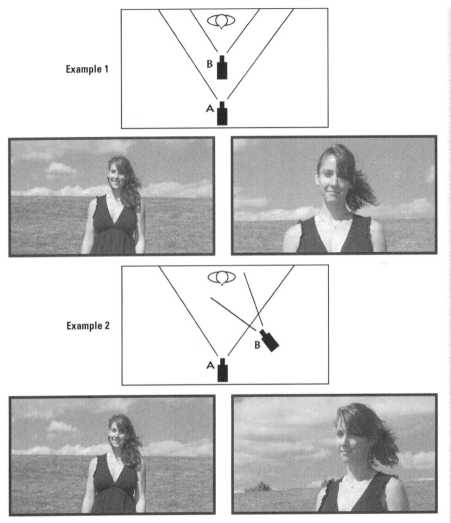

FIGURE 8.9 Example 1 shows a cut-in or an axial punch-in. Example 2 shows a more traditional shot option for the cut. A new angle and focal length help to lessen the chance of a jump cut for the audience.

In Example 2 in Figure 8.9, Camera Position B has moved to the right, creating an angle on the subject that is more 3/4 frontal. If a shot from this position were available, the cut to the new angle would be more traditional and the risk of a jump cut would be reduced.

In the case where a shot from an alternative angle does not exist, then a cutaway could be used to separate the medium shot and the medium close-up of the same character on the same lens axis. This cutaway (of something appropriate to the scene) would allow the audience a visual break and the jump cut effect would not be experienced. This practice is more or less acceptable if you cut out to the medium shot from the medium close-up.

15. With a Single Subject, Try to Avoid Cutting to the Same Camera Angle

Exception

One exception to this practice is when cutting two shots together that are *very* dissimilar, such as when a great distance is covered between the two shots set up along the same lens axis. Of course, for creative reasons, you could edit a series of cut-ins along the same lens axis to achieve a quick punching-in effect – a zoom without the zoom, as it were.

16. Beware of Screen Placement Issues with an Object of Interest

Reason

Even when the human subjects are on the correct sides of the screen in the coverage shots, the audience will have an additional visual reference, sometimes called the object of interest or the point of interest.

For example, a two-shot of a man and a woman (Shot 1 in Figure 8.10) shows a painting that is framed center screen. Cutting to the man (Shot 2) will show the painting screen left. Cutting now to the woman (Shot 3), the object of interest (the painting) has jumped to screen right. Even though the edit is technically correct, the point of interest jumps, and this can be visually distracting.

Solution

Where an object of interest is evident, either keep it in the same area of the frame, or select the shots that either eliminate it altogether or minimize its on-screen presence (Shot 4).

Exception

An exception to this working practice is where the object of interest is so small as to be negligible, where it is far in the background, or where it is out of focus. You may also find that some other subject in the action of the scene obstructs the object of interest, either partially or totally.

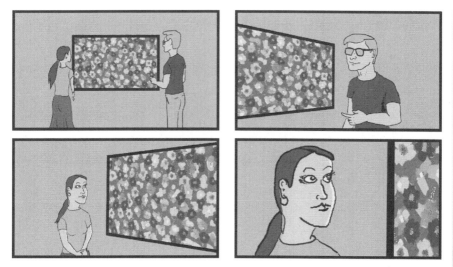

FIGURE 8.10   Much like a person can jump sides of the frame in a three-person back-and-forth dialogue, objects of interest can do the same thing. Tighter shots may hide the object jumping left, then right, and back again.

17. Edit in a Wide Shot as Soon as Possible After a Series of Close-Up Shots in a Group Scene

Reason

It can be easy for the audience to forget the exact location of subjects in the film space, especially during a fast-moving production. After a series of medium shots, medium close-ups, and close-ups, particularly those with out-of-focus backgrounds, it becomes important to re-establish the scene's and the subjects' location. If you choose to introduce a series of characters, all in close-up, then you should show them all again grouped together in the wide shot.

Solution

Be careful about editing an entire sequence with only close-ups — unless there is a need to do so.

Even one quick cut to a long shot, showing the relationship of the subjects to each other and to their surroundings, gives a much better grounding to the scene for the viewing audience.

17. Edit in a Wide Shot as Soon as Possible After a Series of Close-Up Shots in a Group Scene

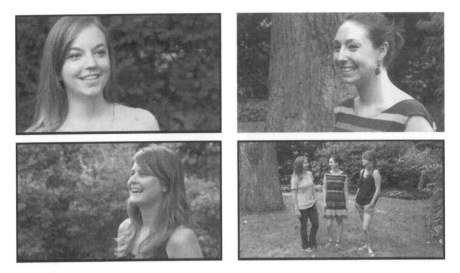

FIGURE 8.11 After a series of closer shots, it may be helpful to show a wide shot to re-establish the scene in the viewer's mind.

Exception

The exception to this practice is where the location or scene is well known to the audience, such as the main set of a popular TV show.

18. Cut to a Close Shot of a New Subject Soon After He or She Enters a Scene

Reason

This may be the first appearance of this subject and the audience will want to know who he or she is. The audience should be shown the new information as soon as is practical.

A long shot will only show the new subject in relationship to other subjects and to the location, but someone new entering the wide scene needs to be shown in a closer shot to be more properly identified.

Solution

Edit in a closer shot of the subject at the earliest opportunity. This also applies if the character is not new but has not been seen by the audience for some time. Support

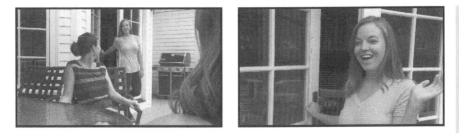

FIGURE 8.12   Inform the audience by showing them a closer shot of a new character entering a scene.

the audience's understanding of the story by reminding them of events and people through tighter shots that provide the necessary details.

Exception

The obvious exceptions are when the character is an extra or a "bit" player, needs a delayed introduction for comedic reasons, or needs to be kept secret for narrative purposes.

19. Use an Establishing Shot to Set Up a New Scene's Location

Reason

The audience not only like to know what is happening in a new scene, but also where it is happening. They benefit from seeing some form of visual "geography" that establishes the relationship between the environment and the subjects in the scene that unfolds there.

Solution

Some form of wide shot – for example, a long shot, a very long shot, or an extreme long shot – will be helpful. This wide shot should serve a number of purposes, such as to give some geography of the scene, to show time of day or season of year, to establish the relationship of the character(s) to the surroundings, and/or to establish a general impression of the movement of the subjects.

In documentary or non-fiction motion media productions, these types of establishing shots should be among the **B-roll** footage. For any kind of project that lacks these shots in its original, visual material, consider using **stock footage** libraries or still photographs of locations – perhaps with a motion effect to provide some energy.

Exception

You may opt, for creative reasons, not to show an establishing shot but rather to cut right in to the scene, perhaps in a close-up shot of some element within the set. Then you could pull back and show a wider shot of the location of the scene. This method creates more of an **anti-establishing shot**. It stresses audio ambience over exterior imagery while you are grounding the viewer in the new location, and makes for a refreshing change. If the scene is shown in closer shots and seems to take place in an unknown location, the actual establishing wide shot could be shown last as a sort of reveal and a surprise for the audience – perhaps for shock, perhaps for comic intent, or perhaps purely as information.

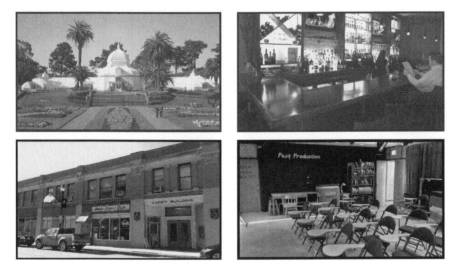

FIGURE 8.13 Using a wider shot to open a new sequence of scenes at a new location can help to ground the audience and provide much-needed information with one image. This holds true for both exterior and interior locations within your story.

20. Use Close-Ups of Subjects in a Scene for the Greatest Emotional Effect

Reason

A close-up of anyone's face is a very intimate shot. It carries with it a great deal of visual information and, depending on the expression of the face and the context within the story at that point, it can easily sway the audience emotionally. Using such a powerful shot too early in a scene's development could dilute the efficacy of close-ups when they are used later to make an emotional point or underscore a certain counter-current in the storyline through a **reaction shot**.

Solution

Save the close-up shot of the character or characters for when the audience will benefit most from seeing the actors' faces in such intimate detail. The close-up will yield a clearer assessment of a character's emotional or mental state to the viewer. If the drama or tension of the scene is rising, cutting to closer shots toward the climax will provide the audience with more emotionally engaging visuals. This effect will be watered down if you go to the close-up shots too soon in a scene's development – or, perhaps even worse, if you allow the energy to dissipate by cutting back out to the wide shot too frequently.

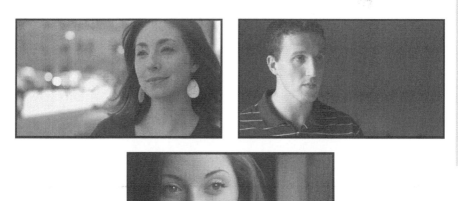

FIGURE 8.14   The close-up conveys much emotional detail. Use where appropriate, but often later in the scene is preferable for the greatest emotional effect on the audience.

Exception

Documentary and news talking-head interviews will be recorded mostly in medium shots and closer. You will have to use these shots right away in the sequence. Often, fictional narrative television and web programming will have significantly more coverage with close shots of individuals due to the smaller screen on which they get displayed. Cutting to such close-up shots sooner in each scene could be encouraged for television and internet programming. Additionally, if the lighting on a close-up of the character partially or entirely obscures the face for narrative purposes (to protect an identity, create mystery, etc.), then these shots should be edited in the sequence as required.

21. Cut Away from Subjects Soon After Their Look Rests upon Their Object of Interest

Reason

A shot depicting a subject looking at some object of interest off screen is the perfect set-up for a reveal to the audience. In general, you would cut to the shot of the object of interest next. The motivation for this edit arises out of the character's look and initial facial reaction to the yet-to-be-seen object off screen. Once the physical movement of head and eyes has come to a rest, the audience will likewise wish to see what is now being focused upon – hence the cut to the shot of the object which reveals the new information (Figure 8.15).

Solution

The editor hopes that the actor was instructed during production to look off screen and react to some object. He or she further hopes that the actor achieves the look with a final solid head placement and eye-line to some object off screen. It is the solidity of the final look – the focusing of the eyes along a particular line – and a facial reaction of recognition that create the strongest cut point.

Exception

Clearly, if no take of the "looking" shot ends with a solid, strong gaze from the actor, then you cannot cut away at the moment of the eyes' focus. You will have to find the most acceptable point of recognition on the actor's face and then cut. Faster action sequences

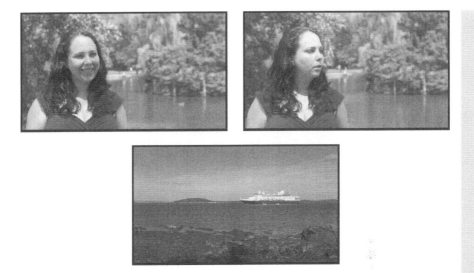

FIGURE 8.15   Allowing the actor's eyes to lock onto the off-screen object of interest generates a need within the viewer to also see this new object. This motivated cut to the object of interest is often called a reveal.

or scenes that involve multiple objects off screen do not necessarily call for a static head and focused eye-line from the actor.

22. Use J-Cuts and L-Cuts to Smooth Over Transitions

Reason

Straight cuts on all picture and audio track edits can feel rather staccato – especially in dialogue scenes. It can really improve the flow of a scene if sometimes the incoming sound starts under the outgoing picture clip (a J-cut), or, conversely, the outgoing sound carries on under the incoming picture clip (an L-cut).

Solution

Sound bridges are useful both within scenes and between scenes or segments of a video. The idea behind the J-cut stems from real life where a person will hear a sound and then look to see what is making that sound – audio information leading to new visual information. The L-cut allows the audience to acclimate to new visual data while they are momentarily carried forward by the familiar audio that they have already been experiencing in the

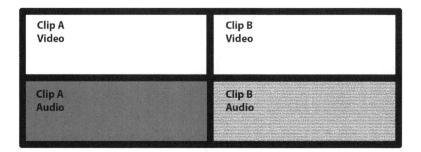

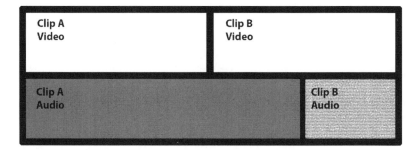

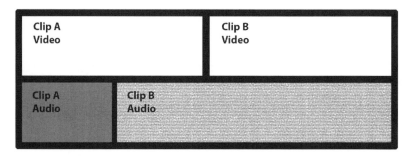

FIGURE 8.16 Simply by trimming the audio track cut point for Clip A and Clip B, you can turn a straight cut into an L-cut or a J-cut split edit or sound bridge.

preceding clip. Rather than an abrupt changeover in both picture and sound information, this staggered approach can smooth over edit points and propel the audience forward with a little more finesse.

Exception

Some moments of a video, depending on the genre, can actually benefit from the hard, simultaneous cut between picture and sound clips in the timeline. Abrupt changes in audio levels (usually from quiet to loud) can "wake up" the audience with a sudden burst of sound energy. This is often accompanied by a changeover in the brightness of the video clips or the amount of visual movement within the imagery at the same time.

23. Create Continuous Motion Action Edits by Matching Physical Movements

Reason

The audience typically expect continuous motion when they watch a scene from a story that was shot in the continuity style of filmmaking. The movements of subjects and objects would be constant and uninterrupted in reality, so they should appear to have the same fluidity in a movie of this style. The various shots, from different angles and with different framing, should be cut together to present this illusion of continuous motion. The "blink" of the actual edit is masked by the matching movements from one shot of the coverage of the action to another shot of the continuation of that same action. The cut goes unnoticed by the audience (Figure 8.17).

Solution

Perhaps this can be best demonstrated with an example. The simple scene involves a woman sitting at a patio table. As she enjoys the morning, she lifts a mug of coffee and drinks. Shot A is a medium shot of the woman at the table and she lifts her mug of coffee – CUT TO – Shot B, a close-up shot continuing the coffee mug lift and showing the actual sipping of the beverage.

As you near the end of Shot A (the medium clip), you would cut somewhere along the motion path of the woman's arm rising – not before the arm begins to move and not after it has fully brought the mug up to her mouth. This new tail frame, cut during the motion, will inform you where to begin Shot B.

You may start by trying to match the mug's position in the first frame of Shot B exactly to the frame at the end of Shot A. This may or may not work. It is often suggested to begin Shot B three to five frames prior to the "ideal" visual frame for "perfect" physical continuity. Those fractions of a second of action are lost on viewers as they acclimate their eyes and minds to the new information on the screen in the second shot. Remember to always back up toward the beginning of Shot A and watch the edit at normal playback speed (scrubbing across the cut will not give you the true timing of the actions even

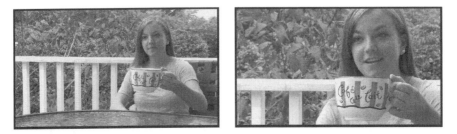

FIGURE 8.17 Cutting on the action of subject movement (about two-thirds completed) will most often make for a smoother transition across the action edit. Viewers ignore the matching action cut as they absorb the new information in the second shot.

though the object placement may seem correct on the screen at the two frames around the cut point).

If there is a jump of some kind (not smooth movement), then experiment with cutting action a little earlier or a little later, and judge for yourself. The Trim Tools in your video-editing application will make this editing process easier. Most continuous action will benefit from trimming just a few frames at either the tail or the head, or sometimes a bit from both.

Exception

Any project that calls for a special visual style, such as jump cuts, or playing with the space/time continuum of actions and reactions, etc., does not always need to follow this practice.

Additionally, if the performance of an actor's dialogue delivery during this scene is particularly engaging and dynamic, then allowing minor gaps in motion continuity may be fine because the audience will most likely be so attentive to the character's words that the glitch in motion may go unnoticed.

24. When Cutting a Rise as an Action Edit, Cut Before the Subject's Eyes Leave the Frame

Reason

A "rise" is any movement of a subject from within the frame to up and out of the top of the frame and then across the edit point in continuous action. In these shots, the camera does not tilt up to properly follow the movements of the subject and the head gets cut off. For example, the subject sits on a park bench and then stands up, someone climbs the rungs of a ladder, or a subject walks up steps. The action edit point could occur anywhere within the actor's total movement up until the eyes are about to break the top of the frame.

It would be advisable to keep the actor's eyes on screen for as long as possible in the first shot. The subject's eyes are the natural focal point of the viewer's attention. When they leave the frame, the audience lose that connection with the subject. Additionally, with no tilt up to maintain proper framing, the subject's head is cut off and this just looks odd to the viewer. This gets worse in close shots when the rise occurs very quickly due to the magnification of the head within the shot's framing.

Solution

A woman is seated at a park bench (Figure 8.18). The edit point in Shot 1 will be when her eyes approach the top of the screen (Frame 1B), cutting to Frame 2B in Shot 2. This may seem only a short distance, but actually the subject leans forward before rising. This happens naturally.

If the subject's head is off screen when the cut is made (Frame 1C), then the edit will appear to be "late." If the editor cuts before movement (Frame 1A), so that all of the movement is seen on the medium long shot (Frame 2A), then the edit may be deemed an "early cut."

In these examples, early cuts are not normally as disturbing as late cuts. Watching most of the action from the second (wider) shot is not so wrong, especially if the woman continues up and out of the frame. However, the late cut example of Shot 1C and Shot 2C presents the issue of what the audience get to look at during the last few moments of Shot 1. Granted this transition will occur relatively quickly, but once the entire head clears the top of the frame, the audience are seeking some new information. They want to see the character's face again and watch the continuous action of the move.

Exception

One exception to this practice is when the first shot is closer than a medium close-up. It is rather difficult to cut smoothly away from a close-up or big close-up on a rise. An early cut is almost inevitable due to the size of the face within the frame and the lack of physical space for the upward movement.

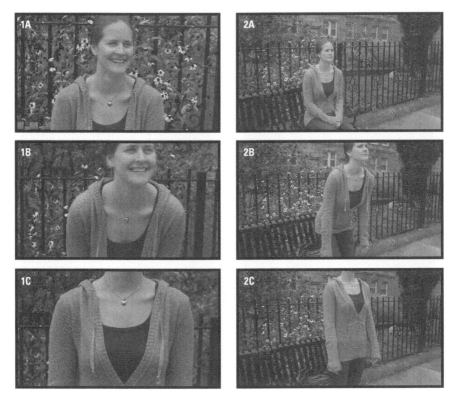

FIGURE 8.18 Examples of cutting on the rise. Column A shows the medium close-up of the character rising off the bench. Column B shows the medium long shot of the same action. Best practice may be to leave the subject's eyes on screen for as long as possible and then cut away from Shot 1B to Shot 2B.

25. When Cutting to a Close-Up of an Action, Select a Version of the Close-Up Where the Action Is Slower

Reason

If the action of the close-up happens at the same speed as that of the wider shot, then the speed of the action, as seen on the close-up, seems faster. This is due to the relative size of the object within the closer framing. It is now a large object so it has very little screen space to move within the close-up frame. Any quick or even "normal" movement would appear to happen too quickly because the object has less distance to travel around the screen before it breaks out through an edge. You hope that the production team understood this phenomenon and got some of the close-up takes at a slower speed of object movement.

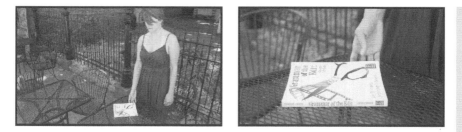

FIGURE 8.19 Be aware of speed of action in closer shots where the magnified object's movement clears the frame very quickly. Shot 1 is a medium long shot of a woman picking up a book. Shot 2 is a close-up highlighting the book's movement out of the frame.

For example, in Figure 8.19, the subject is picking up a book in the wide shot. The close-up shows the hand also picking up the book. The action on the long shot is at normal speed and the book never leaves the frame. But in the closer shot, the book moves out of the frame very quickly. So, if the close-up action is carried out at the same speed, it seems faster.

Solution

You hope that the director has provided an additional close-up with a slightly slower action. The slower version will appear to move at a "normal" speed. If necessary, your video-editing software may have motion effects built in that can slow down a shot just enough to be effective. Be forewarned, however, because a keen audience may easily detect this slight slow-motion effect.

Exception

This practice does not apply to close shots of moving machinery.

26. Understand the Visual Differences Between a Dolly-In and a Zoom

Reason

Many consider a "zooming" image to be a very unnatural visual effect due to its uniform magnification of distant objects. The camera does not move and the lens optically enlarges all visual elements within the frame. It has no change in perspective. The horizon (or far distance) and the middle distance will come toward you at the same speed as any objects in the foreground. As our eyes do not zoom, the "movement" through film space can seem unnatural and stand out to a viewer.

Solution

Unlike a zoom shot, a **dolly-in** shot (sometimes called a **truck-in** or a **push-in**) is considered a more natural movement that will have a perspective change analogous to what our normal vision would produce. The camera lens, like our eyes, is moved closer to the subject, who appears to grow larger while the background remains "further away."

The two sequences of shots in Figure 8.20 show the difference between the zoom and the dolly-in. Note the differences in size and apparent "nearness" of the doorway awning at the corner of the building in the background frame left.

It is also a common practice for filmmakers to combine lens and camera support movement within a complex shot. A shot containing a zoom may also be used if it contains another camera movement at the same time that helps to camouflage the zoom.

Examples of such shots include:

- a tilt with a zoom
- a pan with a zoom
- a crab dolly with a zoom
- a pedestal or boom elevation with a zoom, etc.

Exception

An example of a non-traditional zoom is when it "creeps," i.e., when it is so slow that you actually do not realize it is a zoom. Slow zooms during long takes of slowly paced action or dialogue-driven shots will evolve the composition over a longer time and the subtle changes in framing happen so gradually that viewers will most likely not notice as they pay attention to the actors, etc. As an editor, you will find this type of shot relatively easy to cut into the program in its entirety, or to cut up with other reaction shots as necessary, because the zoom will be so slow that cutting on the lens movement will most likely not be noticed.

A zoom in TV news or other "reality"-type programming or sports coverage is another exception as it is more accepted within those genres. Obviously, a detail of the content or action is the motivation to make the zoom.

In addition, a zoom used in a shot without any discernible background, (e.g., a white wall, sky, or flat ocean) might possibly go unnoticed.

ZOOM   DOLLY-IN

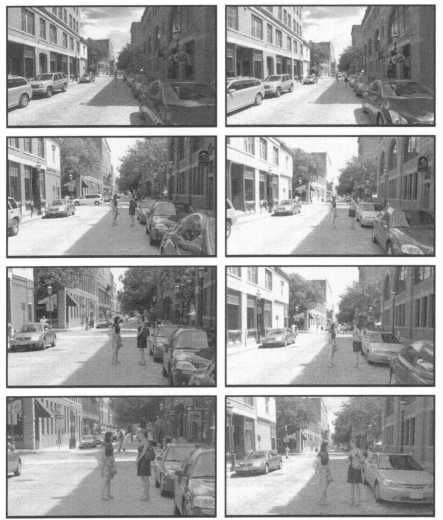

FIGURE 8.20 Zoom movements will alter perspectives on the film space, especially the background. The left column shows zoom movement and the right column shows dolly-in movement. Subjects receive similar magnification, but notice the differences in size and proximity of background elements, chiefly that triangular doorway awning seen in the background frame left.

27. Beware of Shots that Dolly Out without Motivation

27. Beware of Shots that Dolly Out without Motivation

Reason

A dolly **track-out** (sometimes called a **truck-out** or a **pull-out**) can often initiate a scene to show more of the location, or signal the end of a sequence or a scene. It may precede either a dissolve or a cut to another scene or even a fade-to-black. If no subject movement comes toward the camera initiating the track-out (backward, away from the established angle of view on the scene location), then the camera takes on a consciousness of its own. The audience may not be accustomed to the camera suddenly moving as if it were motivated by its own thoughts or desires (Figure 8.21).

Solution

The motivation for the dolly track-out will usually be included in the shot. In the case where no motivation is evident, or where motivation does not exist in the previous shot, see if the scene can still run without that tracking shot. Typically, dolly shots take a long time and can cost a production a lot of money, so it might not be an option to leave it out of the final edit.

Exception

If this is a visual treatment that has already been established in the motion picture (a free-moving camera with its own "motivations"), then it would be part of the style of the film and, therefore, appropriate to use. Another exception may be when a track-out precedes a narrative jump in time, location, or tempo, or where the dolly-out is the final shot of the production.

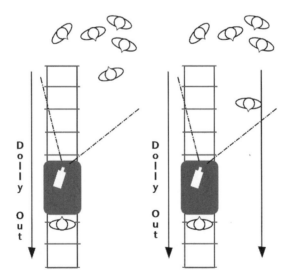

FIGURE 8.21 Understand when track-out dolly shots are motivated by subject movement and when they are not. A camera moving away from the location of a scene on its own appears to have a certain consciousness that may not be evident among the other scenes in the program.

28. Select the Best Version of a Pan or Crab Dolly Shot

Reason

Dolly moves and panning shots that follow talent movement are often rather tricky to record during production. Several variables and different crew members, plus the talent, are involved in their creation and it is easy for things to not quite flow as intended. When reviewing the takes of complex or developing shots like these, watch for the one with smooth camera movement, adequate lead room for the subject's movement, proper focus, and good pacing. An audience watching a bumpy move, a bad composition, or a blurry moment in the shot may have their viewing experience compromised.

Solution

Again, an editor cannot change the quality of the shots that he or she is given, but must work with the material presented as best as possible. Seek out the best takes that are available that meet the criteria for such a shot. In some cases, you may use just the good portions of multiple takes and stitch them together with some cutaways. If there are a number of takes, a shot should be selected where the camera has "led the subject" (i.e., where there is more frame space before the subject than behind – as shown in Figure 8.22), has good focus throughout, and is smooth, with good pacing appropriate for the entire scene.

Exception

The exceptions to this practice may be found in fast-paced action shots, or even hand-held **cinéma vérité** style shooting where the slightly jerky camera adds to a sense of immediacy, danger, or reality.

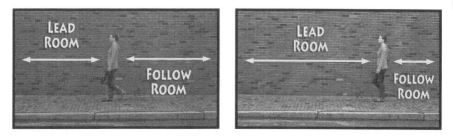

FIGURE 8.22 Select the crab dolly shots that provide stability, good focus, and ample lead room for talent movement.

29. Begin and End Each Pan, Tilt, or Dolly Shot on a Static Frame

Reason

Cutting into a shot that is already in motion can cause a jump cut effect within the mind of the viewer. Cutting away from a shot that is in motion to a static shot can also be jarring, but it may be more acceptable if the narrative calls for such a visual treatment.

Solution

The production team should provide pan, tilt, and dolly shots that begin with a static frame, move for the duration of action, and then end on a static frame. This is not always the case, but as an editor you would hope for this scenario (Figure 8.23).

If Shot 1 is a static, simple shot and you wish to cut to the complex moving shot (Shot 2), then you should keep those static frames at the head of Shot 2. This allows you to cut from static frames to static frames. The audience will treat this as an invisible edit because movement comes after the static transition.

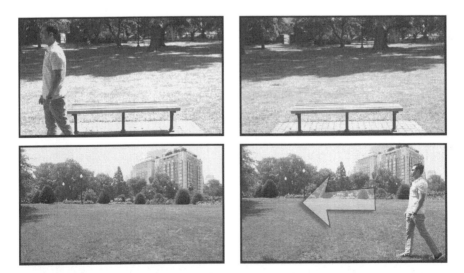

FIGURE 8.23 The locked-off camera at the end of Shot 1 will help to create an invisible cut into the static start frames in dolly Shot 2.

At the end of Shot 2, after the tilt, pan, or dolly move, you would most likely wish to finish that shot on a static frame as well. You can then cut to Shot 3, the next static shot. This again provides an invisible edit for the audience: static to static.

Exception

If you decide to string several complex movement shots together, perhaps in an action sequence, then you can cut not static to static but moving to moving to keep the pace of the action going. One thing to watch out for in this scenario, however, is the speed of the camera movement and of the subject movement within the shots that you are cutting together. If the speeds are not matching or at least similar, this can cause visual interruptions to the flow of images and the audience may sense the shift in tempo.

30. Avoid Editing a Stationary Simple Shot After a Moving Complex Shot of the Same Subject

Reason

A cut from or into a camera movement may appear as a jump to the eye. A subject who is in motion in a dynamic Shot 1 but who is then shown as stationary in a static Shot 2 will appear to jump in time or space.

Solution

Take, for example, a subject who is moving across film space (right to left). The shot calls for her movement to be paralleled by a crab dolly (Figure 8.24). It is possible to cut to a static shot of the subject, but only when the subject has cleared the frame for a reasonable time prior to the cut. The end dolly of complex Shot 1 should be static prior to the cut to the simple static medium Shot 2 of the stationary subject.

There are two reasons for this. First, you may want to finish or clear the action in the shot before cutting out of the shot. Second, the pan or dolly is likely to be a complex shot. As such, like a developing shot, it should have a beginning (the initial static frame), a middle (the pan with another movement, tilt, or zoom), and an end (the final static frame).

The preferred place for the cut is on the static frame, where the camera is not moving even though the subject may be.

So, unless the camera stops, and/or the subject stops, and/or the subject is no longer in the frame, then it is better if the next shot does not show the same subject as stationary.

Exception

There are many scenarios where this guideline may be overruled. Depending on the material involved, the program type, the pacing of the footage, and the pacing of the scene being cut, you may choose to experiment with cutting into and out of action and stationary shots. Most likely, however, you will succeed in proving to yourself that it just does not look or feel right the majority of the time.

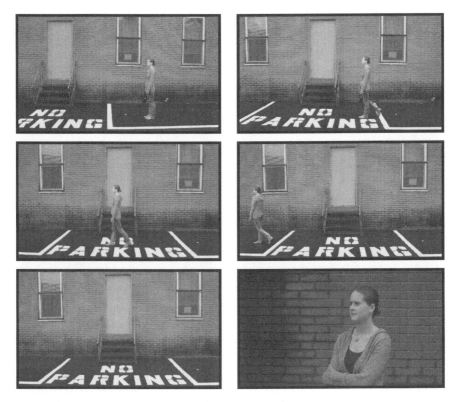

FIGURE 8.24 Allow the dolly action and subject movement to finish before cutting to a static shot of the same subject who appears stationary.

31. Avoid Cutting Pans and Tilts that Reverse Direction at the Cut Point

Reason

Screen direction and flow of motion have a continuity of their own. When object movement motivates a leading camera pan or tilt in Shot A and then Shot B reverses that object's movement, a visual "crash" will occur at the cut point. Screen directions will have suddenly switched and the viewer will feel this reversal as a disorientation of visual flow.

Solution

You hope that the production team maintained screen direction and visual continuity while they were shooting the coverage for the scene. If you do not have a continuous direction in the footage between Shot A and Shot B, then you can either not use Shot B or insert some other shot between the two to distract viewers and re-orient their sense of movement so that when Shot B comes on the screen, they are not disturbed by the alteration in the pan or tilt's direction of movement.

You can also employ a flip effect to switch left/right direction of movement (if no text or numbers appear on the screen during the flipped shot).

Exception

As a creative practice, it may be worthwhile, given the appropriate topic in a program, to attempt to marry reversing pan or tilt shots to *cause* the visual crash for effect. A story with strong conflicting themes, an experimental film, a non-fiction promotional video, or a music video may exhibit such crash cuts.

32. Avoid Crossing the Action Line or the Screen Direction Will Be Reversed

Reason

Refer to the section on screen direction in Chapter Four.

In Diagram 1 of Figure 8.25, a conveyor belt moves boxes from frame left to frame right as seen from Camera Position A. The shot itself is shown in Image 2. If the line is crossed — i.e., if the next shot is taken from Camera Position B (see Diagram 1) — then the belt appears to be moving the boxes from right to left (Image 3).

Solution

Select shots from one side of the line only, or use a neutral cutaway between the shots if the line must be crossed. A close-up of part of the machinery not showing the belt movement would be suitable. In documentary or reality programming, you could also use a wipe to get from one side of the belt to the other.

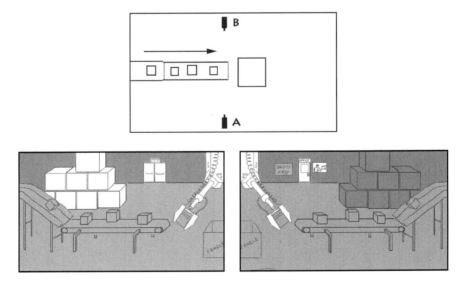

FIGURE 8.25   The moving machinery establishes an action line and a screen direction. Shooting from the opposite side of the initial 180-degree arc would reverse the flow and flip directions, so try to avoid editing such conflicting shots.

Obviously, if the camera were to move from one side of the belt to the other during the shot, a jump cut would not appear, but the direction of the belt would still be reversed.

Exception

Shots (especially B-roll for a non-fiction program) recorded from the opposite side of the action line could certainly be edited together in a fast-paced montage sequence.

33. Avoid Cutting an Action Edit from a Two-Shot to Another Two-Shot of the Same Subjects

Reason

An action edit requires closely matching continuity of placement, movement, and general performance. With two moving subjects involved in the shots, it becomes that much more difficult for the editor to match the movements of each (Figure 8.26).

Solution

When cutting out of the two-shot, cut to a closer shot of one of the two characters, cut to some form of reaction shot, or possibly cut to a very long shot if it exists among the footage. Trying to match the action for all concerned parties would be difficult if you went for another two-shot from a different angle.

Exception

A much wider shot of the entire environment, including the two subjects, is more likely to hide any incongruous body movements, etc. Any event shot with multiple cameras may also avoid this issue because action would match across a multi-camera edit. If the action concerned is frenetic enough (a fight scene, extreme sports, fast dancing, etc.), then cutting from two-shot to two-shot may be perfectly acceptable with that sort of energy, confusion, or movement, although it would still appear as a jump cut.

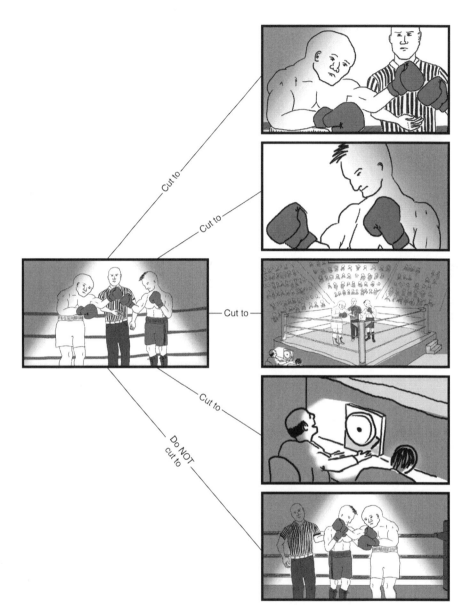

FIGURE 8.26 Cut from the first medium long shot to any other coverage shot except another medium long shot still showing all subjects. An unwelcome jump cut will result if you do not follow this guideline.

34. Allow a Subject to Exit the Frame Completely Prior to Showing Him or Her Entering the Next Shot

Reason

In the "classic" screen-direction continuity action edit, it is advisable to allow the subject to leave the frame entirely in Shot A – especially when Shot B shows that same character, but at a new location and at a later film time. It is customary to cut away once the actor's eyes have cleared the edge of the frame, because the face and eyes of the actor are what the audience will be watching, but showing the whole body clear the frame allows for a cut to any new location with no need for matching continuous body placement. Screen direction may still be maintained, however. If an emotional note has just played out in the scene and the characters depart, then you may want to linger on the empty location in Shot A for a beat or two to allow the audience time to soak in that quiet moment.

Solution

As seen in Figure 8.27, Shot A ends with the body no longer visible just prior to the cut. Introducing Shot B, the viewer will find an empty frame of a new location, and possibly a

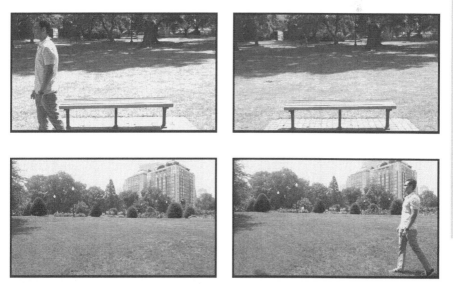

FIGURE 8.27 If you wish to jump a subject in place and time at a cut point, allow him or her to clear the frame entirely and have the new or incoming shot start empty. The new empty frame of Shot B will provide new visual data (place and time) to the viewer before the character strides in from the edge of the frame.

new time, to analyze. Then the actor or object will enter the frame. This allows something of interest to the viewer to remain on the screen at all times.

Exception

Extremely fast-paced action sequences may allow for portions of the subject's body to remain on screen at the end of Shot A and appear already on screen at the start of Shot B. The increased speed of subject movement covers the jumps in subject screen placement at the cut point. If the pacing is too slow, however, the portions of the subject visible at opposite ends of the screen might cause a jump cut.

35. Maintain Screen Direction Across an Action Edit

Reason

This is a very basic practice for any moving subject within the accepted film grammar. The continuity of screen direction, even across the transition, should be constant. It helps to establish the directions of left and right within the film space and keeps the audience properly oriented within this fictional landscape (Figure 8.28).

Solution

The appropriate coverage with proper screen direction should be provided to you for the edit. If you do not get footage with proper screen direction maintained, then you had better seek a diverting cutaway shot to place in between shots. You may also choose to establish this "inconsistency" as a visual motif for this character or for the overall project.

Exception

The exceptions to this practice are when:

- the direction is actually seen to change on screen;
- there is a suggested change of direction on screen followed by a cutaway;
- the change of direction is caused by the cutaway (e.g., in the haunted house, running in one direction, seeing the ghost, then running the opposite way).

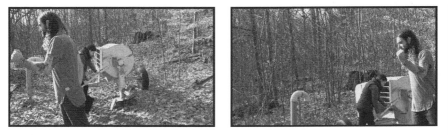

FIGURE 8.28 Screen direction of moving subjects should be maintained across action edits. (Photo credits: Zach Benard)

36. Avoid Making an Action Edit from a Long Shot of a Subject to a Close-Up of the Same Subject

Reason

It is a jump cut to be avoided, unless a shock effect is required or unless the character is recognizable and identifiable in the long shot and there is not much action to physically match when the close-up shot cuts on screen.

Solution

In Example 1 of Figure 8.29, the overhead schematic shows a man walking up to a car in a wide shot. He stops beside the car door to unlock it with his key. In two shots, it may look as it does in the images in the example.

It will cut together, but it is too much of a jump to the eyes of the audience, and the visual reaction may be, "Who is this new man?" or "Where have the first man and the car gone?" Unless this character and vehicle are extremely well known to the viewing audience, this edit can break the visual flow and is therefore discouraged.

It would be better to use three shots, as shown in Example 2: (1) the wide shot to set the scene; (2) the medium long shot at a different angle to show more details; and (3) the close-up shot from the first angle. The result of having the extra shot between the wide shot and the close-up is to make the scene flow more smoothly. Now the audience know who the man is, where he is going, and what he is doing.

Exception

This practice may be overruled if the established editing style of the program calls for such a visual treatment of the material.

Example 1

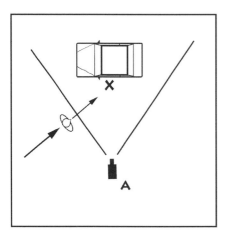

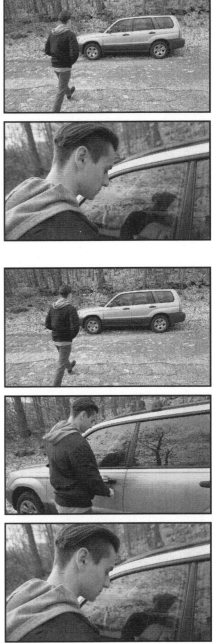

Example 2

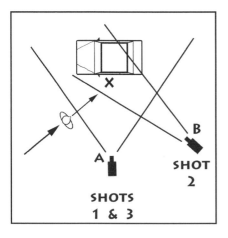

FIGURE 8.29 If the coverage has been provided, you may find it beneficial to cut three shots (long, medium, close) rather than just two (long, close) so that the audience follow along with this series of action edits. (Photo credits: Anthony Martel)

37. Beware of Editing a Cut-to-Black Followed by a Cut-to-Full-Picture

Reason

A straight cut-to-black is a very serious statement in narrative film production. Because it is an abrupt change-over from visible picture to full black, it carries with it a very dramatic weight, especially when you cut straight out of that black to a new, full image in the next shot. Reserve this bold treatment for an appropriate project whose visual style can absorb this dramatic editing practice.

Solution

Some possible combinations for the end of a sequence or scene and the start of another are:

- cutting to the next picture;
- dissolving to the next picture;
- fading to black and then fading up to the next picture (dipping to black);
- cutting to black and then fading up to the next picture;
- fading to black and then cutting to the next picture.

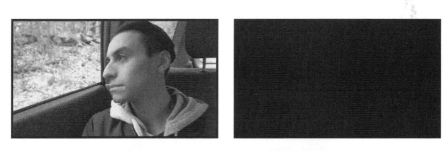

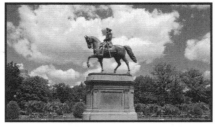

FIGURE 8.30 A hard cut from a full picture to a full screen of opaque black can be jarring for the audience. Treat this dramatic transition with respect and use it appropriately.

Exception

The cut-to-black and cut-to-picture are used to break two entire programs, two productions, or two complete items from each other, or for a very dramatic effect. Cuts-to-black are often used in editing feature film trailers because the shots that are joined together to advertise the movie were not meant to be joined together and cuts-to-black add to the drama and mystery of the story. Also, the cut-to-black may quickly lead into a title (typically white font over black, opaque background).

38. Take Advantage of the Transition Point that Natural Wipes Offer

Reason

Natural wipes occur any time that an object moves past the camera lens and momentarily blocks the composition of the frame before it clears out of the way. The movement (typically horizontal, but sometimes vertical) provides the perfect motivation to make a cut or a wipe to a new shot in the same scene, or to transition into a new scene.

Solution

Really thoughtful filmmakers will actually pre-plan the talent blocking of main characters, or more often "extras," to create the natural wipe moment for the editor to use. Other times, a simple happenstance like a van driving through the foreground of the shot on a long-lens exterior set-up can provide the motivation and the physical "image blocker" for the editor to create the natural wipe on his or her own initiative.

Regardless of who constructs it, a natural wipe is "natural" because it occurs during the shot while it is recorded – the wiping of the image on screen is inherent to the footage. Sometimes, during a complex dolly shot, the camera may crab past columns or pillars in a hotel lobby or a parking garage structure. Even though the objects are solid and unmoving, the camera's movement past them will create a natural (solid vertical) wipe across the recorded images. These may become convenient or clever transition points for the editor to use (Figure 8.31).

It may be helpful to have several of these natural wipes within one scene but certainly within the entire motion media piece, as only one may stand out as awkward or uncharacteristic of the established visual style of the program. Multiple natural wipes create a visual motif for the show.

Also be watchful for production footage that may allow for (or require, if scripted that way) a natural wipe that occurs on vertical camera movement. A camera may rise up in Shot 1 (via a tilt, a jib arm boom, a crane, etc.) and move past a solid horizontal object, such as a ceiling, the wall over a doorway, heavily leafed tree branches, or even a star-filled night sky. Shot 2 of this mini-sequence would typically also have matching upward vertical movement, such as up from behind a desk or counter, or even "through" the floor. Join these two shots together to make it seem as though the camera has gone "up" to a new place, in both space and time.

Exception

Just because a natural wipe occurs within the footage, it does not mean that you must avail yourself of it and cut or wipe at that point, especially if it does not add to the overall scene or story flow.

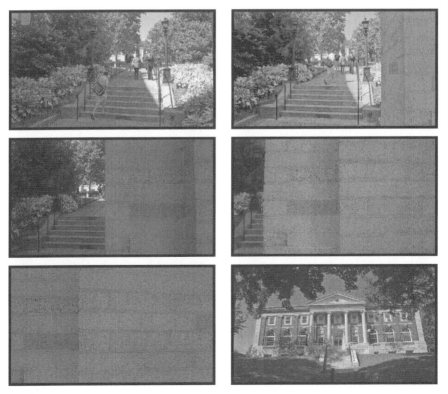

FIGURE 8.31   An editor can take advantage of a natural wipe within the footage and either cut or wipe to a new shot at that time.

38. Take Advantage of the Transition Point that Natural Wipes Offer

39. Take Advantage of the Transition Point that Whip Pans Offer

Reason

Much like the natural wipe, the **whip pan** (or **flash pan**) offers a very convenient and visually interesting motivation to transition from one shot to another. If planned by the filmmaker ahead of time, the fast motion blur generated at the end of a shot as the camera quickly spins horizontally will match with a corresponding motion blur at the start of another shot that is supposed to follow. The editor will join the tail blur of Shot A to the head blur of Shot B and the illusion, when watching the transition play itself through, will be that the motion of the blurring whip hurtles the viewer into a new location, time, or entirely different scene.

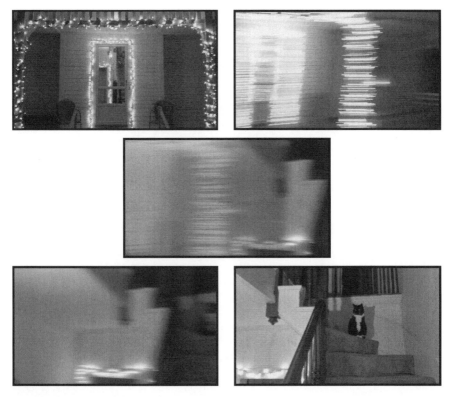

FIGURE 8.32 An editor can take advantage of the whip pan contained within two clips that were planned to be joined in this way. If no such whip pan occurred in either clip, then most video-editing software allows you to add blur effects and an editor could create the transition from scratch.

Solution

These whip pans (and, much less frequently, whip tilts) are usually designed and shot on purpose by the filmmaker during production. Unless there is a great deal of handheld footage that whips quickly left or right, then there will be little opportunity for an editor to create his or her own whip pans, although editing software may provide a cheat with some transition blur effects. Highly stylized shows or those with frenetic space/time jumps (like children's programming, travel shows, or home & garden DIY shows) often employ these constructed pan/blur shot transition effects in post-production.

Exception

Not all whip pan transitions will play correctly. The tail of Shot A and the head of Shot B must be whip panning in the same direction and roughly at the same speed for this transition trick to work.

40. Do *Not* Use Video Track Dissolves During a Dialogue Scene

Reason

Dissolves typically represent a passage of time between the two video clips that are joined by that transition effect. Dissolves are also associated with a slowing of story time or a blending together of related visual elements to create a more profound, romantic, or otherwise "emotional" moment in the story. Dialogue scenes, typically, happen at one moment in continuous story time and should not need a transition effect to join the coverage shots together.

Solution

Straight cuts will most often be your safest bet when it comes to editing together the coverage shots of a dialogue scene. The pacing of the conversation is set by the timing between the video/audio clips of each character saying his or her lines or reacting to the lines of the others present. Time is usually immediate and continuous. A dissolve would suggest to the viewing audience that a more significant passage of time has somehow elapsed between clips. Additionally, as dissolve effects also act like audio cross-fades, there is a risk of compromising the outgoing and incoming lines of dialogue on the associated audio tracks.

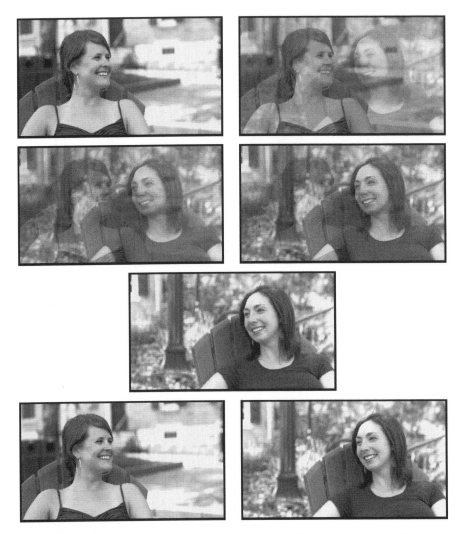

FIGURE 8.33 Stay clear of using dissolve transition effects between dialogue coverage shots within a single scene, as shown in the first five images above. Unless the dialogue happens across a very long span of time, just use straight cuts within the dialogue scene edit.

Exception

Using dissolves to join video clips within a dialogue scene may be appropriate if the dialogue scene actually happens across a longer period of time. Example: Two friends lounge around their apartment on a lazy Sunday afternoon – only speaking occasionally – and the dissolves cover up the gaps in time between their spoken words to one another. It may also be appropriate to use dissolves during a dialogue scene if the scene also contains a short montage sequence of the subjects involved in the conversation simultaneously doing things and speaking across a longer period of time. Otherwise, stick to straight cuts.

41. Use a "Soft Cut" or Mini-Dissolve to Mask a Cut in Interview Footage

Reason

It is inevitable that an editor will have to cut down or in some way condense or "clean up" the spoken-word responses of an interviewee. This extraction of unusable words and picture will often result in a jump cut for the image. If the editor is lucky enough, the person being interviewed moved very little while speaking on camera in his or her medium shot or MCU. A short dissolve effect can smooth over this minor visual discrepancy.

Solution

Rather than using B-roll or some other cutaway to layer over the very subtle jump cuts, the editor may use a two- to four-frame dissolve across the cut to quickly but gently morph the two almost exactly matching video images of the speaker. A dissolve of such a short duration will either go entirely unnoticed (if the talent remained very still) or appear as a "soft cut" or minor melding effect rather than a hard jump in picture alignment.

Exception

Obviously, if the interviewee changed his or her body positioning or facial expression too much at the cut point, the dissolve, no matter how brief or long, will not success-fully morph the two video clips together. A B-roll clip over audio would be preferable, or perhaps a **noddy** of the interviewer, if that is how the show is constructed.

42. Use a Dissolve Between Simile Shots

Reason

As you may know, a **simile** is a comparison of two unrelated subjects using the words "like" or "as" (e.g., "She's as tough as nails"). Two shots that may not have anything in common within the context of the present scene or story can behave like a simile.

The dissolve will unite the two different shots and a new meaning is created in the mind of the audience. A straight cut would not unite the subjects of the two different shots as blatantly; therefore, the audience might not understand the filmmaker's "literary" intentions. Although a very old and slightly heavy-handed method of visual storytelling, the dissolved simile shot is still effectively used today, particularly in comedies and animations.

Solution

Sometimes, a filmmaker wishes to make a visual simile with two distinctly different shots. In our example, we compare the young man with a dog. Although the dog is part of the narrative, a cut to him may not create the sought-after visual connection. A dissolve to the dog and back to the young man would unite them and allow the audience to understand the visual simile connection.

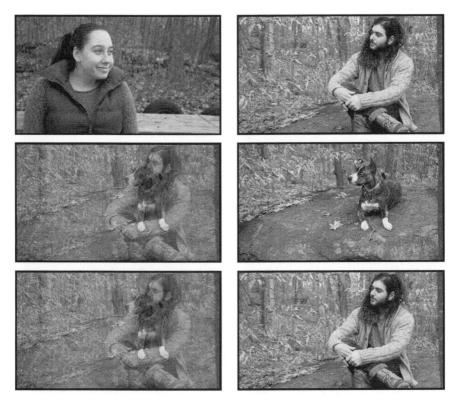

FIGURE 8.34 A dissolve across these two shots of the man and the dog will help to make a connection between them in the mind of a viewer. A simile is formed: the young man is like a watchful dog. (Photo credits: A – Anthony Martel; B, D & F – Zach Benard)

The composition of these two simile shots need not be matching (as in a form edit) but it can help to "meld" these disparate objects and generate a sort of intellectual form of simile edit.

Exception

This sort of visual simile treatment has its origins in silent cinema and, if used today, can often feel heavy-handed. Through the use of sound and other, less obvious, visual elements, you might be able to convey a similar connection.

43. Handle Continuity, Time, or Information "Gaps" with an Insert Shot

Reason

There will arise a moment in every editorial process where continuity of action, direction, or dialogue is not quite right across certain edits. There will also be a need for the editor to condense or expand time to help the pacing of a scene. Insert and cutaway shots will help with this (Figure 8.35). They divert the audience's attention enough from the previous shot without breaking out of the content of the scene in which they appear. The momentary distraction usually serves as enough of a visual break to reset the attention of the audience on the next cut that continues the action or dialogue after the hidden glitch. If a particular person or object needs to be highlighted as "important" to the audience, it can be shown as an insert.

Solution

The editor will hope to have footage specifically shot for insert or cutaway use, or he or she will have marked certain shots that contain usable insert moments: a close-up of a dog, a clock, or a photograph; a reaction shot from another character in the scene, etc. Keeping these insert/cutaway clips available will help the editor to mask over the continuity issues or to lengthen a moment or condense a longer event by providing a momentary, narratively related, and believable distraction to the minds of the audience.

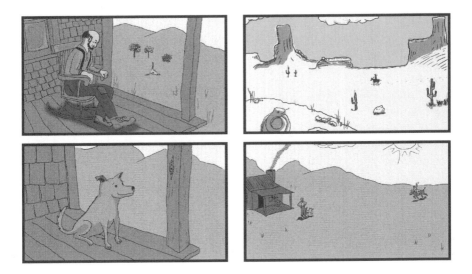

FIGURE 8.35   The insert shot of the dog close-up allows time to be condensed so that the rider can arrive at the cabin that much sooner.

Exception

Certain footage – for example, from long-winded talking-head interviews – that has no B-roll or other related visual material may not offer any opportunity for insert or cutaway shots. If the project does not have the footage and does not call for the use of full-frame graphics or titles, then you may be in an editorial quandary. Again, stock footage or still photographs may help here.

44. Cut to Reaction Shots During Phrases or Sentences Rather than at the End

Reason

Each consecutive shot should convey some new information to the viewing audience. During a dialogue scene, just because one person is speaking does not mean that he or she is always providing new visual information. To help to keep the audience engaged, it can be useful to cut to something new, such as the reaction shot of the other character listening. Breaking up a long line delivery with the reaction shots of the other character(s) involved in the scene can provide a certain rhythm and show new information about the response of those listening.

If you show only one person speaking, then cut to the other person's reaction over silence, then cut back to the first person who starts speaking again, etc., it will become rather monotonous for the viewer – too much straight back and forth, like a tennis match.

Solution

Look at and listen very carefully to the footage to find a motivation, however small, to insert a cutaway of the listener reacting. The reaction shot of Character B is visible over the continuing dialogue of Character A. If the cutaway is close to the end of Character A's words, then this clip may become the next shot where Character B will actually be seen to speak as well. This type of dialogue editing with lapping picture and character line delivery is more interesting to the audience because it shows communication between the subjects, with both actions and reactions.

Exception

There are times when a single character does the majority of the speaking in a scene. If the performance is powerful enough to "carry" the scene, then by all means leave the line delivery uncut for the stronger emotional effect on the audience. Also, there may be a monologue delivered by one individual. If that performance is powerful enough, let it ride. For comedic purposes, it might underscore the monotony of the conversation to keep it in the form of a "he says, she says" back and forth, and not lap the listening character's reactions over the off-screen dialogue.

45. When Editing Dialogue, Avoid Automatically Removing a Performer's Pauses

Reason

There are some things that can really disrupt a performance, and this is one of them. The performer will have rehearsed the script to achieve a certain emotional state in the scene. Actors rightly claim that the space between words is just as important as the words themselves. Most of the time, the pauses are used to create weight and signifi-cance, or to add a dramatic element to the words or the scene in general. To automatically edit out these spaces (or beats or pauses) in a monologue or dialogue can completely change the intended meaning of the scene.

Solution

Accept the pauses as a guide for your edits and, perhaps, use them as a motivation to incorporate a cutaway. Seeing some other subject, as in a reaction shot or noddy, will maintain visual interest while keeping true to the pace of the actor's spoken performance. Accept the pauses as an important integrated element in the dialogue and not just as a moment when someone is not speaking.

Exception

The exceptions may have to do with the lack of time. In non-fiction programming like news, documentary, short-form commercial, and current affairs, where the maximum amount of visual and verbal information must fit into the minimum amount of time, the editor may choose to edit out unnecessary pauses.

It is very important to note that an editor may also remove, add, shorten, or lengthen pauses for the purposes of reconstructing the scene with a new rhythm and pacing of line delivery. Although the subject's performance is highly valued, the editor has the responsibility of sculpting the best story and character representations in the scene and across the entire motion picture. Playing with time, word order, and word placement can be beneficial.

---

46. In Documentary Programming, Edit Out "Ums" and "Ahs" in Interviewee Speech

Reason

Often, your goal as an editor, especially in documentary and other non-fiction programming about real people, is to make them look and sound as good as possible on screen. A fourth grader, a diplomat, or a scientist may all have certain verbal pauses in their vocalized speech patterns. They may say "um" or "ah" to fill the space between their thoughts. While listening in person, these verbal pauses often go unnoticed unless they are extremely excessive. Watching a short answer filled with "ums" and "ahs" will be more noticeable and less appealing to the viewer, and it can waste valuable time to get to the point.

Production Audio Says:
Yeah, so like in essence we ah you know we just sat down and like started to do the work.

Edited Version Now Says:
So in essence we just sat down and started to do the work.

FIGURE 8.36   For reasons of clarity or program timing, it can be advantageous to edit out the "ums," "ahs," and "likes" from a speaker's dialogue.

Solution

Edit out these verbal pauses in documentary or non-fiction material whenever possible. If the mouth does not move very much while the sound is made, lift the "um," "ah," or "gulp" and let the room tone or ambience track mask the hole. If the offense is more visually noticeable, then you may have to cutaway to a graphic or some B-roll, or to an interviewer noddy shot if such a thing exists. The B-roll cutaway is a staple of documentary monologue editing so that the verbal points of the person speaking sound clear, concise, and coherent. When the "ums" and "ahs" are removed from the clip, the picture track will look very choppy but the sound track will flow smoothly. B-roll and other cutaways will mask the jump cuts and also provide the audience with additional visual story information.

Exception

Occasionally, someone's speech pattern and the verbal tics that he or she exhibits are inextricably tied to his or her persona. It will be best to keep these inherent pauses or sounds to provide the viewer with the full "flavor" of the individual's true character.

46. In Documentary Programming, Edit Out "Ums" and "Ahs" in Interviewee Speech

47. Use a Character's Cleanly Recorded Dialogue under His or Her Off-Screen or Over-the-Shoulder Line Delivery

Reason

During production, the sound recordist may not have the boom operator favor the off-screen actor or the over-the-shoulder's "shoulder" talent, which means that this "hidden" actor's dialogue will sound weak on the recording while the favored talent's line delivery, given closer to the microphone, will sound stronger.

Solution

Traditional master scene shooting technique should provide multiple shots of the same dialogue delivery as covered from different camera angles. Any wide or two-shot should provide strong audio levels from both characters. Single shots (MS, MCU, CU, etc.) of each character should also yield strong audio recordings of line delivery. Whenever a character needs to say lines but is either not on screen or has the back of his or her head visible in an OTS shot, the editor should cut in clean, clear audio track lifted from some other source if the production track is not good for that "off-screen" character. The bad-sounding audio for the "off-screen" character is cut out and replaced with good versions of the same script lines. This way, the person whom the audience are watching gets clean dialogue and the "off-screen" character also gets clear, clean dialogue with proper levels, albeit from different takes and different audio sources of that performer.

Exception

There really should be no exceptions to this guideline. You should always strive to start with the cleanest, clearest, strongest audio signal when you are editing the sound elements for a program. If the sound needs to be modified (made worse) for a special effect within the story, then you should still start with clean sound and degrade it yourself in a controlled fashion using audio software effects, etc.

48. Do Not Be Too Bound by Dialogue When Looking for a Cut Point

Reason

In dialogue footage, there are two major motivations for cutting: vision and sounds. During a two-person dialogue, actions and reactions will take place. If you only cut when one character's words are finished, then it can become predictable or boring. While one person is talking, the other will be listening and may show facial reactions, provided the production team shot such footage. These reactions are very important and can be used as the motivation for the back-and-forth editing for the scene.

Solution

In fictional narrative shooting, it is common to record the close shots of one character's dialogue delivery with an off-screen performance of the lines for the unseen character. The audio for the off-screen character will most likely not be used, but the visuals of the on-camera talent will be useful. It will be during these non-speaking moments that an editor should be able to find the reaction shots for cutaways in the scene. Also, it may be possible to lift some frames out of the beginning of the shot before "Action" was called, or from the end after "Cut" was called, if the talent did not break character too early.

In documentary, news, and other talking-head programming, if no facial reaction is evident during the question and answer period, then the director or producer will hopefully have shot what some people call a reaction noddy of the listener as safety coverage. Noddies are additional, close shots of the listener simulating a reaction to what was said – usually a slow head nod. A noddy may show other movements of the head or eyebrows, a smile, etc. When noddies are cut into the dialogue with a motivation, they can look quite natural, but they do tip the scales of artifice in non-fiction editing.

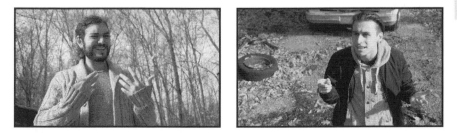

FIGURE 8.37   If cut in at the right moment, a reaction shot may have greater significance to the audience than the dialogue that they are hearing coming from the other character. (Photo credits: A – Zach Benard; B – Anthony Martel)

Noddies are also useful to edit out parts of verbal information. For instance, they can be used to reduce the duration of an interviewee's answer or cover for the numerous "ums" and "ahs" that inevitably need to be edited out of the replies. There is no written rule about the duration of a noddy, so it more or less depends on the circumstances. Adding a cutaway shot that is too short (maybe under two seconds) may seem jarring; adding one that is too long may leave the audience wondering why they are not watching the speaker again.

Exception

An exception could be when the primary shot is a monologue. There will be no other character or subject present in the scene to use as a cutaway. Also, for comic timing, a delay in the cut to other characters may build the tension/release dynamic of the "pregnant" pause.

49. Do Not Leave Any Holes in Your Audio Tracks

Reason

Non-linear digital video-editing software applications allow you to place video and audio clips wherever you wish on their respective tracks. Unless it is purposefully planned, no editor will want to have a blank black screen in his or her video. Care is usually taken to ensure that there is some sort of video clip on every frame from the start to the end of the sequence. The same goes for the audio tracks. A section of the sequence that contains no audio data whatsoever will play back as total silence – an audio hole that sounds really "dead" when encountered in an otherwise sound-filled timeline.

Solution

Make sure that you have some kind of sound clip in place on each frame of your sequence. If your program calls for silence, place an audio clip in your timeline that has some level of recorded "silence" – like the tone of a "completely silent" room. There will be some sound data present that will typically mix better with the other clips of actual sound (sync source tracks, NATS, SFX, music, etc.) in your sequence. This way, the quiet, in-between moments will sound like relative silence in comparison to the rest of the audio and not like total dead silence.

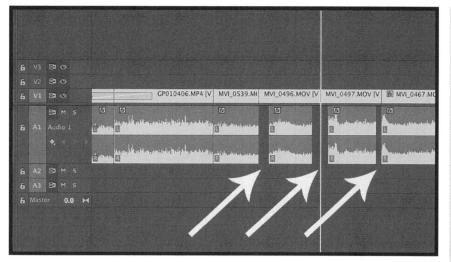

FIGURE 8.38 A hole in the audio track will play as absolute silence and will be rather conspicuous to the listener. Try to have an audio clip (even of "silence"), on some track, at every frame across the entire sequence.

Exception

There can be certain creative uses of total dead silence in almost any kind of program, but it will play as rather dramatic to the audience. Be cautious with this technique and be sure to handle the transitions into and out of this dead audio hole with care.

50. When Appropriate, Edit Video Tracks to the Beats of Music in Your Sequence

Reason

Most people respond well to music and the structure of much of the music from around the world has beats that count off particular intervals of time. When the audience hear the beats, they "get into the groove," as it were, and become more susceptible to having the visuals of the picture track change over at these unique beat moments. The beats and cuts follow along together in time. Faster-tempo cutting may be more "fun" or "exciting" and slower-tempo cutting may feel more "peaceful" or "sad."

Solution

If your music video, promotional video or commercial, montage sequence, or non-fiction programming contains a soundtrack (especially a pop music song), then it can be relatively easy (and effective) to make your straight cuts on the picture track(s) when the music beats occur. Most editing apps allow you to add virtual markers to clips. You can manually add markers to your song clip at each frame where the pronounced beat occurs. Aligning your timeline position indicator (playhead) with one of these markers, you can then edit in a video clip starting at the correct beat moment. Some software can also do audio clip analysis and pre-mark the beats for you.

Exception

Obviously, an editor would (most likely) not wish to edit an entire video directly on the same matching beat interval. This would become too predictable and, perhaps, repetitively boring for the audience. Perhaps save this technique for certain key moments in the song and in the visual material.

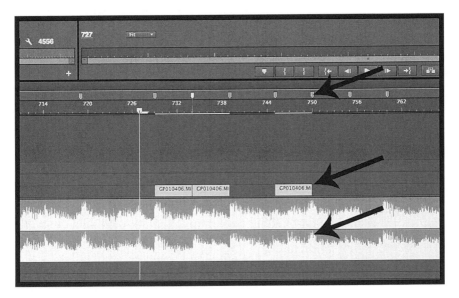

FIGURE 8.39 Most software will allow you to add markers to the sequence at the beats of your music clip. This allows you to edit short video clips IN to OUT precisely between the beats.

51. If Appropriate for Your Story, Make a Cut at a Loud Sound on the Audio Track

Reason

Loud sounds are known to cause many people to blink their eyes. It's like a crash cut.

Solution

An editor may be able to find a point in a scene's development where a loud sound occurs on the audio track. If the picture edit is made with discretion at this point, it is likely that the cut transition will be hidden during the blinking process of the audience members who are reacting to the loud sound. This is a bit of a cheat and a bit of a gamble, but it may be effective at the right moment.

Exception

You should not cut just any time that there is a loud sound on the audio tracks. This is a poor way to construct a good story flow. However, a music video could benefit from this editing pattern if a cut were to be made on the strong drumbeats, for example.

52. Hold Off on Adding Music to Dialogue Scenes

Reason

Dialogue should most often convey important information about the story, the characters, or the topics of discussion. Carefully performed and cleverly edited dialogue will have a rhythm or cadence all of its own that can feel like the flow found in music. Adding actual music under spoken-word audio tracks can sometimes be a distraction for the audience, especially if the song has lyrics.

Solution

As an editor trying to get a feel for a scene from a film or a segment from a documentary, etc., you should keep your own distractions to a minimum. As much as there is value in editing to music (to help you to find the pacing), it would be best to cut dialogue scenes without any music present. This way, you can judge the technical qualities of the actual sync sound production audio files, and you can construct your own rhythm for the material.

Exception

If a diegetic musical soundtrack needs to be present in the scene, then add and mix it appropriately after the picture lock stage. The same goes for an original musical score.

---

53. During the Audio Mix, Make Sure that Music Track Levels Do Not Overpower Dialogue

Reason

Music is a very powerful creative device. It can propel a scene forward, slow it down, make the audience feel sad, happy, tense, etc. Once you get your program to the point where your music bed is in place, it is important to regulate the sound levels so that the music does not compete with the dialogue or other audio elements in your sequence.

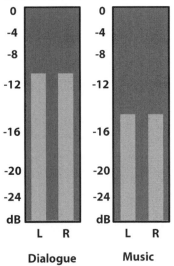

AUDIO TRACK DECIBEL LEVEL SCALE

Dialogue   Music

FIGURE 8.40 Your dialogue and music tracks will most often be separate and independently controllable clips in your timeline sequence. Make sure that you lower the volume of your music to appropriate levels whenever important lines of dialogue are being delivered.

Solution

Attend to the proper audio level mixing for all audio elements, especially the music. If the music is "source" or diegetic (generated within the film world by a radio, live band, .mp3 player, etc.), then be aware that it should play continuously under that scene until either the music or the scene ends. If dialogue is delivered on top of the music bed, then make sure that you lower the music level under the spoken words. The audience will accept the fact that the music level drops into the background sounds because they are usually more interested in what the characters have to say.

Exception

If the location sound is recorded during the documentation of a live event (concert, benefit gala, etc.), then it will be difficult or impossible to lower the captured music levels in the background. Also, if the fictional narrative story calls for the loud music to drown out the spoken word, then keep it hot in the mix for this special purpose.

54. Consider Using a Sound Element Before Active Picture at the Start of a Program

Reason

Some claim that a picture without sound is dead, but sound without a picture is not. The audience, upon hearing sound (possibly spoken words, music, or ambience), will begin to imagine what is happening even before they know anything about it. The imagination is triggered. As the pictures then come onto the screen, the multi-sensory experience begins. This harkens back to those old-time radio programs where the listening audience heard dialogue, sound effects, and music but found engagement and entertainment in the aural experience – much as with podcasts of today.

Solution

If the type of program warrants it, sound elements important to the narrative (such as ambience, SFX, or music) may begin underneath the opening credit sequence, which can incorporate a fair amount of black screen space. The location and mood of the story are set by this leading audio information. Obviously, this practice depends upon what the sounds are and what the opening imagery will be in the program.

Exception

The exceptions to this guideline are short-form (30 to 60 seconds) television advertisements, where the picture is obviously on screen as early as possible for time reasons. In general, those who produce television and streaming web programming do not like to incorporate full black screens for too long because the viewing audience could mistake this for an actual technical error at the broadcasting station, with the cable signal, with the display device or video stream, etc.

55. For the End of a Program, Use the End of the Music

Reason

Music, of whatever nature, usually is divided up into different phrases, verses, or movements and has a distinct structure. Part of this structure will be an ending, fade-out, or climax. This climax should be used to match the shots that end your video. It would be confusing to show the final pictures of a program with an opening musical passage that awkwardly fades down. They would probably not match well.

Solution

The music should be **back timed** to find its correct start point relative to the visuals of the sequence. If the timing is correct, the last bars of the musical piece should match the final shots of the sequence. This is especially true at the end of a program when the last bar of the music would be timed with the fade-to-black, either at the conclusion of the story action or at the end of the closing credit sequence. Those more skilled in music editing may cut out the middle of a song and mix together the start and the end to jive better with the end of the motion picture.

Exception

The main exception to this practice is where the music is faded gradually into or under other sound, dialogue, or music that is stronger in the mix.

56. Make Appropriate Font Choices for Your Titles

Reason

Whether you have access to fonts just from your computer's operating system or you have downloaded a larger collection of font libraries, you should choose sans serif fonts for most titling purposes in your video-editing software. Serifs are those little extra flourishes extending off the major structures that form each letter in an alphabet and number sequence. Fonts with serifs, particularly when used within interlaced standard-definition video projects, do not look very good at lower resolutions or when compressed into media files for streaming or on small-screen playback. The thinness in the design of some of those serif attributes gets lost (Figure 8.41).

Solution

Select sans serif fonts. You may even wish to make your chosen font bold and of a point size appropriate to the purpose of the title. Too small and the titles may not be legible on screen, especially if viewers will be watching your video on tablets or smartphone screens. Spell-check your words and names also. Crazy colors, drop shadows, or strokes may complicate things visually. White fill color over black background may often be the simplest and best choice for full-screen, opaque titles.

Exception

You are free to use any fonts recognized by your video-editing software and its titling tool, but the look should fit the show and be technically correct (sans serif most often). If you are sharing projects with editing partners across computer systems, you should guarantee

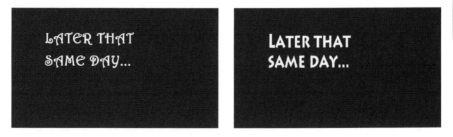

FIGURE 8.41 The font in Title A has serifs and other thin attributes that may not play well on video screens. The font in Title B is sans serif and may look better when used in titles.

that the fonts that you have selected for your titles also live on the other editing systems. Most often, the font data of your titles originates on your local host computer and does not travel with your project.

57. Be Aware of Proper On-Screen Durations for Inter-Title and Lower-Third Graphics

Reason

Just as a recorded shot of a person can stay on screen for too long, so can a title or other graphic element. The audience absorb visual information from the shots as a product of composition, lighting, character facial expressions, colors, etc., but they absorb information from **inter-titles** and identifying **lower thirds** by reading it. If a title is not on screen long enough, it cannot be read and understood. If a title is left on screen for too long, the audience may become vexed waiting for the next shot or the next bit of information to appear.

Solution

An inter-title that says, "Later that same day . . ." (only four words) may be on screen for as little as two seconds. An inter-title that consists of several short phrases may require five, ten, or more seconds, depending on how many words there are and how complex the visual presentation is. A general guideline for the editor is to leave a title on the screen for as long as it takes to read through the words three times in a row. This is dependent upon the length of the written words, of course, and may have to be averaged down or up depending on the importance of the title information within the motion media piece and the overall timing of the edited program. Inter-titles, which are traditionally white lettering over a solid black background, are often preceded by a fade-to-black and followed by a fade-from-black.

Lower thirds are superimposed identification titles, usually showing a person's name, occupation, or location in news, documentary, and non-fiction programming. They appear in the bottom lower third of the screen shortly after a close shot of the person speaking is edited into the sequence. The title should stay on screen long enough for the information to be read and digested by the average person, and then it should go away. Often, lower-third identifying titles like this dissolve onto the screen, stay solid, and then dissolve off – a bit less harsh than a straight cut on and off. You may also have seen fancier lower-third treatments that slide onto, type onto, or otherwise animate onto the screen. It is also customary to use the lower-third identifying title on the first appearance of a

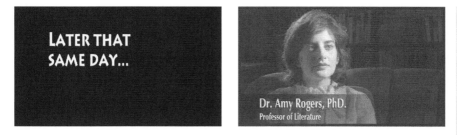

FIGURE 8.42 Titles and lower-third graphics require appropriate timing for each edited piece. Too short and the audience may miss out on information; too long and they may get impatient waiting for the next visual element to appear.

person in a program. There often is little need to show the title again if the same person is shown again later in your sequence, although this may happen if you wish – especially if your program is broken down into sections and the audience will need a reminder of who is speaking on screen.

Generally, a title can live on screen at full opacity for as long as needed. The actual duration will be determined by watching the end of the preceding clip and seeing how the title comes onto the screen and for how long before it cuts out to the next shot.

Scrubbing through the title clip in your timeline will not give you the appropriate sense of time. You must back up your playhead prior to the title's entrance, and then play through its duration in real time in order to feel how long is long enough. It would be advisable for you to get feedback from several other people who know the project so that you can gauge how they feel about the timing of the title elements and lower thirds. Often, half of a second longer or shorter will make a big difference in helping it to feel "right."

Exception

There are no real exceptions to this general practice. As the editor of these created graphic elements, you have total control over how long you wish to leave them on screen. After you know the information has been conveyed, it becomes a question of beats to determine the appropriate duration.

During the construction of your sequence, you can become enamored of a particular portion of a song that is playing on the audio track under the title or graphic. Timing out a visual element (like the inter-title or lower third) to a musical phrase can be a good way to engage an audience with multiple senses, but be aware that if the sound element is too short or too long, the title will be adversely affected also.

57. Be Aware of Proper On-Screen Durations for Inter-Title and Lower-Third Graphics

58. Use Still Digital Photographs Whose Image Resolution Is as Large as or Larger than the Project Format's Pixel Resolution

Reason

Digital images that have a pixel resolution smaller than that of the project settings for the sequence being edited will need to be scaled larger to fit the full frame of video and will, therefore, degrade in quality.

Solution

Acquire still digital image files that match or exceed your sequence's dimensions of pixel rows and columns. Example: An image that is 250 × 250 pixels will have to be scaled up quite a bit to fit nearer the edges of a full HD video frame that is 1920 × 1080 pixels in size. Scaling this small web image up to full HD pixel resolution will cause it to look blocky, chunky, blurry, and all-around bad. Images that have much larger pixel dimensions will easily scale down, retain much of their image data, and look good. Example: An image that is 3543 × 2365 pixels will reduce down to fit within the full HD video frame size.

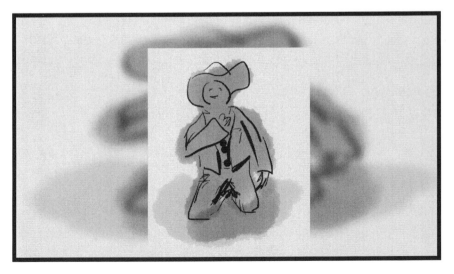

FIGURE 8.43 Imported digital photographs that are too small for the HD or larger video format may need a special treatment such as this to retain image quality.

Exception

If a client must use a lower-resolution image, then design a layout that can highlight the smaller image within the larger frame and do not attempt to scale it up. A common and quick trick is to stretch the smaller image to fit into the larger sequence frame and then soften it with a frame-wide blur effect. On top of this blurred and stretched image, you can place the best version of the imported smaller picture at its original size to maintain full quality (Figure 8.43).

59. If Working for a Client, Complete Rudimentary Color Correction Before Showing a Rough Cut

Reason

Not everyone understands that video sometimes has less than desirable color characteristics. Overall brightness, contrast, and color casts can be quickly corrected with your software tools so that your sequence plays back and looks "normal" to the untrained eyes of your client.

Solution

Although the complete color grading will not be done until the finishing phase of post-production, there can be value in correcting any major luminance and chrominance video signal issues earlier, at the rough cut stage. Individuals who are not accustomed to how video editing and finishing work may have great difficulty seeing beyond the compromised imagery and may be less able to provide proper feedback on the actual edit in progress. With a quick pass on color correction, you are not staring at unsightly video clips all day long and the client will not freak out.

Exception

Some clients trust in the process and will not need to see corrected video early on. Time may not be on your side and even quick drag-and-drop auto-correction effects may be too time consuming for your due date. If you are editing your own personal projects, then follow the more traditional steps and save the real color grading for the finishing stage.

60. When Color Grading, Work Through Shots, Then Scenes, Then Overall Look

Reason

Scenes are made up of individual shots and the entire motion media piece is made up of scenes or segments. If you start small and build to larger chunks of the overall piece, then you'll get the base levels set, match the adjoining scene clips, and be able to tweak an overall look for the entire project – in that order.

Solution

A solid approach to color grading a sequence during the finishing phase of post-production is to start with the shots that need the least help first and move on from there to the more difficult fixes. You should grade an individual shot and then apply that fix to all other clips from the same master clip that also live in the timeline. Next, grade the other shots in that scene so that shots that are supposed to be taking place at the same location and at the same moment of film time have a uniform appearance. Lastly, once all of the video clips have been corrected and graded to look as good as the project needs, then create the final, overall look for the entire show based on the already tweaked base layer.

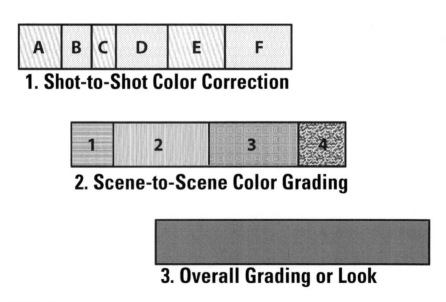

FIGURE 8.44 Color grading should progress from individual shots to shots within scenes or segments of a show and finally end with the creation of an overall look or color treatment for the entire program.

Exception

There really should not be much deviation from this order, because video-editing software applications process the video signal in certain orders. Ensure all of the clips have good contrast, brightness, and color values (across the entire sequence) before you attempt an overall, final look for the show or for segments of the show. Also, even the silliest or quickest of video sequences can benefit from the color correction and grading process, so it is best not to skip this phase of the editing process.

Chapter Eight – Review

1. Pay careful attention to media and project organization.
2. Learn and use the keyboard shortcuts for your video-editing applications and operating systems.
3. Organize your timeline tracks and maintain consistency across projects.
4. Keep your rough cut long; do not be tempted to do a finely tuned edit early in the process.
5. Review each edit or series of edits as you make them.
6. Duplicate your sequence before making major changes.
7. Show your edited motion picture to someone else and get feedback.
8. Put aside your edited sequence for a short time and watch it again with fresh eyes.
9. Use shots with matching headroom when cutting shot–reverse–shot in a dialogue scene.
10. Avoid shots where distracting objects appear to be too close to the subject's head.
11. Avoid shots where the side edges of the frame cut off the heads or bodies of people.
12. Cut matched shots rather than unmatched shots in a back-and-forth dialogue scene.
13. When editing a telephone conversation, the subjects should appear to be looking across the screen at one another.
14. In a three-person dialogue, beware of cutting from a two-shot to another two-shot.
15. With a single subject, try to avoid cutting to the same camera angle.

Chapter Eight – Review

16. Beware of screen placement issues with an object of interest.

17. Edit in a wide shot as soon as possible after a series of close-up shots in a group scene.

18. Cut to a close shot of a new subject soon after he or she enters a scene.

19. When editing a new scene with new backgrounds, show an establishing shot at the earliest opportunity.

20. Use close-ups of subjects in a scene for the greatest emotional effect.

21. Cut away from subjects soon after their look rests upon their object of interest.

22. Use J-cuts and L-cuts to smooth over transitions.

23. Create a continuous motion action edit by cutting during the physical movement in the two matching clips.

24. When cutting a rise as an action edit, cut before the subject's eyes leave the frame.

25. When cutting to a close-up of an action, select a version of the close-up where the action is slower.

26. Understand the visual differences between a dolly-in and a zoom.

27. Beware of shots that dolly out without motivation.

28. When editing in a pan or a crab dolly move, use the best version that is smooth, timed well, and leads the subject's movement.

29. Begin and end each pan, tilt, or dolly shot on a static frame.

30. If a subject is moving within a pan, crab dolly, or tracking shot, avoid cutting to a static image of the same subject if he or she is then stationary.

31. Avoid cutting pans and tilts that reverse direction at the cut point.

32. Objects, like people, moving in a direction have an action line. Avoid crossing it or the screen direction will be reversed.

33. Avoid cutting an action edit from a two-shot to another two-shot of the same people.

34. Allow a subject to completely exit the frame prior to cutting to that same subject in a new film space and time.

35. For any action edit, if a subject exits frame left, then the same subject should enter the next shot frame right.

36. Avoid making an action edit from a long shot of a subject to a close-up of the same subject.

37. Beware of editing a cut-to-black followed by a cut-to-full-picture.

38. Take advantage of the transition point that natural wipes offer when they occur in the footage.

39. Take advantage of the transition point that whip pans offer when they occur in the footage.

40. Do *not* use video track dissolves during a dialogue scene.

41. Use a "soft cut" or mini-dissolve to mask a cut in interview footage.

42. Use a dissolve between simile shots.

43. Use insert shots to cover gaps in continuity, condense or expand time, or reveal important story information.

44. A reaction shot seems more natural during a spoken phrase or sentence than at the end.

45. When editing fiction dialogue, avoid automatically removing a performer's pauses.

46. In non-fiction programming, edit out "ums" and "ahs" in interviewee speech.

47. Use a character's cleanly recorded dialogue under his or her off-screen or over-the-shoulder line delivery.

48. Do not be too bound by dialogue when looking for a cut point.

49. Do not leave any holes in your audio tracks.

50. When appropriate, edit video tracks to the beats of music in your sequence.

51. If appropriate for your story, make a cut at a loud sound on the audio track.

52. Hold off on adding music to dialogue scenes.

53. During the audio mix, make sure that music track levels do not overpower dialogue.

54. At the start of a program, the sound track can lead the visual track.

55. For the end of a program, use the end of the music.

56. Make appropriate font choices for your titles.

57. Be aware of proper on-screen durations for inter-title and lower-third graphics.

58. Use still digital photographs whose image resolution is as large as or larger than the project's pixel resolution format.

59. If working for a client, complete rudimentary color correction before showing a rough cut.

60. When color grading, work through shots, then scenes, then overall look.

Chapter Eight – Exercises

1. Conduct a test of the most usable fonts. With your video-editing application of choice, type the following sentence into the title tool: "The quick brown fox jumps over the lazy dog." Run through a series of fonts, colors, point sizes, borders, and drop/depth shadows. See which ones work best over an opaque background and which ones work best keyed over a video background.

2. Record a quick video interview with a friend, family member, or co-worker. Watch the footage and listen for any particular speech patterns, verbal tics, or padding with extraneous sounds or words. Edit out the time-consuming "ums," "ahs," and extra "likes." Does it make the interviewee's responses sound smoother, tighter, and more to the point? How did you choose to cover over the picture jump cuts?

3. Practice editing a piece of music to see if you can cleanly cut it down and seamlessly mix the pieces together. Try it with rock, pop, jazz, hip-hop, and classical to see which genres, if any, are easier to handle. (Hint: Instrumental pieces may work best.)

4. Based on the script found in Appendix C, record two people performing that scene, then edit it together. Try to incorporate as many of the applicable guidelines that have been presented here in Chapter Eight. If you need to, refer to the shot types discussed in Chapter Two before you record the video.

Chapter Eight – Quiz Yourself

1. What is a traditional "reaction shot" and when and why might you want to edit it into a scene?

2. Why might an axial edit (or punch-in) cause a jump cut with those two shots recorded from the same angle on action? When might this be a good thing to do?

3. What are "simile shots" and what might be the best way to join them together?

4. Why might you want to allow a subject to completely exit the frame before cutting to a new time and location where that same subject then enters?

5. If a car exits frame right in Shot A, then how should it enter the frame of the next shot (if you are following the traditional approach to handling screen direction of action)?

6. What is a "natural wipe" and how might you, as an editor, go about constructing one?

7. What is an "insert shot" and how, when, and where can you use it in your edited sequence?

8. How can B-roll be used to help to cover up the visual jump cuts caused when you edit out the "ums" and "ahs" of an interview subject in non-fiction or documentary programming? If B-roll for the subject of discussion does not exist in the source footage, what might an editor be able to use in its place?

9. Why might an action that is shown in a tight close-up shot appear to happen very quickly on the big screen?

10. Why might it be advantageous to make a picture track edit when a loud sound is heard on the audio tracks?

Chapter Nine
Concluding Thoughts

- Sound and Vision Are Partners
- A New Shot Should Contain New Information
- There Should Be a Reason for Every Edit
- Pacing Has a Purpose
- Observe the Action Line
- Select the Appropriate Form of Edit
- The Better the Edit, the Less It Is Noticed
- Editing Is Manipulation
- The Role of an Assistant Editor
- Editing Is Creating

The material in this last chapter will brief you on some of the key guidelines for any edit session. Regardless of the editing fashion of the day, these ways of thinking about the editing process have been around for quite some time, and although they have changed somewhat over the years, they have stayed true to their purposes. We are looking to provide some basic ideas for you, as new editors, so that you may absorb these concepts and also move forward with your editing careers. We want you to think on your own as well, and learn by doing. The common grammar presented here gets everybody on the same page. Through practice, your editing skills will increase over time as you creatively expand your craft.

Sound and Vision Are Partners

This seems somewhat obvious, but it is surprising how many new editors allow the sound to "fight" the picture. Sound is a partner in the production and must be edited with the same care and attention to detail as the visual elements. The ear and the eye work in unison, supplementing each other's information, so any conflict between the two could cause confusion for the audience.

Information on your audio tracks should reinforce and expand the visual content of the story. On the most basic level, if you show horses galloping down the prairie, then we should hear the sound of horse hooves galloping across matching terrain. We hear what we see. As an example of a more complex editing style, say we see a character get into a taxi, then we have a series of shots that show the taxi maneuvering through city streets and making its way onto a highway. Underneath this exterior montage of the moving taxi, we hear the sounds of the streets, and maybe some musical score for the movie, but we also hear the sound of jet engines warming up, airport intercom announcements, and a boarding call for a flight to New Delhi. This montage sequence may end with us seeing that character either onboard the airplane or even already arrived at the new location. The picture and audio tracks are giving us different moments of story progression at the same time. You are delivering a multi-sensory experience to the audience. There is corroboration between the visual and aural information being presented, yet there is also a layering of space, time, and content. It still helps the audience to accept it as "reality."

Sounds can quickly create more "reality" than vision. The eye tends to take what it sees factually, whereas sounds stimulate the brain's imagination centers. Objects off screen may never be shown to the audience, but the sounds generated by these unseen things can help to establish their presence in the film world. This concept can also hold true for the audience viewing things on screen that they have never directly experienced or that cannot happen in our reality. An object disintegrating as it is hit by an alien ray gun isn't real, but the sound you hear while it's happening on screen makes you believe it is real.

This is why musical scoring and sound design (and the quality of the production recordings of dialogue and natural sounds) can be so important to a motion picture experience. Sounds are connected to emotional responses. We process them "viscerally." As the hero walks through the dark cave and we hear a deep, bass sub-rumble, a sense of foreboding can be felt in our chests. When the little girl is taken away to the orphanage and we hear a single, mournful violin playing, we experience "true" sadness. Never underestimate the manipulative power that sound and music can have over the audience's emotions.

Consequently, stimulating the ear to help the eye is one of the key tasks of the editor. At its most basic, you keep the dialogue clear and clean so that the audience can hear what people are saying. There is little more aggravating than watching a motion media program that has dialogue that seems important to the story but the audio track is so muddled or poorly mixed that you cannot hear the characters' conversations. Frustrating the audience like this is a sure-fire way to get them to "drop out" of the viewing experience.

In more complex manipulations, the audio tracks can provide important narrative details, augment the "reality" of the story's events, or generate emotional reactions in the viewer, and, if sound that directly contradicts the visuals is laid in, it can serve to comment on themes or make an ironic statement. An editor should always remember that sound and vision are both critical elements of motion pictures, often combining their efforts to help to show and tell a better story.

A New Shot Should Contain New Information

The success of a good motion media project is based on the audience's expectation that there will be a continuous supply of visual information. This supply, if it is correctly delivered, will constantly update and increase the visual information of the events of the program that is received by the viewer.

If you are editing an instructional video for a website, such as how to bake a cake, then you have a pretty good understanding of the flow of information. The recipe for the cake batter and the process of mixing, baking, and icing the final product is the pre-built "script" that you can follow. Each shot can show a new step in the process.

Thirty-second television commercials are very exacting in their construction. Airtime is expensive and 30 seconds is a very short window in which to clearly convey your message. The script and storyboards will have been followed very closely during production because many people had to give approval on just those few details. The editor, although having some freedom to play creatively, is initially bound to the script and storyboards. New information has to be present in each shot because you only have so many shots that you can possibly fit, coherently, into a 30-second spot.

This predetermined flow of information can become rather tricky, even with scripted production footage from narrative films and outlined documentaries, etc. Time is precious to both the presenter and the viewer of motion pictures. If you fail to deliver new information with each shot, then you are not being very efficient with screen time, you are failing to progress the story, and you may be losing the attention of your audience. Keep in mind that information can come from the picture track or sound tracks, it can be directly involved with the characters or story, or it can take the form of intellectual or emotional manipulations that you exercise on your audience. Even shots that seem to contain no pertinent story information can exist to help to control pacing, set a mood, or simply allow the audience time to pause and reflect on the presentation thus far. No matter what, you are constructing an experience for the audience, who can readily "tune out" if you do not keep them engaged and "tuned in."

There Should Be a Reason for Every Edit

This convention is linked with motivation, one of the six elements of the cut discussed in Chapter Five.

If the shot is good and complete in itself, with a beginning, a middle, and an end, then it may not serve much purpose to cut a section out and replace it – especially if the overall result is not better or more interesting than the original, complete shot. In short, do your best not to cut apart a shot that stands firmly on its own, intact. Sometimes, the best choice for an editor to make is to not cut a shot at all, but simply time its entrance and exit within the sequence. This happens on occasion but it is not the norm.

Consider the following scenario. Two people are having a conversation until one of the characters launches into a three-minute monologue. As she drones on, the other character is listening and is likely to make some form of facial or body reaction to what is being said. These reaction shots could be shown to help to break up the continual, verbal performance of the one character and to provide new information about the listening party's perceived mental and emotional state (Figure 9.1).

If, however, in a different story scenario, a character is totally alone and talking to himself, and there are no reasons to add flashbacks or insert shots, then this uninterrupted monologue may stand unedited. Cutting up a shot such as this just so the audience can have something else to look at is a poor motivation and may only serve to break the true power of the actor's monologue delivery and disturb the audience. If the shot is boring, the fault may lie in the type of shot or the shot composition, the script, or the actor's performance. Most filmmakers will, however, record such monologues from several different camera angles, so that at least continuity cutting may still be possible. In those instances, it will be your task to find the motivations for the cuts to the same performer throughout the scene.

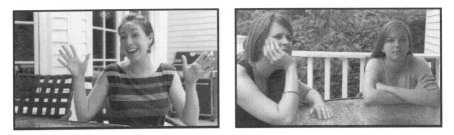

FIGURE 9.1　For long monologues, you may wish to cut in reaction shots to help to keep the viewer interested in the scene.

Pacing Has a Purpose

Back in the days of silent cinema, especially with costume dramas, the pacing of scenes could be excruciatingly slow. Sometimes, it felt like viewing live theater where the camera coverage would not change very much – if at all. This even held true for slapstick comedies where the pratfalls often played themselves out from one camera angle. Tools, techniques, and storytelling practices quickly evolved and the pacing of edits soon grew to reflect the genre of story being shown. In recent history, a very fast-paced editing style has become rather widespread. Some trace this back to the "MTV effect," named after the quick cutting of many of the music videos once found on that cable network. Quickly cut sequences, however, especially of action scenes, had been around for many years before that. This tendency toward very fast pacing has developed alarmingly to the point where a shot lasting more than three seconds is viewed by some producers and directors as boringly long. Quick cuts can be very effective, however, and the reason may have less to do with information and motivation and more to do with the energy or anxiety that they can create in the viewing audience.

Pacing obviously depends on the type of production, the picture content, and the viewing habits of the expected audience. What is acceptable in an action sequence is not acceptable in a love scene – typically. The reason to make the edit should be worthwhile and visible to all. If you capitalize on the motivation and the reason for the edit, the edit will then seem more natural and befitting of the mood of the motion picture.

Finally, in deciding the length of a shot, it is essential to give the eyes enough time to read and absorb the visual information. If you are questioning the "proper" duration for a shot, then you could describe, in your mind, what you are seeing in the shot. When viewing the example in Figure 9.2, you could say to yourself, "There is a woman standing in a polka dotted dress, there is a city skyline behind her, there is a gondola on the water, and it appears to be daytime and maybe summer. Cut!" And that is the length of the shot.

Of course, if you are cutting a very rapid montage in which each shot is only on screen for half of a second, then each image is really just a flash of shape, color, and light. The human visual system can take in and process such rapidly flashing images, but not all data will be absorbed. The eyes and brain will become selective in what they pick up from the pictures. More often than not, what you end up creating is a type of concept edit or intellectual edit where the audience are left to generate an idea or feeling based around the collection of rapidly flashing images. These types of quickly edited montage can be very effective in extreme sports programs, psychological thrillers, horror films, paranormal

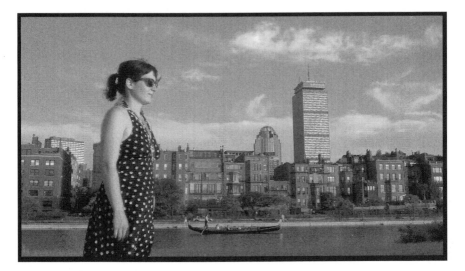

FIGURE 9.2 One method of deciding shot length is to talk out the basic description of the shot content. If your eyes and brain require that much or that little time to digest the image, then most viewers will comprehend the visuals at about the same rate.

non-fiction, and promotional trailers for these sort of stories. The speed can cause excitement or stress and anxiety in the viewer and the desired effect can hinge upon the type of musical accompaniment chosen to go with the very quick montage.

Observe the Action Line

The **action line** (or axis of action) is a mental guide for both directors and editors when using the master scene continuity style of filmmaking. It is the imaginary line that cuts through the area of action along talent sight lines or follows in the direction of an object's movement. With it, you establish the 180-degree arc around the subject. It dictates from which side of that subject you are able to record imagery. Editors must make sure that the shots that they use in the final edited version stay on the correct side of the line and therefore maintain the established screen direction for the scene.

Crossing the line results in a visual contradiction for the audience. They are confronted with a different viewpoint of the action as screen direction is reversed and this will change their perception of what is happening. It will, in essence, flip the orientation of left and right within the film space.

For example, if a car is traveling from right to left across the screen in Shot A, then the action line becomes the direction of movement (Figure 9.3). If another shot is taken from the other side of the line, and that shot is then cut next as Shot B, the car will appear to be going from left to right as if it immediately reversed its screen direction. In the film's reality, of course, the car is actually going the same way all of the time. Cutting these two shots together, the first from one side of the line and the second from the other, will break the visual flow and the viewer may become momentarily confused and ask, "Why is the car now going the opposite way?" Perhaps an insert shot of a police car chasing the hero's car could be placed between Shot A and Shot B in order to break up the screen direction mismatch. Modern viewers of motion imagery are rather adept at assessing visual information, so this type of screen direction shift may not stop them in their tracks. However, even a brief brain "glitch," such as that caused by having to account for the car's change of direction, can lift the viewer out of the immersive viewing experience. And that is something that we, as editors, want to avoid.

The editor should only select shots from one side of the line unless the line is seen to change – for example, if the car changes direction on screen during one of the shots, if a POV from inside the car is shown, or if the car exits a shot and then a new, wider re-establishing shot is cut in.

The line also exists for people. A two-shot will establish frame left and frame right, therefore also establishing screen direction, look room, and lines of attention for the two

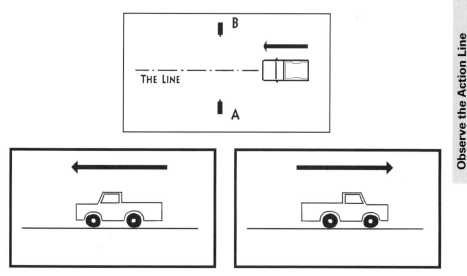

FIGURE 9.3   The camera placement from Shot A establishes the axis of action and the subsequent screen direction for the moving vehicle. When the camera is mistakenly moved to the opposite side of the action line, Shot B records the vehicle's movement again but will reverse screen direction when edited together with Shot A. Edit shots that have respected the 180-degree rule when assembling coverage for a scene.

Observe the Action Line

characters. In Figure 9.4, Character A is looking toward frame right and Character B is looking toward frame left. Any coverage single shot, such as a medium shot or a medium close-up, should keep the characters on the same sides of the screen and looking in their appropriate directions. The two shots would edit together well.

However, if one of the shots – perhaps the single shot of Character B – was shot from the opposite side of the established line, then that person would also appear to be looking toward frame right (Figure 9.5). Clearly, with both characters looking right, they would appear to be talking to some unseen third person just off screen. It would not make sense to the audience, who would only be able to account for the two characters. To follow the traditional guidelines of continuity editing, both shots (of Characters A and B) should come

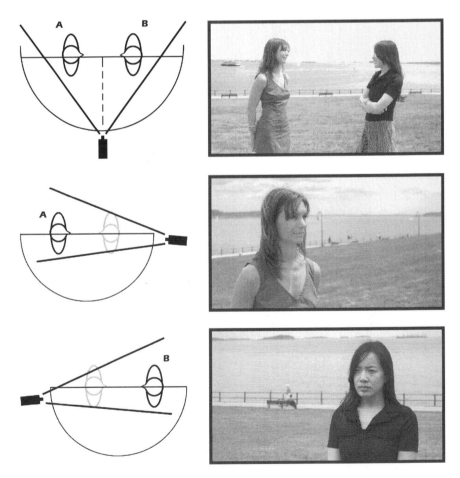

FIGURE 9.4 Shots that respect the action line for people will cut well together. Screen direction is maintained for Character A and Character B.

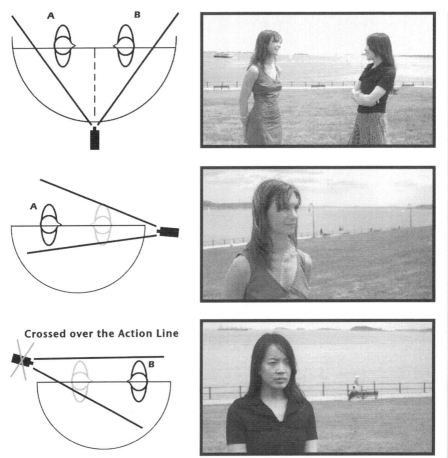

FIGURE 9.5 Shots that do not respect the action line for people will not cut well together. Screen direction is reversed for Character B.

from the established side of the action line, and within the 180-degree arc – not one from each side. Shooting from anywhere around the talent and editing from anywhere around the talent can and is being done all of the time, but it may only work if it is appropriate for your motion picture's style of editing.

Select the Appropriate Form of Edit

If a straight cut does not create a successful transition between two shots, then it is very unlikely that a dissolve or a fade will make it look better. A bad dissolve is no better than a bad cut. Depending on the type of motion media project being edited, it might be possible to use a wipe to make an edit work at an otherwise "sticky" cut point. If a wipe is

Select the Appropriate Form of Edit

not appropriate for the show, then you are back to square one. Of course, different genres of visual media call for different treatments at transitions. You will find, at times, that certain edits will just not work.

If two shots will not go together as a cut, then they will almost certainly not go together as a dissolve. This may be because:

- the angles are too similar;
- the continuity is mismatched;
- there is no new information;
- there is no motivation;
- the shot compositions are conflicting;
- there is a combination of the above,

There is very little an editor can do to improve this because most of the time the fault lies within the production footage.

For example, the action line has been mistakenly crossed in the shots in Figure 9.5. Obviously, Character B is on the wrong side of the frame. As a cut from one shot to the other, there will be a blatant jump. It will jar the audience visually. The technical disjunction between the composition of the two images will cause a narrative interruption for the viewer and it will not flow smoothly as intended or needed. Clearly, the edit as a cut would be incorrect. If, however, you are condensing time during an event where a straight cut would cause a jump cut, then the audience would be more accepting of a dissolve on this occasion. For example, one camera angle covers a student taking a difficult exam in a classroom. The video source clip lasts twelve minutes – way too long. You must cut it down into shorter, digestible chunks, but, rather than having jump cuts at the transitions in this brief montage, you opt to add dissolves, making the otherwise jumpy edits appear smooth and understandable to the audience.

A similar issue is found in the OTS shots in Figure 9.6. If the editor were to treat this transition between these shots as a dissolve, the edit would be as equally confusing for the viewer. First, the faces of the man and the woman would superimpose over one another during the dissolve, which would make the viewer wonder whether this visual treatment were somehow symbolic of the couple's union, or perhaps there is some supernatural activity at play, etc. Second, it would be extremely rare for an editor to use a dissolve during any traditionally edited back-and-forth dialogue scene. There is no reason for it – it just does not make sense.

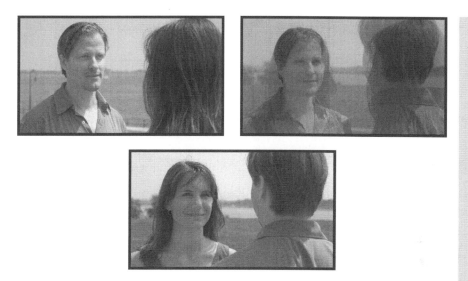

FIGURE 9.6   The incorrect framing of coverage shots will not work as a straight cut and it is made more complicated and questionable by the use of a dissolve.

If an edit should be a straight cut and it fails as such, then the failure might be
compounded by the use of a dissolve.

The Better the Edit, the Less It Is Noticed

This is the ideal situation for most motion media projects. A program that is well edited
will result in the edits going unnoticed by the viewer. If the edits are not seen, or just feel
like the natural flow of events, then the story progresses more smoothly from beginning
to end and keeps the audience engaged.

Sometimes, the edits can be very powerful as a result of the images of the edited shots,
the category or type of edit, the timing, or the information conveyed. Because they
keep the audience engrossed in the experience, they will still not be seen and as such
will help the visual flow. This is the work of a creative editor.

It is equally true that one bad edit can ruin an entire sequence of shots. No one from the
general public (excluding filmmakers and those familiar with the technical side of motion
picture creation) is likely to stand up, point at the screen, and shout, "Hey! That was a
terrible edit." What is more likely to happen is much more subtle and also much more
problematic. The average viewer, when experiencing a bad edit, will acknowledge the "glitch"
– perhaps not consciously, but that visual or auditory blip will register in his or her brain or

gut as something "not quite right." As the viewer watches the program after the bad edit, his or her brain may still be trying to justify what it has earlier experienced at the bad cut. The viewer's ability to absorb the new information presented after the bad edit will be compromised.

This is not to say that creating edited imagery that draws attention to itself is going to be bad. On the contrary, there are many types of programs whose style of editing is meant to attract attention to itself. The audience may or may not appreciate why it is being done, but the presence of "self-aware" editing practices will not bother them. Of course, the audience may also really enjoy the focus on and value the assembly of the piece more than the actual content. You never know.

Remember that it is your job, as the editor, to create a motion media project that will be accepted by the audience. If what you do is not to their liking, or presents picture and sound elements that go outside of or transgress the traditional film grammar that they expect for your type of program, they have the right to reject it. If your editing style fits the content of the story, then they are much more likely to be accepting of it. As many people are very familiar with this "invisible" technique of film editing (cutting that does not purposefully draw attention to itself), you will not go wrong by working in this fashion. Some of the best edits are the ones that no one notices but you, the editor.

Editing Is Manipulation

The very nature of the process – constructing a story from separate and potentially unrelated sources – is very manipulative. Top that with the goal of providing a particular experience to the audience and it seems like all you are doing is manipulating something or someone. But it's all for a good cause.

A core goal with fictional narrative motion pictures, as opposed to informational and certain fact-based, educational, non-fiction programming, is to engage the audience, get them to care about the lives of others, and have them willingly suspend their disbelief in the actions and events that they experience on screen. The content of the shots that you edit together, the pacing that you provide to those clips, and the sounds and music that you lay underneath the imagery all lead to mental, emotional, and, often, physical reactions in the viewer. It's part of why people go to the movies and watch television: to be transported somewhere else, to relate to or even care about other "people," and to have their emotions manipulated for a short time in a controlled, safe way. When all of the sources of motion picture creation come together in the right way (story, shots, performance, editing, music, etc.), they will combine to make something very special. Edit for the emotional experience, and you will win over your audience.

The Role of an Assistant Editor

As with many trades over the centuries, knowledge is passed down from the more experienced editor to the apprentice or assistant editor. One day, the assistant knows enough and has proven himself or herself skilled enough to branch out on his or her own and become a full-time editor. Many who start out in the field of video editing get their first job as an assistant editor and work their way up from there.

Responsibilities for assistants can vary widely depending on the type of show produced, the size of the budget, the type of post-production facility, etc. Generally speaking, the assistant is assigned to an editor or an edit suite (the physical room where the editing process takes place). He or she may be responsible for acquiring the raw footage, setting up a project in the editing software, capturing the picture and sound files onto the computer and media drives, organizing the bin or folder structure within the project, and helping the editor to output any final versions of the edited program for approval copies or eventual mastering of the completed product. The assistant may even get to take a first pass at a pre-edit version of a scene or sequence for the full-time editor to polish — but this is usually done during off hours such as overnights and weekends.

There are numerous nitty-gritty details that go along with any editing facility, such as standardized naming conventions, particular media formats or media drive allocations, etc. The assistant editor works with others behind the scenes, as well as in the edit suite, to keep the post-production workflow smooth and easy for the editor. This way, the editor can perform the edit free from stress or worry about the organizational and technical elements and focus more energy on the storytelling aspect of the job. Exposure to both sides of the editing process (technical and creative) is a great training ground for the assistant. Observe, ask questions at the appropriate moments, and practice editing. You will be in a good position to transition into the editor's chair when the time comes.

Editing Is Creating

As stated earlier in this book, the editor is one of the last people in the creative chain of a motion picture's production. It is his or her job to craft the final version of the program from all of the rough picture and sound materials provided by the production team. Furthermore, it is the editor's responsibility to make sure that the types of edits fall within the accepted grammar of the program's genre. If the editing style falls outside the audience's traditional understanding, then the program may not be well received. The audience simply may not get it.

The general terms, topics, and working practices presented in this book offer, to the new editor, numerous guidelines for basic motion media editing. Everyone should start out understanding why these guidelines exist and then move forward into the realms of play, experimentation, and innovation with their own editing styles. There are very well-known, experienced directors who, along with their editors, have produced very interesting results by breaking the fundamentals of editing. Some directors use the jump cut to a creative end, others purposefully break the 180-degree rule, and still others choose to provide shots with radical framing, shaky camera, or bad color. These are usually creative choices motivated and informed by some years of experience and they are applied to particular sequences for storytelling purposes.

The basic advice and working practices presented in this book are designed to offer new editors some exposure to the many learning points found in the grammar of motion picture editing. It will be important for you to understand these conventions, why they were put into practice, and when you might need to use them. But perfect editing grammar is not an end in itself. Breaking the guidelines to achieve a special result is valid under nearly all circumstances. At least it is worth a try. Certainly, when an editor is seeking to achieve these special results, some general working practices may be changed, ignored, or subverted. Look upon each edit as an opportunity for you to find the most effective and creative way to show your story. If you don't like the results, the fix is only an "Undo" away.

Chapter Nine – Final Thoughts: Key Take-Aways

No matter what computer software you end up using to perform your digital video edit, remember that you are the editor and the software is just the tool that helps you to execute your decisions. As an editor, you are, most likely, the last creative person to touch the visual and auditory components of a project in a major way. As such, you have an incredible opportunity to help to form or re-form the story being told. Whatever you end up cutting, you should strive to combine your picture and sound elements in the best way possible. The shots that you select, the rhythm and pacing of the individual edits, and the transition choices that you make should all serve the story well and keep the viewing audience engaged, informed, and entertained. In the end, the grammar of the edit is the underlying language used to splice it all together.

Thank you.

Chapter Nine – Review

1. Use sound creatively. It can underscore and enhance the visual data or subvert it in some ironic way. You will provide the audience with a better multi-sensory experience.
2. Keep the viewer interested by providing new visual or aural information in each new shot that you edit in a sequence.
3. Find the motivation for each edit. There should be a reason to leave a shot at a certain time and a reason to transition into the beginning of the next shot when you do.
4. Pacing creates energy in the movie. Use the timings of shots to engage and influence your audience.
5. Observe the action line by editing material that holds true to the established screen direction, lines of attention, and lines of motion.
6. Select the appropriate form of edit. Learn when a cut or dissolve or wipe is best and know that sometimes nothing may work to your liking.
7. Good editing often goes unnoticed. This is a compliment, so be grateful.
8. Editing is manipulative in its nature. Cut your movies for emotion and performance and you will score every time.
9. An assistant editor performs a variety of important and necessary tasks that help to make the entire post-production process possible for the editor. Assisting an established editor is a great way to learn while you work and to become recommended when a new job comes along for you.
10. Learn and understand the basic guidelines and techniques of editing grammar and film language, but be prepared to creatively innovate when you know how and why.

Chapter Nine – Review

Chapter Nine – Exercises

1. Go edit as many projects as you can, learn a lot, and have fun doing it.

Chapter Nine – Quiz Yourself

1. What is the best job in the whole world? (Answer: video editor.)

Appendix A
Helpful Resources for the New Filmmaker

Websites

www.artoftheguillotine.com
www.cinema5d.com
www.cinematography.com
www.cinematography.net
www.colorgradingcentral.com
www.dofmaster.com
www.filmcontracts.net
www.filmmakeriq.com
www.googleartproject.com
www.joyoffilmediting.com
www.lightsfilmschool.com/blog
www.newsshooter.com
www.precinemahistory.net
www.premiumbeat.com/blog
www.theasc.com
www.videomaker.com
www.wga.hu/index1.html

(All website URLs accessed on March 1, 2017.)

Books

Cinematography: Theory and Practice
Image Making for Cinematographers and Directors, 3rd Edition
By Blain Brown
(Focal Press, 2017)

Voice & Vision
A Creative Approach to Narrative Film and DV Production, 2nd Edition
By Mick Hurbis-Cherrier
(Focal Press, 2011)

Grammar of the Shot
4th Edition
By Christopher J. Bowen
(Routledge, 2018)

DSLR Cinema
Crafting the Film Look with Video 2nd Edition
By Kurt Lancaster
(Focal Press, 2013)

The Visual Story
Creating the Visual Structure of Film, TV, and Digital Media 2nd Edition
By Bruce Block
(Focal Press, 2008)

Motion Picture and Video Lighting
2nd Edition
By Blain Brown
(Focal Press, 2007)

Light: Science and Magic
An Introduction to Photographic Lighting, 4th Edition
By Fil Hunter, Paul Fuqua, and Steven Biver
(Focal Press, 2011)

The Art Direction Handbook for Film & Television
2nd Edition
By Michael Rizzo
(Focal Press, 2014)

If It's Purple, Someone's Gonna Die
The Power of Color in Visual Storytelling
By Patti Bellantoni
(Focal Press, 2005)

The Screenwriter's Roadmap
21 Ways to Jumpstart Your Story
By Neil Landau
(Focal Press, 2012)

Directing
Film Techniques and Aesthetics, 5th Edition
By Michael Rabiger and Mick Hurbis-Cherrier
(Focal Press, 2013)

Changing Direction
A Practical Approach to Directing Actors in Film and Theatre
By Lenore DeKoven
(Focal Press, 2006)

Directing the Story
Professional Storytelling and Storyboarding Techniques for Live Action and Animation
By Francis Glebas
(Focal Press, 2008)

The Technique of Film and Video Editing
History, Theory, and Practice, 5th Edition
By Ken Dancyger
(Focal Press, 2010)

FilmCraft: Editing
By Justin Chang
(Focal Press, 2011)

Make the Cut
A Guide to Becoming a Successful Assistant Editor in Film and TV
By Lori Coleman and Diana Friedberg
(Focal Press, 2010)

The Camera Assistant's Manual
6th Edition
By David E. Elkins
(Focal Press, 2013)

Experimental Filmmaking
Break the Machine
By Kathryn Ramey
(Focal Press, 2016)

Appendix B
Crew Members Commonly Needed for Motion Picture Production

Assistant Director (AD) – Responsible for setting and maintaining the production schedule. The assistant director will verify with all departments that they are ready for a take, call the actors to the set for the director, and call the roll to begin the recording process for a take.

Boom Operator – In charge of holding or rigging a microphone from a boom pole (a telescoping rod that supports the sensitive microphone suspended over the actors as they speak). Works with the sound mixer and camera operator to find the best placement of microphones for sound levels and picture integrity.

Camera Assistant (AC) – Technician responsible for all camera equipment (bodies, lenses, accessories, batteries, media, etc.). Ensures that everything is clean, cabled, and running correctly. During the take, usually controls the follow focus apparatus. Also often the keeper of the camera report and logs. On smaller productions, the camera assistant may also do the head slating of each take for picture and sound.

Camera Operator – In charge of running the camera. Responsible for ensuring proper framing and double-checking focus during a shot. Sometimes starts and stops the recording process of the camera as well.

Digital Imaging Technician/Data Wrangler (Media Wrangler) (DIT) – On productions exclusively using digital video cameras that generate media files, the digital imaging technician is the person in charge of calibrating the digital imaging sensors of the cameras and doing on-set color grading in cooperation with the director of photography. The data wrangler also copies media from camera memory cards, backs them up, and transports them to the hard drives of the post-production team. Without film or tape original sources, these media files are extremely important and their careful replication and preservation is paramount.

Director – In charge of interpreting the written words of the screenplay story and turning them into viewable motion pictures. Responsible for selecting shots and working with actors to achieve desired characterizations. Collaborates with many other members of the production and post-production teams to help to realize her or his overall vision for the piece.

Director of Photography/Cinematographer (DP/DOP) – Responsible for creating the overall look of the film. Chief member of the camera department. Works with the director to select the shots. Creates the lighting scheme for each set-up. Collaborates with the electric, grip, and art department heads. Often consults on color correction and grading during post-production.

Dolly Grip – A grip specifically assigned to build, maintain, and move the camera dolly around the film set. May set up and level any tracks or rail needed for the dolly move.

Editor – The person, during post-production, responsible for editing picture and sound elements into the final story that will be experienced by the audience. Depending on the project, the editor may also occasionally be on set during production to edit together scenes from the digital "dailies" made each day.

Electric – Responsible for running the power lines of electricity to all departments on a film set.

Gaffer – Chief electric in charge of the entire electric department. In consultation with the director of photography, chooses and sets the lighting fixtures that illuminate the film's sets or locations. Responsible for achieving the desired look and levels of light for exposure.

Grip – Member of the grip department. Grips have many responsibilities and are capable of performing many tasks on a film set that involve moving and supporting things.

Key Grip – Chief grip in charge of all grips on the crew. Works closely with the director of photography and gaffer to get the necessary support equipment (for camera and lighting) placed for each shot.

Lighting Technician – Hoists, strikes, and angles the film lights on set.

Production Designer – In charge of the design elements of a film's overall look. Generates the concepts for and oversees set design, costuming, make-up, etc. Collaborates closely with the director, director of photography, and art director.

Screenwriter – Writes the screenplay, which is either an original idea or an adaptation of an existing property. Not typically involved during the production or post-production phases of the project.

Script Supervisor – Responsible for monitoring each take during production and noting how closely it follows the written script. Takes notes on all significant aspects of the set, props, actions, line delivery, etc. Keeps track of scene and take numbers and provides that data to the camera and sound departments for the organization of slate information.

Sound Recordist/Sound Mixer – Audio technician in charge of running any audio-recording equipment on set. Maintains good levels of sound during recording. Coordinates the best microphone placement with the set boom operator.

Appendix C
Practice Script

The following is a very simple short fiction sample script that you may use to practice recording coverage of dialogue and action using the shot types (found in Chapter Two) and all of the editing techniques presented throughout the book. It is referred to as a "content-less scene," meaning that it is purposefully vague and does not follow strict screenplay formatting so that you may interpret freely and maximize your creativity. It may be helpful if you first read the script, then make some decisions about who these characters are, what their story is, and where and when it should take place. Those decisions will then inform how you approach recording and editing the two brief scenes. Have fun.

> CHARACTER A
> Hey.

> CHARACTER B
> Hey.

> CHARACTER A
> How's it going?

> CHARACTER B
> Good.

> CHARACTER A
> Cool. Cool. Um, listen – I'm really
> sorry about the—

> CHARACTER B
> Yeah. It's no big deal.
> What are you going to do about it, right?

> CHARACTER A
> Right.

> CHARACTER B
> Well, I've got to get going.

CHARACTER A

Yeah. Yeah. Me too.

Character B exits – cut to new location. Character B enters followed by Character A.

CHARACTER A

Hey. Wait up. You forgot this.

CHARACTER B

That's not mine.

(A few hints about this particular script: it should happen in at least two different locations; Character A must be sorry about something that can be represented visually, in some way, in the scene; Character A must try to present Character B with some "forgotten" item, in either a literal sense or in a figurative or symbolic fashion.)

Remember that although the script does not call out locations or specific items, your shot list should allow for such things as establishing shots, detail shots, inserts/cutaways, and a variety of shot compositions. This variety will provide you plenty of editing options during post-production practice.

Glossary

4K – A shorthand reference to the 4096 x 2160 pixel image of digital cinema projection.

4:3 – The aspect ratio for standard-definition television. Four units wide by three units tall – more square in its visual presentation than the widescreen high-definition 16:9 video display.

16:9 – The aspect ratio for high-definition video. Sixteen units wide by nine units tall – a widescreen display.

30 Degree Rule – A cousin to the 180-degree rule, this rule suggests that when recording coverage for a scene from differing camera angles within the film set, the camera should be moved around the 180-degree arc by at least 30 degrees from one shot to the next to create enough variation on the angle on action so that the two different shots will edit together and appear different enough in their framing. A focal length change between set-ups will also help.

50–50 – A profile two-shot, typically in a medium shot or closer, where both subjects look across the screen at one another. Used especially in dialogue scenes.

180-Degree Line/Action Line/Axis of Action/Imaginary Line – The imaginary line established by the sight lines of objects within a shot that determines where the 180-degree arc of safe shooting is set up for the camera coverage of that scene. Traditionally, the camera should not be moved to the opposite side of this action line because it will cause a reversal in the established screen direction when the shots are edited together. See also 180-Degree Rule, Sight Line.

180-Degree Rule – In filmmaking, an imaginary 180-degree arc, or half-circle, is established on one side of the shooting set once the camera first records an angle on the action in that space. All subsequent shots should be made from within that same semicircle. As screen direction, left and right, for the entire scene is already established, the camera cannot photograph the subject from the other side of the circle without causing a reversal in the screen direction.

Act (noun) – Much as in stage plays, in long-form programming (feature films or episodic television, etc.), the story is broken down into several major sections known as acts. In fictional narrative filmmaking, a story will traditionally have three acts, loosely termed the set-up, the confrontation, and the resolution.

Action – What the director calls out to signify that the acting for the shot being recorded should begin.

ADR (Automated Dialogue Replacement) – A process where actors record lines of dialogue in a recording studio. Used to replace poor-quality or altogether missing production audio. An editor may then use these clean recordings for the actual edit.

Aesthetics – A way of creating and analyzing art and art forms for their beauty.

Ambience/Atmosphere (sound) – The general background sounds of any location where a scene for a film is shot. Examples: school cafeteria, football stadium, subway car, remote forest.

Analog – Not digital in nature. Composed of or designed with a more free-form variant not specifically limited to a single, quantifiable range.

Angle of Incidence – The angle from which incident light falls upon a film set. A single lighting fixture directly overhead will have a 90-degree (from horizon) angle of incidence.

Angle of View – The field of view encompassed by the light-gathering power of a camera's lens. A wide-angle lens has a wide angle of view. A telephoto lens has a narrower angle of view on the world.

Angle on Action – The angle from which a camera views the action on the film set.

Aperture – In motion picture equipment terms, the aperture refers to the iris or flexible opening of the camera lens that controls how much or how little light is used to expose the image inside the camera. A wide aperture or iris setting lets in a larger amount of light. A smaller aperture lets in less light. On many camera lenses, the aperture can also be fully "stopped down" or closed all of the way for total darkness on the image.

Artificial Light – Any light generated by a manmade device such as a film light, a desk lamp, or a neon sign.

Aspect Ratio – The numerical relationship between the dimensions of width and height for any given visual recording medium. In the example 16:9, the first number, 16, represents the units of measure across the width of a high-definition video frame. The second number, 9, represents the same units of measure for the height of the same frame.

Assembly Edit – The phase during the post-production process when an editor first assembles the raw footage into a basic story structure.

Assistant Editor – A support position within a post-production environment. The duties and responsibilities of an assistant editor change with the complexity of the program being edited, the budget, and the facility in which the edit is completed. General tasks include capturing and organizing footage within an editing project, attending to the chief editor's needs, authoring proof copies for review and approval, etc.

Atmospherics – Any particulates suspended in the air around a film set or location, such as fog, mist, or dust, which will cumulatively obscure the distant background or "catch" and "show" the light in the air.

Attention – The direction in which a subject looks within the film space. The attention of a subject may be drawn by another subject, an inanimate object, or anything that attracts his or her gaze. An imaginary line connects the eyes of the subject and the object of his or her attention and, most often, the audience will trace this line to also see what the subject is observing. See also Sight Line.

Audio Mix – The process of blending together the many different audio tracks used in an edited program such that their levels (volumes) work appropriately together. Spoken dialogue, voice-over narration, music, sound effects, etc. are all blended so they sound good with one another under the picture track.

Axial Edit – Cutting two shots together that view the subject from the exact same angle on action but only change the magnification of the subject. See also Cut-In, Punch-In.

Background – The zone within a filmed frame that shows the deep space further away from the camera. The background is often out of focus, but serves to generate the ambience of the location.

Back Light – A light used on a film set placed behind an object but pointed at its backside. It generally serves to help to separate the object from the background by providing a rim or halo of light around the edges of the body, head, and hair. It may also illuminate the reflective surfaces around the subject such as wet pavement or polished floors.

Back Timing – Laying in audio from a known and desired end point with a yet-to-be-determined starting point in your program.

Beat – A moment in time. A pause of no precise timing but appropriate for the needs of the edited piece. When strung together, several beats can account for the editor's gut instinct in proper timing of shots, titles, transition effects, etc.

Binocular Vision (human visual system) – Having two eyes located at the front of the head. The slight distance between the two eyes causes humans to see nearby objects from two distinct vantage points. The brain then combines the two distinct images into one picture where the overlapping elements take on a 3D aspect.

Blocking – The planned movement of subjects within the film space and the corresponding movement, if any, of the camera to follow the actions of the moving subjects.

Boom Arm – Deriving its name from the armature on a sailing ship's mast, a boom arm is used to swivel and extend the camera's placement to get sweeping shots or keep the camera buoyant without a tripod directly beneath it.

Boom Operator (audio recording) – The crew member whose job it is to hold and manipulate the audio-recording microphone suspended from a long, telescoping pole usually over the heads of the acting talent.

Break Frame – When an object being recorded accidentally moves to the edge of the frame and falls outside the visible area of the image.

B-Roll – Any visual material acquired for a project (especially news, documentary, and reality) that visually supports the main topic of discussion but does not include important human subjects. Often used to "mask" edits in an interviewee's answers or commentary when used as a cutaway on the picture track.

Business – Any busy work performed by an actor with his or her hands while acting in a scene.

Butt-Cut – A straight edit between two video clips in a sequence with no transition effect such as a dissolve, wipe, or fade. See also Straight Cut.

Camera Angle – The angle at which a camera views a particular scene. Camera angles can be based on horizontal camera positioning around the subject or vertical camera positioning below or above the subject.

Camera Person/Camera Operator – The person who physically handles the camera during the shooting, whose main responsibility is to maintain proper framing and composition and to verify good focus.

Camera Set-Up – A place on the film set where a camera is positioned to record a shot. Each time the camera is physically moved to a new position, it is considered a new camera set-up. The camera set-up is often associated with a particular shot from the shot list for scene coverage.

Camera Support – Any device or piece of film equipment that is used to support the motion picture camera. Tripods, dollies, and car mounts are all examples of various kinds of camera support.

Charge-Coupled Device (CCD) – The electronic light sensor built into many video cameras that turns light wave energy into electronic voltages. These voltages get recorded as brightness and color values on a tape, hard drive, or memory card in the camera.

Chiaroscuro – Italian for light/dark, this term is used in the visual arts to talk about the high contrast ratio between light and dark areas of a frame. Filmmakers, as well as painters, use this technique to show or hide certain visual elements within their frames.

Clapper Board – This is the visual record of the shot that is to be filmed. On the clapper board is marked the scene and take number, together with other information about the production. The sound of the board "clapped" together is the point at which sound and vision are synchronized together during post-production. If the board is clapped, it indicates that sound and vision are being recorded. If the board is held open, it indicates that vision only is being recorded. If the board is shown upside down, it indicates that it was recorded at the end of the shot and is called an "end board" or "tail slate." An end board can be also either clapped or mute. See also Slate.

Clean Single – A medium shot to a close-up that contains body parts of only one person even though other characters may be part of the scene being recorded.

Clip – Any piece of film or segment of digital video media file that will be used in an edited sequence.

Close-Up – Any detail shot where the object of interest being photographed takes up the majority of the frame. Details will be magnified. When photographing a human being, the bottom of the frame will just graze the top part of the shoulders and the top of the frame may just cut off the top part of the head or hair.

Color Bars – In video, these are the thick, colored vertical lines that are recorded first on a tape. They are used to calibrate or "line up" the editing machines, so that each time a picture is copied, the color is the same. The colors are, from the left of the screen, white, yellow, cyan, green, magenta, red, blue, and black.

Color Temperature – Often referenced on the degrees Kelvin scale, color temperature is a measurement of a light's perceived color when compared to the color of light emitted from a "perfect black body" exposed to increasing levels of heat. The color temperature for tungsten film lighting is generally accepted as around 3200 degrees Kelvin. Noontime

Glossary

sunlight is generally accepted as around 5600 degrees Kelvin. The lower numbers appear "warm" orange/amber when compared to white, and the higher numbers appear "cool" blue.

Complementary Metal-Oxide Semiconductor (CMOS) – A type of image sensor used in many smaller devices such as smartphones and in both consumer- and professional-grade digital video cameras.

Complex Shot – Any shot that involves both talent movement and movement of the camera (pan or tilt).

Composition – In motion picture terms, the artful design employed to place objects of importance within and around the recorded frame.

Continuity – In motion picture production terms: (1) having actors repeat the same script lines in the same way while performing similar physical actions across multiple takes; (2) making sure that screen direction is followed from one camera set-up to the next; (3) in post-production, matching physical action across a cut point between two shots of coverage for a scene.

Contrast – The range of dark and light tonalities within a film frame.

Contrast Ratio – The level of delineation between strong areas of dark and strong areas of light within a film frame, as represented in a ratio of two numbers: Key+Fill:Fill.

Coverage – Shooting the same action from multiple angles with different framing at each camera set-up. Example: A dialogue scene between two people may require a wide, establishing shot of the room; a tighter two-shot of both subjects; clean singles of each actor; reciprocal over-the-shoulder shots favoring each actor; cutaways of hands moving or the clock on the wall, etc.

Crab – When a dolly moves the camera sideways or parallel to the movement/action recorded. The camera lens is most often actually perpendicular to the subjects.

Crane – Much like the large, heavy machinery used in construction, a crane on a film set may raise and move the camera or have large lighting units mounted to it from high above the set.

Critical Focus – As with the human eye, there can be only one plane or physical slice of reality that is in sharpest focus for the motion picture camera. The plane of critical focus is this slice of space in front of the lens, at a particular distance, that will show any object within that plane to be in true focus. Example: When recording a person's face in a medium close-up, his or her eyes should be in sharpest focus, in which case the plane of critical focus is the same distance away from the lens as the actor's eyes.

Cross-Cutting/Parallel Editing – A process in film construction where one plot line of action is intercut with another, potentially related plot line. The audience are given an alternating taste of each action sequence as the "single" scene progresses toward resolution.

Cross-Fade – An audio treatment applied to audio edits where the end of one piece of audio is faded down under the rising audio level of the next piece of sound.

Cut (noun) – An edit point.

Cut (verb) – To edit a motion picture.

Cut Away (verb) – Editing out of one shot to another shot that is different in subject matter from the previous one. Example: "Cut away from the postman coming through the gate to the dog inside the house, waiting."

Cutaway (noun) – Any shot recorded that allows a break from the main action within a scene. The editor may place a cutaway into an edited scene of shots when a visual break is necessary or when two other shots from the primary coverage will not edit together smoothly.

Cut-In – A tighter shot taken either with a long-focal-length lens or a closer camera position but along the same lens axis as the original wider shot. See also Axial Edit, Punch-In.

Daylight Balance – Emulsion film stock and video cameras may be biased toward seeing the color temperature of daylight as "white" light. When they are set this way, they have a daylight balance of approximately 5500 degrees Kelvin.

Degrees Kelvin – The scale used to indicate a light source's color temperature, ranging roughly from 1000 to 20,000 degrees. Red/orange/amber-colored light falls from 1000 to 4000 and bluish light falls from 4500 to 20,000.

Depth – The distance from the camera receding into the background of the set or location. The illusion of 3D deep space on the 2D film plane.

Depth of Field (DOF) – In filmmaking terms, the DOF refers to a zone, some distance from the camera lens, where any object will appear to be in acceptable focus to the viewing audience. The DOF lives around the plane of critical focus, appearing one-third in front of and two-thirds behind the plane of critical focus instead of being centered equally. Any object outside the DOF will appear blurry to the viewer. The DOF may be altered or controlled by changing the camera-to-subject distance or by adding light to or subtracting light from the subject and adjusting the lens iris accordingly.

Desaturation – In filmmaking, the removal of colors (hues) from an image such that only gray-scale values (blacks, grays, whites) are left in the pixels of the image.

Developing Shot – Any shot that incorporates elaborate talent movement: a zoom, a pan or tilt, and a camera dolly.

Diegetic – Generated by something within the film world, usually associated with sound elements in a fictional motion picture. Example: a song playing on a jukebox in a diner.

Digital Zoom – A camera lens function that digitally enlarges an image, based on a magnification of the existing pixel data by the camera's processor. The result is often blurry or "pixelated" due to this expansion of limited picture information. A digital zoom is a digital blow-up, and differs from an optical zoom, which uses glass lenses to record an actual magnified image of a distant object.

Direct Address – A subjective style of recording motion pictures where the subject looks (and speaks) directly into the camera lens. Used in news reporting, talk shows, game shows, etc.

Director of Photography (DP/DOP) – The person on the film crew who is responsible for the overall look of a motion picture project's recorded image. He or she primarily creates the lighting scheme but may also help in planning the angles, composition, and movement of the camera as well as design details such as color palettes and object textures.

Dirty Single – A medium shot to a close-up that contains the main person of interest for the shot but that also contains some visible segment of another character who is part of the same scene. The clean single is made "dirty" by having this sliver of another's body part in the frame.

Dissolve – A treatment applied to the visual track of a program at an edit point. While the end of the outgoing shot is disappearing from the screen, the incoming shot is simultaneously resolving onto the screen.

Dolly – Traditionally, any wheeled device used to move a motion picture camera around a film set, either while recording or between shots. A dolly may be three or four wheeled; travel on the floor, or roll (with special wheels) along straight or curved tracks; or have a telescoping or booming arm that lifts and lowers the camera.

Domestic Cutoff – The outer 10% of analog-transmitted picture information that is cut off at the outside edges of a cathode ray tube television set and not viewable by the in-home audience. Although not as common in the digital age, this phenomenon should be taken into account when composing shots for a project that will be broadcast on television or viewed as a standard-definition DVD. Videos encoded for web playback will display full frame.

Dutch Angle/Dutch Tilt/Canted Angle/Oblique Angle – In filmmaking terms, any shot where the camera is canted or not level with the actual horizon line. The Dutch angle is often used to represent a view of objects or actions that are not quite right, underhanded, diabolical, or disquieting. All horizontal lines within the frame go slightly askew diagonally and, as a result, any true vertical lines will tip in the same direction.

Edit (noun) – The actual cut point between two different clips in a sequence.

Edit (verb) – To assemble a motion picture from disparate visual and auditory elements.

End Frame – Any time that the camera has been moving to follow action, the camera should come to a stop before the recorded action ceases. This clean, static frame may be used by the editor to cut away from the moving shot to any other shot that would come next. In a filmed sequence, viewing moving frames cut to static frames can be a jarring visual cut, and this static end frame may help to prevent this visual glitch.

Establishing Shot – Traditionally, the first shot of a new scene in a motion picture. It is a wide shot that reveals the location where the immediately following action will take place. The audience may quickly learn place, rough time of day, rough time of year, weather conditions, historical era, etc. by seeing this shot.

Exposure – In motion picture camera terms, the light needed to create an image on the recording medium (either emulsion film or a video light sensor). If you do not have enough light, you will underexpose your image and it will appear too dark. If you have too much light, you will overexpose your image and it will appear too bright.

Exterior – In film terms, any shot that has to take place outside.

Eye Light/Catch Light/Life Light – A light source placed somewhere in front of the talent that reflects off the moist and curved surface of the eye. This eye twinkle brings out the sparkle in the eye and often informs the audience that the character is alive and vibrant. Absence of the eye light can mean that a character is no longer living or is hiding something, etc.

Glossary

Eye-Line – The imaginary line that traces across the screen from the talent's eyes to some object of interest. See also Attention, Sight Line.

Eye-Line Match –The attention line from a subject (eye-line) should match in direction and angle to the object of interest in the reveal shot. Example: When shooting clean single coverage for a two-person dialogue scene, the eyes of each character should be looking out of the frame in the direction of where the other character's head or face would be. Even though the actors may not be sitting next to one another as they were in the wider two-shot, the eye-line of each "looking" at the other must match from shot to shot so that there is consistency in the edited scene.

Eye Trace – The places on a screen that attract the viewer's eyes. As the motion picture plays on the screen, the audience will move their focus around the composition to find new pieces of information.

Fade – A treatment of an edit point where the screen transitions from a frame of solid color into a fully visible image or from a fully visible image into a frame of solid color.

Fade-In/Fade-Up – A transition from a solid black opaque screen to a fully visible image.

Fade-Out/Fade-Down – A transition from a fully visible image to a solid black opaque screen.

Fill Light – A light, of lesser intensity than the key light, used to help to control contrast on a set but most often on a person's face. It "fills" in the shadows caused by the dominant key light.

Film Gauge – In the world of emulsion film motion pictures, the physical width of the plastic film strip is measured in millimeters (e.g. 16mm, 35mm). This measurement of film width is also referred to as the film's gauge.

Film Space – The world within the film, both that which is currently presented on screen and that which is "known" to exist within the film's manufactured reality.

Fine Cut – A later stage in the editing process where the edited program is very near completion. Any further changes will be minor.

Fisheye Lens – A camera lens whose front optical element is so convex (or bulbous, like the eye of a fish) that it can gather light rays from a very wide area around the front of the camera. The resulting image formed when using such a lens often shows a distortion in the exaggerated expansion of physical space, object sizes, and perspective – especially with subjects close to the camera.

Flashback – A device in film construction that jumps the narrative from the present time of the story to an earlier time. Usually used to explain how the current circumstances came about.

Flash Pan – A very quick panning action that blurs the image across the film or video frame horizontally. Flash pans are often used in pairs as a way to transition out of one shot and into the next.

Focal Length – The angle of view that a particular lens can record. It is a number, traditionally measured in millimeters (mm), that represents a camera lens' ability to gather and focus light. A lower focal length number (e.g., 10mm) indicates a wide angle of view. A higher focal length number (e.g., 200mm) indicates a narrower field of view where objects further from the camera appear to be magnified and fill more of the frame.

Focus – The state where objects being viewed by the camera appear to be sharply edged and well defined, and show clear detail. Anything out of focus is said to be blurry.

Foley – A sound-recording practice where "artists" make noises in a studio while they watch the edited motion picture. The sounds that they record will replace or augment the sound effects of the film, such as footsteps, leather creaks, door knob jiggles, etc.

Following Focus – If a subject moves closer to or further away from the camera but stays within the film frame, often the camera assistant or camera operator must manually control the focus of the recording lens to keep the moving subject in clear, crisp focus. If a subject at the plane of critical focus moves away from that plane and outside the corresponding depth of field, he or she will get blurry unless the camera assistant follows focus and shifts the DOF.

Footage – The raw visual material with which the editor works. It is a general name given to the recorded images on the film or video that were created during production, even if the media file counts in timecode and not feet.

Foreground – The zone within a filmed frame that starts near the camera's lens but ends before it reaches a more distant zone where the main action may be occurring. Any object that exists in the foreground of the recorded frame will obscure anything in the more distant zones out to the infinity point that would normally have been visible behind it.

Foreshortening – In the visual arts, it is a way that 3D objects are represented on the 2D plane. When pictured from a certain view or perspective, the object may appear compressed and/or distorted from its actual shape: the closer end will appear larger and the further end will appear smaller or tapered.

Fourth Wall – In fictional narrative filmmaking, this term means the place from which the camera objectively observes the action on the film set. Because it is possible for the camera to record only three of the four walls within a film set without moving, the fourth wall is the space on set where the camera lives and it is from that privileged place that it observes the action. "Breaking the fourth wall" means that the actor has directly addressed the camera lens and therefore the audience.

Frame – The entire rectangular area of the recorded image with zones of top, bottom, left, right, center, and depth.

Front Lighting – Any lighting scheme where lights come from above and almost directly behind the camera recording the scene. The talent, when facing toward the camera, will have an overall even lighting, which often causes flatness to their features but may also smooth out surface imperfections.

Geared Head – A professional piece of camera support used on dollies, cranes, and tripods that has two spinning geared wheels that allow for very fluid vertical and horizontal movements of the camera. The camera operator must crank each gear wheel manually to maintain the appropriate framing during tilts or pans.

Gel – Heat-resistant sheet of flexible, thin plastic that contains a uniform color. Used to add a "wash" of color on a film set. Example: If the feeling of sunset is required for a shot, an orange/yellow gel can be placed between the lights and the set to give the impression of a warmer sunset color.

Genre – A French term meaning a category within some larger group. In film, the term applies to types of movies such as comedy, drama, action, musical, etc.

Golden Hour/Magic Hour – The moments just after actual sunset but before the ambient light in the sky fades to night-time darkness. Filmmakers often appreciate the visual quality that the soft top light of dusk creates on exterior scenes.

Grip – A film crew member whose job is to move, place, and tweak any of the various pieces of film equipment used for the support of camera and lighting units, or devices used to block light, among other duties. A special dolly grip may be used to rig the dolly tracks and push or pull the dolly or camera during the recording of a shot.

Handheld – Operating the motion picture camera while it is supported in the hands or propped upon the shoulder of the camera operator. The human body acts as the key support device for the camera and is responsible for all movement achieved by the camera during the recording process.

Hard Light – A quality of light defined by the presence of strong, parallel rays being emitted by the light source. Well-defined, dark shadows are created by hard light.

Head – The common film term for the beginning of a shot, especially during the post-production editing process.

Headroom – The free space at the top of the recorded frame above the head of the subject. Any object may have headroom. Too much headroom will waste valuable space in the frame, and not enough may cause your subject to appear cut off or truncated at the top.

High-Angle Shot – Any shot where the camera records the action from a vertical position higher than most objects being recorded. Example: The camera, looking out of the third-floor window of an apartment house, records a car pulling into the driveway down below.

High Definition (HD) – A reference to the increased image quality and wider frame size (16:9) of the digital video format, compared to the standard-definition format used for television in the 20th century. The increase in vertical line resolution per frame (720 or 1080) increases the sharpness and color intensity of the playback image. All HD formats use square pixels.

High-Key Lighting – A lighting style in which a low contrast ratio exists between the brightly lit areas and the dark areas of the frame. Overall, even lighting gives proper exposure to most of the set and characters within it. There are no real dark shadow regions and no real overly bright regions.

HMI – A film lighting fixture in which the internal lamp burns in such a way as to emit light that matches daylight/sunlight in color temperature (5500–6000 degrees Kelvin).

Hood Mount – A device used to mount a tripod head and camera to the hood of a motor vehicle such that the occupants of the vehicle may be recorded while the vehicle is in motion. Often, a large suction cup is employed to help to secure the camera rig to the hood.

Horizon Line – The distant line that cuts across a film frame horizontally. It is used to help to establish the scope of the film space and define the top and bottom of the film world.

Incoming Picture – At a cut point, there is one shot ending and another beginning. The shot that is beginning after the cut point is the incoming picture.

Glossary

Insert Shot – Any shot inserted into a scene that is not part of the main coverage but relates to the story unfolding.

Interior – In film terms, any shot that has to take place inside.

Inter-Title – A title card or opaque graphic that appears on the screen to convey written information.

Iris – In motion picture equipment terms, the iris refers to the aperture or flexible opening of the camera lens that controls how much or how little light is used to expose the image inside the camera. Some modern video cameras use an electronic iris that controls the amount of light automatically. Most high-end HD and emulsion film lenses use an iris of sliding metal blades that overlap to make the aperture smaller or wider. A marked ring on the lens barrel can manually control the size of the opening.

J-Cut – A particular kind of split edit where the outgoing and incoming video and audio tracks are offset in their actual cut points. The audio tracks cut first and the video tracks cut a few moments later. Also referred to as sound leading picture. The clip segments around this edit will take on a "J" shape. See also Split Edit, Lapping, Sound Bridge.

Jib Arm – A piece of motion picture camera support equipment that allows the camera to move around a central fulcrum point, left/right/up/down/diagonally. It may be mounted onto tripod legs or on a dolly.

Jump Cut – An anomaly of the edited film when two very similar shots of the same subject are cut together and played. A "jump" in space or time appears to have occurred, which often interrupts the viewer's appreciation of the story.

Jump the Line/Cross the Line – Based on the concept inherent to the action line or 180-degree rule, this expression refers to moving the camera across the line and recording coverage for a scene that will not match the established screen direction when edited together.

Key Light – The main light source around which the remaining lighting plan is built. Traditionally, on film sets, it is the brightest light that helps to illuminate and expose the face of the main subject of the shot.

Kicker Light – Any light that hits the talent from a 3/4 backside placement. It often rims just one side of the hair, shoulder, or jawline.

Lapping (picture and sound) – The practice of editing where corresponding outgoing picture and sound tracks are not cut straight, but are staggered so that one is longer and the other is shorter. The same treatment must therefore be given to the incoming picture and sound tracks. See Split Edit, L-Cut.

L-Cut – A particular kind of split edit where the outgoing and incoming video and audio tracks are offset in their actual cut points. The video tracks cut first and the audio tracks cut a few moments later. Also referred to as picture leading sound. The clip segments around this edit will take on an "L" shape. See also Split Edit, Lapping, Sound Bridge.

Legs – An alternative name for a camera tripod.

Lens Axis – In motion picture camera terms, the central path cutting through the middle of the circular glass found in the camera's lens. Light traveling parallel to the lens axis is collected by the lens and brought into the camera that is exposing the recording medium. You can trace an imaginary straight line out of the camera's lens (like a laser pointer) and have it fall on the subject being recorded. That subject is now placed along the axis of the lens.

Light Meter – A device designed to read and measure the quantity of light falling on a scene or being emitted from it. Often used to help to set the level of exposure on the film set and, consequently, the setting on the camera's iris.

Line of Attention – The imaginary line that connects a subject's gaze to the object of interest viewed by that subject. Example: A man, standing in the entryway of an apartment building, looks at the nameplate on the door buzzer. The "line" would be traced from the man's eyes to the nameplate on the wall. The next shot may be a close-up of the nameplate itself, giving the audience an answer to the question, "What is he looking at?" See also Sight Line.

Locked Off – The description of a shot where the tripod head pan and tilt controls are locked tight so that there will be no movement of the camera. If there were a need to make adjustments to the frame during shooting, the pan and tilt locks would be loosened slightly for smooth movement.

Log – Generally, all shots are written down while shooting. This list is called a shooting log. During the creation of an editing project, shots that are going to be used from original sources are also logged. After the entire sequence is completed, an edit decision list (an edit log) can also be created to keep track of the shots used and the timecodes associated with their clip segments.

Long Shot/Wide Shot – When photographing a standing human subject, his or her entire body is visible within the frame and a large amount of the surrounding environment is also visible around him or her.

Look Room/Looking Room/Nose Room – When photographing a person, it is the space between his or her face and the furthest edge of the film frame. If a person is positioned frame left and is looking across empty space at frame right, then that empty space is considered the look room or nose room.

Looping (audio recording) – An audio post-production process in which actors re-record better-quality dialogue performance in a controlled studio. This new, clean audio track is then edited into the motion picture and appears in sync with the original picture.

Low-Angle Shot – Any shot where the camera records the action from a vertical position lower than most objects being recorded. Example: The camera, on a city sidewalk, points up to the tenth floor of an office building to record two men suspended with rigging cleaning the windows.

Lower Third – A title or graphic that appears as a superimposed visual element across the bottom lower third of the screen. Usually used to identify a person or place in a factual news piece or a documentary interview.

Low-Key Lighting – A lighting style in which a large contrast ratio exist between the brightly lit areas and the dark areas of the frame. Example: Film noir used low-key lighting to create deep, dark shadows and single-source key lighting for exposure of the principal subjects of importance.

Mastering – The process of creating the final version of an edited program or film that looks and sounds the best and will be used to create other copies for distribution.

Match Dissolve – A dissolve between two shots whose visual elements are compositionally similar. Shape, color, mass, or brightness of the outgoing shot will dissolve into visually similar shape, color, mass, or brightness of the incoming shot.

Matching Shots/Reciprocating Imagery/Answering Shots – When shooting coverage for a scene, each camera set-up favoring each character being covered should be very similar if not identical. You should match the framing, camera height, focal length, lighting, etc. When edited together, the matching shots will balance one another and keep the information presented about each character consistent.

Medium Shot – When photographing a standing human subject, the bottom of the frame will cut off the person around the waist.

Middle Ground – The zone within the depth of a filmed frame where, typically, the majority of the important visual action will take place. Objects in the middle ground may be obscured by other objects in the foreground, but middle-ground objects may then also obscure objects far away from the camera in the background.

Monocular Vision (camera lens) – A visual system in which only one lens takes in and records all data. The 3D aspect of human binocular vision is not present in the monocular vision of the film or video camera.

Montage – (1) The French word for editing; (2) a series of edits that show an event or events that happen over time but are condensed into a brief episode of screen time and usually edited to music; (3) a sequence of edited film clips that generates a new meaning for the viewer based on the juxtaposition of the individual shots' contents.

MOS – A term applied to shots recorded without sound. It should be noted on the clap slate and on the camera report and camera log. Although originating in the early days of sync sound emulsion film production, it may be used on any project where a camera records the visual images and a separate device records the audio signal. The post-production team know not to search for a sync sound clip that corresponds to that MOS picture clip.

Motivated Light – Light, seen on a film set, that appears to be coming from a light source within the film's pretend world.

Natural Light – Any light that is made by a non-manmade sources such as the sun or fire.

Natural Sound (NATS) – Audio ambience or background sounds recorded on the film set at the time of the picture being recorded.

Natural Wipe – Any large visual element that can move across and obscure the frame while recording a shot on a film set or location. This object naturally wipes the frame and blocks the view of the main subject or object of interest.

Negative Space – An artistic concept wherein unoccupied or empty space within a composition or arrangement of objects also has mass, weight, and importance, and is worth attention. Used to help to balance actual objects within the frame.

Neutral-Density (ND) Filter – A device that reduces the amount of light entering a camera (density), but does not alter the color temperature of that light (neutral). It is either a glass filter that you can apply to the front of the camera lens or, with many video cameras, a setting within the camera's electronics that replicates the reduced light effect of neutral-density glass lens filters.

Noddy – Any reaction shot of a person used as a cutaway. Most often associated with news interviews and some documentary pieces, these shots of heads nodding are usually recorded after the main interview and are edited in to cover up audio edits.

Normal Lens – A camera lens whose focal length closely replicates what the field of view and perspective might be on certain objects if those same objects were seen with human eyes.

Objective Shooting – A style of filmmaking where the subjects never address the existence of the camera. The camera is a neutral observer, not actively participating in the recorded event but simply acting as a viewer of the event for the benefit of the audience.

Outgoing Picture – At a cut point, there is one shot ending and another beginning. The shot that is ending prior to the cut point is the outgoing picture.

Overexposed – A state of an image where the bright regions contain no discernable visual data but appear as glowing white areas. The overall tonality of this image may also be lacking in true "black" values so that everything seems gray to white in luminance.

Overheads – Drawings or diagrams of the film set, as seen from above like a bird's-eye view, that show the placement of the camera, lighting equipment, talent, and any set furnishings, etc. These overheads will act as a map for each department to place the necessary equipment in those roughed-out regions of the set.

Overlapping Action – While shooting coverage for a particular scene, certain actions made by the talent will have to be repeated from different camera angles and framings. When cutting the film together, the editor will benefit from having the talent making these repeated movements, or overlapping actions, in multiple shots so that when the cut is made, it can be made on the matching movement of the action across the two shots.

Over-the-Shoulder (OTS) Shot – A shot used in filmmaking where the back of a character's head and one of his or her shoulders create an "L" shape in the left/bottom or right/bottom foreground and act as a "frame" for the full face of another character standing or seated in the middle ground opposite to the first character. This shot is often used when recording a dialogue scene between two people.

Overwrite – Mostly associated with video editing, this is an edit command that actually writes new frames of picture and/or sound over the top of, and replacing, existing video.

Pan – Short for "panoramic," this is horizontal movement of the camera, from left to right or right to left, while it is recording action. If you are using a tripod for camera support, the pan is achieved by loosening the pan lock on the tripod head and using the pan handle to swivel the camera around the central pivot point of the tripod to follow the action or reveal the recorded environment.

Pan and Scan – A process used in standard-definition television broadcasting where an original widescreen motion picture image is cropped down to fit into a 4:3 aspect ratio window (the screen size of SDTV) and slid or panned left and right to help to maintain some degree of picture composition. If a widescreen image did not have the pan-and-scan treatment, it would have to have the letterbox treatment (black bars at the top and bottom) to show the entire widescreen aspect ratio inside the squarer 4:3 TV screen.

Pan Handle – A tripod head with a horizontal pivot axis allows for the panning action of the camera, either left or right. The pan handle is a stick or length of metal tubing that extends off the tripod head and allows the camera operator to control the rate of movement of the camera pan by physically pushing or pulling it around the central axis of the tripod.

Pedestal – A camera support device that has vertical boom and 360-degree freewheel capabilities. Most often used on the floor of a television studio.

Picture Lock – The phase of editing a motion picture where there will be no more additions to or subtractions from the picture track(s). The duration of the movie will no longer change. From this point forward, the remaining audio track construction and tweaking may take place.

Point of View (POV) – In filmmaking terms, any shot that takes on a subjective vantage point. The camera records exactly what one of the characters is seeing. The camera sits in place of the talent, and what it shows to the viewing audience is supposed to represent what the character is actually seeing in the story. It can help the audience to relate to that character because they are placed in that character's position.

Point Source – A light source derived from a specific, localized instance of light generation/emission. A non-diffused light source.

Post-Production – The period of work on a motion picture project that occurs after all of the action is recorded with a camera (also known as production). Post-production can include picture and sound editing, title and graphics creation, motion effects rendering, color correction, musical scoring and mixing, etc.

Practical – A functional, on-set lighting fixture visible in the recorded shot's frame that may actually help to illuminate the set for exposure. Example: A shot of a man sitting down at a desk at night. Upon the desk is a lamp whose light illuminates the face of the man.

Pre-Production – The period of work on a motion picture project that occurs prior to the start of principal photography (also known as production). Story development, script writing, storyboards, casting, etc. all happen during this phase.

Production – The period of work on a motion picture project that occurs while the scenes are being recorded on film or video. This could be as short as a single day for a commercial or music video or last several months for a feature film.

Proscenium Style – In theater as well as motion pictures, a way to stage the action such that it is seen from only one direction. The audience or, for the film, the camera view and record the action from only one angle.

Pulling Focus – Camera lenses that have manual controls for the focus will allow a camera assistant or camera operator to move the plane of critical focus closer to the camera, therefore shifting the distance of the zone that appears to be in sharp focus within the depth of the frame. This is often done to shift focus from an object further in the frame to one closer within the frame.

Punch-In – When two or more separate shots of differing frame sizes cover the same subject along the same camera axis. See also Axial Edit, Cut-In.

Pushing Focus – Camera lenses that have manual controls for the focus will allow a camera assistant or camera operator to move the plane of critical focus further away from the camera, therefore shifting the distance of the zone that appears to be in sharp focus within the depth of the frame. This is often done to shift focus from an object near in the frame to one further away within the frame.

Racking Focus – During the recording of a shot that has a shallow depth of field, the camera assistant or camera operator may need to shift focus from one subject in the frame to another. This shifting of planes of critical focus from one distance away from the camera to another is called racking focus.

Reaction Shot – A shot in a scene that comes after some action, event, or line of dialogue. The first shot is the catalyst for the reaction depicted in the second shot. It lets the viewer know how the other characters are reacting to the action, event, or dialogue just shown.

Reformat – Changing the shape, size, and sometimes frame rate of a motion picture so that it will play on different-sized screens or in different countries with different standards for motion picture display.

Reveal – Any time that the filmmaker shows new, important, or startling visual information on the screen through camera movement, talent blocking, or edited shots in post-production. The reveal of information is the pay-off after a suspenseful expectation has been established within the story.

Rim Light – Any light source whose rays rim or halo the edges of a subject or an object on the film set, often placed somewhere behind the subject but directed at him or her.

Room Tone – The sound of "silence" that is the underlying tone present in every room or environment where filming takes place. Most sound recordists will capture at least 30 seconds of room tone at every location where filming has occurred. Editors use this tone to fill in gaps of empty space on the audio tracks so it has a continuous level or tone throughout.

Rough Cut – An initial stage of program editing that usually comes just after the assembly stage. The story is roughed out during this construction phase of the edit.

Rule of Thirds – A commonly used guideline of film frame composition where an imaginary grid of lines falls across the frame, both vertically and horizontally, at the mark of thirds. Placing objects along these lines or at the cross points of two of these lines is considered part of the tried and true composition of film images.

Running Time – The actual time that an entire edited program or film takes to play through from start to finish.

Safe Action Area – Related to the domestic cutoff phenomenon, the safe action area is found on many camera viewfinders and is used to keep the important action composed more toward the inner region of the frame. This prevents important action from being cut off.

Scene – A segment of a motion picture that takes place at one location. A scene may be composed of many shots from different camera angles or just one shot from one camera set-up.

Screen Direction – The direction in which a subject moves across or out of the frame. Example: A person standing at the center of the frame suddenly walks out of frame left. The movement to the left is the established screen direction. When the next shot is cut together for the story, the same person should enter the frame from frame right, continuing his or her journey in the same screen direction – from right to left.

Sequence – A number of shots joined together that depict a particular action or event in a longer program. Sometimes likened to a scene, but a longer scene may have several key sequences play out within it.

Shooting Ratio – The amount of material that you shoot for a project compared to the amount of material that makes it into the final edit. Example: You shoot 14 takes of one actor saying a line, but only use one of those takes in the final movie. You have a 14:1 shooting ratio for that one line of dialogue.

Shot – One action or event that is recorded by one camera at one time. A shot is the smallest building block used to construct a motion picture.

Shot List – A list of shots, usually prepared by the director during pre-production, that acts as a guide for what shots are required for best coverage of a scene in a motion picture project. It should show the shot type and may follow a number and letter naming scheme (e.g., Scene 4, Shot C, or simply 4C).

Shot–Reverse–Shot – A term applied to an editing style where one shot of a particular type (e.g., medium close-up) is used on one character and then the same type of shot is edited next in the sequence to show the other character in the scene. You see the shot, "reverse" the camera angle, and see a matching shot of the other character.

Side Lighting – A method of applying light to a subject or film set where the lights come from the side, not above or below.

Sight Line – The imaginary line that traces the direction in which a subject is looking on screen. The sight line also establishes the line of action and sets up the 180-degree arc for shooting coverage of a scene. See also Line of Attention, 180-Degree Line.

Silhouette – A special way of exposing a shot where the brighter background is correct in its exposure but the subject (in the middle ground or foreground) is underexposed and appears as a black shape with no detail but the hard edge "cut out."

Simple Shot – Any shot that only contains minor talent movement but uses no zoom, no tilt/pan, no camera dolly, and no booming actions. Locked-off framing.

Slate (noun) – The clapboard used to identify the shot being recorded. Often, the name of the production, director, and director of photography, the shooting scene, and the date are written on the slate.

State (verb) – Using the clapboard sticks to make a "clapping" sound, which serves as a synchronization point of picture and sound tracks during the editing process.

Slop Edit – An assembly edit done very early on in the editing process where speed of creation overrides the precision of the actual cut points. The general structure of the story is hastily assembled.

Slow Motion – Any treatment in film or video where the actual time taken for an event to occur is slowed down considerably so that it lasts longer in screen time and more detail of the action can be analyzed by the viewer.

Smash Cut – An abrupt and often jarring transition between two contrasting actions or moods that happen at different times and/or places.

Soft Light – Any light that has diffused, non-parallel rays. Strong shadows are very rare if you use soft light to illuminate the talent.

Sound Bridge – An audio treatment given to a cut point where either the sound of the outgoing shot continues underneath the new image of the incoming picture track or the new audio of the incoming shot begins to play before the picture of the outgoing shot leaves the screen.

Sound Design – The process of building audio tracks that act to augment and enhance the physical actions seen on the screen and the sounds from the environments in which the story's action takes place. These sounds may be actual sounds or fabricated to generate a hyper-reality of the audio elements in a program.

Sound on Tape (SOT) – Most often associated with the spoken word from news reporters or documentary interviewees. SOTs are the sound bites.

Sound Recordist/Sound Mixer – The person on a film crew responsible for recording spoken dialogue, ambience, and room tone.

Sound Track – An audio track. A place in the motion media sequence where audio clips are edited.

Soundtrack – (1) A music performance recorded during production; (2) the entire mix of audio clips from a motion media sequence; (3) the collection of music and orchestral score played throughout a motion media piece that is sold separately for listening enjoyment.

Splice (noun) – The cut point where two shots are joined together at an edit point. The term originated when physical strips of film were actually taped or glued together.

Splice (verb) – To cut two shots together.

Splicer – In film, the footage is physically cut with a small machine called a splicer and the pictures are spliced together with glue or special transparent tape.

Split Edit – A transition between clips where the video tracks and audio tracks are offset and not cut at the same frame in time. Either the video tracks will last longer and play over the new incoming audio tracks or the new video tracks appear first and play over the continuing audio tracks from the outgoing shot. See also J-Cut, L-Cut, Lapping, Sound Bridge.

Spot – Slang for a television commercial advertisement.

Spreader – The three legs of a tripod are often attached to a spreader, a rubber or metal device to keep them from splaying too far apart while the heavy camera sits atop the tripod head. This three-branched brace allows for greater stability, especially as the tripod legs are spread further and further apart to get the camera lower to the ground.

Staging – The placement of set dressings and objects within the film set.

Standard Definition (SD) – A reference to the normal image quality and frame size of most televisions around the world during the 20th century. Limitations in broadcast bandwidth, among other technological reasons, required a low-resolution image (525-line NTSC or 576-line PAL) of the 4:3 aspect ratio for television reception in the home.

Start Frame – Any time that the camera needs to move to follow action, the camera should begin recording, stay stationary for a few moments while the action begins, and then start to move to follow the action. The start frame can be useful to the editor of the film so that the shot will have a static frame to start on at the beginning of the cut. Static frames cut to moving frames can be a jarring visual experience and this static start frame may help to prevent this.

Sticks – (1) An alternative name for a camera tripod; (2) the clapboard or slate used to mark the synchronization point of picture and sound being recorded.

Storyboards – Drawings often done during pre-production of a motion picture that represent the best guess of what the ultimate framing and movement of camera shots will be when the film goes into production. These comic book-like illustrations act as a template for the creative team when principal photography begins.

Straight Cut – An edit point where the picture track and the sound track(s) are cut and joined at the same moment in time. See also Butt-Cut.

Subjective Shooting – A style of filmmaking where the subjects address the camera straight into the lens (as in news broadcasting) or when the camera records exactly what a character is observing in a fictional narrative, as with the point-of-view shot.

Suite – A small room in which editing machines are kept and used. The actual editing of the program will often occur in this private, dark, quiet room so that the editor can stay focused on the footage and the sound elements without outside disturbances.

Superimposition – When an image of less than 100% opacity is placed on top of another image. This is like a dissolve that lasts for a longer time on screen.

Sync – Short for "synchronous" or "synchronized." In film work, it refers to how the audio tracks play in corresponding time with the picture track. When you see a character's mouth move, you hear the appropriate audio play at the exact same time.

Tail – The common film term for the end of a shot, especially during the post-production editing process.

Tail Slate – Often used while recording documentary footage, a tail slate is the process of identifying the shot and "clapping" the slate after the action has been recorded but before the camera stops rolling. The slate is physically held upside down to visually indicate a tail slate.

Take – Each action, event, or line of dialogue recorded in a shot may need to be repeated until its technical and creative aspects are done to the satisfaction of the filmmakers. Each of the times the camera rolls to record this repeated event is called a take. Takes are traditionally numbered, starting at one.

Taking Lens – The active lens on a motion picture or video camera that is actually collecting, focusing, and controlling the light for the recording of the image. On certain models of emulsion film motion picture cameras, there can be more than one lens mounted to the camera body. Most video cameras have only one lens, which would be the taking lens.

Talking Head – Any medium close-up shot or closer that frames one person's head and shoulders. Usually associated with documentaries, news, and interview footage.

Three-Point Lighting Method – A basic but widely used lighting method where a key light is employed for main exposure on one side of the talent, a fill light for contrast control on the opposite side, and a back light for subject/background separation.

Tilt – The vertical movement of the camera, either down/up or up/down, while it is recording action. If you are using a tripod for camera support, the tilt is achieved by loosening the tilt lock on the tripod head and using the pan handle to swing the camera lens up or down to follow the vertical action or reveal the recorded environment.

Glossary

Timecode – A counting scheme based on hours, minutes, seconds, and frames that is used to keep track of image and sound placement on video, digital media files, and editing software.

Tracking In/Trucking In – Moving the camera into the set, usually atop a dolly on tracks.

Tracks/Rail – Much like railroad tracks, these small-scale metal rails are used to smoothly roll a dolly across surfaces, either inside or outside, to get a moving shot.

Tripod – A three-legged device, often with telescoping legs, used to support and steady the camera for motion picture shooting. The camera attaches to a device capable of vertical and horizontal axis movement called the tripod head, which sits atop the balancing legs.

Tripod Head – The device, usually mounted on top of tripod legs, to which you attach the camera. The head may have panning and tilting functionality.

Tracking Out/Trucking Out – Pulling the camera out of the set, usually atop a dolly on tracks.

Tungsten Balance – Film and video cameras may be biased toward seeing the color temperature of tungsten lamps (also known as film lights) as "white" light. When they are set this way, they have a tungsten balance at approximately 3200 degrees Kelvin.

Two-Shot/2-Shot – Any shot that contains the bodies (or body parts) of two people.

Underexposed – A state of an image where the dark regions contain no discernible visual data but appear as deep black areas. The overall tonality of this image may also be lacking in true "white" values so that everything seems gray down to black in luminance.

Vanishing Point – A long-established technique in the visual arts where opposing diagonal lines converge at the horizon line to indicate the inclusion of a great distance in the image's environment. It is an illusion used to help to represent 3D space on a 2D surface.

Varifocal Lens – Another name for a zoom lens. A lens that has multiple glass elements that allow it to catch light from various focal lengths or angles of view of a scene.

Video Format – A video combines recorded electronic voltage fluctuations or digital bit data that represent picture and sound information. Video cameras are manufactured to record that data onto a tape or memory card in a particular way. The shape, amount of data, frame rate, color information, etc. that get recorded are determined by the technologies inside the video camera. Examples include NTSC-525 line, PAL, HD-1080i, and HD-720p.

Visible Spectrum – The zone in electromagnetic energy waves that appears to our eyes and brains as colored light.

Voice-Over Narration – An edited program may require the voice of an unseen narrator who provides important information or commentary about the story that is unfolding. The voice is heard "over" the pictures and the natural sounds.

Voice Slate – A practice used at the head of a shot after the camera is rolling and before the director calls "Action." Often, a camera assistant will verbally say the scene and take number so as to identify the audio data that may be recorded separately from the picture.

Whip Pan – An extremely quick panning action that will cause severe motion blur on the recorded image. Often used to exit a scene and then quickly begin another at a different time or place.

Wipe – An editing transition where an incoming shot's image literally wipes the existing outgoing shot's image from the screen.

Workflow – A plan or methodology that maps the flow of picture and sound data from production through numerous post-production phases and ultimately to a finished product that is distributed for viewing. Managing a clear digital media file workflow is very important to the efficient completion of any project.

Zoom Lens – A camera lens with a multiple glass lens element construction and telescoping barrel design, allowing it to gather light from a wide range or field of view and also from a very narrow (more magnified) field of view. The focal length of the lens is altered by changing the distances of the optical elements contained within the lens barrel itself. Most modern video cameras have built-in optical zoom lenses that can be adjusted from wide to telephoto with the touch of a button or a twist of the focal length ring on the lens barrel.

Index